RADIO'S
MORNING SHOW
PERSONALITIES

RADIO'S MORNING SHOW PERSONALITIES

*Early Hour Broadcasters
and Deejays from the
1920s to the 1990s*

by
PHILIP A. LIEBERMAN

McFarland & Company, Inc., Publishers
Jefferson, North Carolina, and London

British Library Cataloguing-in-Publication data are available

Library of Congress Cataloguing-in-Publication Data

Lieberman, Philip A., 1948–
    Radio's morning show personalities : early hour broadcasters
and deejays from the 1920s to the 1990s / by Philip A. Lieberman.
        p.   cm.
    Includes bibliographical references and index. ∞
    ISBN 0-7864-0037-4 (lib. bdg. : 50# alk. paper)
    1. Radio broadcasters — United States — Biography.   2. Disc
jockeys — United States — Biography.   3. Radio broadcasting —
United States — History.   I. Title.
PN1991.4.L46A4   1996
791.44′028′092273 — dc20
[B]   95-45032
                                                        CIP

Manufactured in the United States of America

McFarland & Company, Inc., Publishers
    Box 611, Jefferson, North Carolina 28640

This book is dedicated to the memory of
fellow Northeastern Pennsylvanian Hugh Brannum
a.k.a. "Uncle Lumpy," a.k.a. "Mr. Green Jeans,"
friend, organic farmer, and bass player,
who worked along with many of the greats
in morning radio before there was television

Contents

Acknowledgments

Considering the hundreds of letters, telephone calls, faxes, and live interviews which have taken place over the almost four years of preparation required for this work, I undoubtedly will omit the names of some persons to whom I owe an expression of gratitude for helping make this the most comprehensive work available on the subject. I shall try to list the more salient ones.

First and foremost are the following contributing authors who helped me write a generous percentage of the entries in Part V: John Hargrave, Nicholson, Pennsylvania; Marion Melnyk, Trucksville, Pennsylvania; Mary Ellen Alu, Allentown, Pennsylvania; Rita Fitzgerald, Tunkhannock, Pennsylvania; Theresa Klimchak, Duryea, Pennsylvania; Roxanna Pote, Tunkhannock, Pennsylvania; the Reverend William Reid, Tunkhannock, Pennsylvania; Maryse Quinn, Conklin, New York.

Deep thanks are due to Bill Fromm, publisher of *Radio Programming Profile*, who granted me permission to use material from rare back issues. On a smaller scale, I want to thank Bill Earl of Montebello, California, for granting me permission to quote from his exhaustive treatise on Los Angeles radio, and Paul Bhaerman of Staten Island, New York, who generously offered his time to conduct research at the Museum of Television and Radio in New York City, where he perused microfilm archives.

Other persons who were kind enough to provide materials and information at their own expense include the following: Bill Eckart, Mustang, Oklahoma; Chuck Southcott, Granada Hills, California; Ken Cosset of the Radio Advertising Bureau, New York, New York; former radio and television performer Sandy Becker, New York, New York; and Dennis Burns, Concord Township, Ohio.

Special thanks must be given to Theresa A. Klimchak, who transcribed the vast majority of material in this book in WordPerfect for submission to the publisher. She also suggested numerous editorial changes to make the language clearer for people without an extensive background in media. Also, Michael Skowronski provided technical support in formatting and merging the various incompatible word processing formats that I used in the three years this book took to prepare.

The keen recollection of my parents, David and Maria Lieberman, helped steer me on the right course for dredging up obscure radio history.

And, finally, thanks are due to my wife, Rosalind, who fielded numerous telephone calls from total strangers in a businesslike manner, and accompanied me with my daughter Michelle and son Joseph on several journeys to gather information. They have all learned more about radio than they ever cared to know.

Introduction

Despite the television and radio nostalgia craze of the past two decades, with books now available on virtually every subject from the art of Hanna-Barbera to an 800-page directory of *Gunsmoke* episodes, few words have been written about a subject that is more a part of our daily lives than almost any other media presentation. What Americans have not, at some point in their lives, gotten into the habit of tuning in their favorite "morning man" on the radio? He is that friendly local deejay who helps listeners get ready to face the day with information on weather, traffic, transit, and school and plant delays.

Morning men, or "morning personality" now that a few women are on the scene, come in all shapes and sizes. In the 1940s and early 1950s, the typical morning deejay such as "Buffalo" Bob Smith and, later, Johnny Andrews at WNBC in New York City, sang and played the piano to segue into the recorded music. In the 1980s and 1990s, there emerged new deejays who trived on dirty jokes and outrageous character assassinations. In between were morning men with political commentaries, morning men with zany contests, and morning men with homespun anecdotes.

With the advent of television and the gradual demise of prime-time radio listeners in the evening, and with the increasing number of people who drive to work rather than walk or use mass transit, the early morning period has been the prime time for radio for quite some time. In most markets, the morning show has the most listeners and carries the highest advertising rates. It therefore behooves each station to put its best talent in that slot. Furthermore, if a station can hook its listeners when they first arise, it has the edge for later programs, too, as many listeners leave their dials set in that position. Even some nonpersonality FM rock stations are aware of this fact, and put personalities in the drive-time slot. An example would be the wisecracking Daniels and Webster comedy team on WEZX FM in Scranton, Pennsylvania.

Nevertheless, it should be obvious to any radio listener over the age of 30 that the prevailing style of morning deejays has been changing since the mid–1950s. The public generally has become less folksy,

1

faster paced, and more specialized in its demands. Some people want all news, some want all soft music, and some want business data. This trend away from individuality has been exacerbated by radio station takeovers and by conglomerate managers who are more interested in the bottom line than in providing a quality entertainment package. Someone can be hired to spin records or read news copy for a considerably lower salary than that of a comedian like Gene Rayburn or a musical scholar like Jonathan Schwartz. A return to quality programming will occur only when the public demands better talent from its local stations and commercial sponsors, and supports those programs by patronizing their advertisers.

Parts I–IV of this book focus on 32 trendsetting morning men from four historical periods: the early period, when playing records was not the major thrust of a morning show; the golden age, when recorded music was important, but not as important as the personality playing it; the top 40 era, when personalities had less time to spend with the audience; and the post–top 40 era, when stations began to target specific audiences. Part V provides information on hundreds of other morning personalities.

I have defined the morning drive-time show as any program occurring wholly or in part on a daily basis between 5:00 and 10:00 a.m. The vast majority of these programs aired either Monday through Friday or Monday through Saturday.

I have been as thorough as possible in researching each radio station; however, many radio stations were omitted, particularly those no longer in business. Readers are encouraged to write to me in care of the publisher reporting any omissions or errors in this book so that I will be able to correct the situation in any future edition.

One final note about the book: Although there have been a few "morning women" on the air in recent years, the position has historically been dominated by men, and the front portion of this work reflects this historical reality. No women are profiled in Parts I, II, III, or IV. However, concise biographical information for the most prominent female morning personalities is provided in Part V.

Part I

The Early Years

In the earliest years of radio, the mid–1920s, there were no morning shows. It was assumed that people had time to listen to the radio only at night. As a result, most stations did not broadcast at all during the day. A few had a midday show, then would sign off in the afternoon and return in the evening. But it took only a few years for stations to realize a tremendous potential at breakfast time, and by 1930, most stations broadcast from at least sunrise until midnight.

A little known fact, even among people who lived through the period, is that women announcers were quite common in the earliest days of radio, but by the 1930s they had virtually disappeared. One of the first morning personalities was a woman, Halloween Martin, whose program on KYW in Chicago, "The Musical Clock"—which bore the same name as John Gambling's program in New York—established light and lively music as being most suitable for these hours. Other stations tried different formats. John Gambling's program began as an exercise routine. Pittsburgh's KDKA had the same format. "The idea of canned music during the early morning hours would not have been very popular in the '20s," writes George Douglas in his book, *The Early Days of Radio Broadcasting*. While some programs featured calisthenics, others featured health talk, farm news, or live piano solos. But a few did play music: Norman Ross on WMAQ in Chicago and "Frank Cope's Alarm Klok Klub" on WGBS in Philadelphia are two notable examples. While these men never gained great fame, they were early pioneers of a format that would endure for decades to come.

While musical tastes have changed enormously, and some of today's deejays get away with comments and humor that would have been considered unacceptable in a nightclub 70 years ago, there are some enduring features about wakeup programs. As George Douglas aptly stated, "There are many people who can tolerate the disembodied sound of radio at times of the day when they cannot endure the flashing light of the television screen; thus, there are many who will listen religiously to a morning radio wakeup show who would not dream of turning on the television at that hour."

THE GAMBLINGS

"Rambling with Gambling," the longest running morning show on radio, began on WOR when the station was in its infancy, and continues to date with John R. Gambling, grandson of the program's founder, John B. Gambling.

When WOR first signed on in 1924, from Newark, N.J., radio was still an unfamiliar medium to most people; the concept of a "morning man" to wake up listeners with news and events was not yet established. The station's broadcast day began at 6:30 a.m. with an exercise program, hosted by Arthur Bagley, who was succeeded by Bernarr McFadden. One day in 1925, McFadden called in ill. The young engineer and announcer on duty, John Bradley Gambling, called chief engineer Jack Poppele in a panic. Poppele asked him if he had the exercise chart and knew the routine. Gambling said he did, so Poppele told him to substitute for McFadden. Within minutes, people began calling in, complimenting Gambling's clear voice and precise diction.

A few weeks after calling in ill, McFadden quit the station, and Gambling agreed to take over his position until a replacement could be found. Instead of just dryly calling out the calisthenics, Gambling worked in old British Navy jokes and horsed around, singing with the live orchestra. Then he added time checks, weather reports, and news from the morning papers. It was the birth of morning radio. "WOR forgot all about replacing me," reflected Gambling. The show was retitled "The Musical Clock," and the first sponsor was Colgate toothpaste. In 1929, the Illinois Meat Company used the program to introduce a new product appropriately named Broadcast Corned Beef Hash.

Recognizing that sound gags would work in radio as well as sight gags did in film, Gambling had his pianist "cuckoo" with the time checks, while Gambling himself made cat and hen noises. Live canaries were used on the show until 1950. In 1934, a survey revealed that only a small fraction of listeners cared about the exercises, so they were dropped.

"The Musical Clock" was a true morning show, with only one major difference from today's shows: there was no recorded music. "The World's Greatest Little Orchestra," which had played background for the calisthenics, provided all the music until the 1940s, when Gambling began playing records to supplement the live music.

In 1948, Gambling's slot was expanded to begin at 6:00 a.m. Monday through Saturday. The first hour was titled "Rambling with Gambling." "The Musical Clock" continued until 8:00 a.m., but in the 1950s it was expanded to 9:00 a.m. For a brief time, another 15 minutes, "Gambling's Second Breakfast," were tacked on at 9:15 following Harry Hennessy's crisp, smooth newscast.

A dispute with the musicians' union in 1954 was the death knell for Gambling's orchestra; the program switched to recorded music only in a "middle-of-the-road" format which Gambling defined as "no boogie-woogie and no opera, either." However, Strauss waltzes on a morning show were a conservative format even in 1954.

In March 1955, Gambling filled Madison Square Garden with his 30th anniversary show, featuring celebrities from radio, opera, and politics. His son, John Alfred Gambling served as emcee. John A. had a pleasant personality, but he lacked the baritone voice of his father; he sounded too much like a kid to some. Nevertheless, John B. wanted to retire, and pushed WOR executives to let his son prove himself by doing other shows. So, in 1956, WOR cleared a huge block of time in the evenings and on Sundays for a soft music program in "hi-fi" called "Music from Studio X," with John A. as host. John A. also substituted for his father on most Saturday mornings. In preparation for his retirement in 1959, John B. shared the microphone on his morning show with his son for about a year. Then, on March 5, 1959, John B. quietly left the show, returning only as vacation substitute for his son.

"Rambling with Gambling" in the early 1960s was expanded to begin at 5:30 a.m., then in the late 1960s expanded again to 10:00 a.m. In the mid–1960s, WOR experimented with a less talkative prerecorded "second breakfast" portion from 9:15 to 11:00 a.m. Saturdays and added Sundays from 7:15 to 11:00 a.m. In the early 1970s, after newsman Peter Roberts took over the Sunday shows, the starting time was standardized at 5:15 a.m., immediately following the day's first newscast with Jack Allen, with a quitting time at 10:00 a.m.

John A. moved the music format away from the classics and toward Sinatra, but not toward rock 'n' roll until the late 1960s. In fact, until the late 1970s, John A. continued to air artists like Percy Faith and Frank Chacksfield, which met with his father's approval. But to

RUDOLPH FROSINI   VINCENT SAMMY MEPHESTO   IGNATZ   JOHN B. GAMBLING   RASTUS CUCKOO

hold on to younger listeners, Gambling began playing songs by Carole King and Simon and Garfunkel. Soon, the traditional soft music was shelved.

In 1962, WOR had hired Peter Roberts away from WINS to broadcast 5-minute newscasts on the half-hour, supplementing the 15-minute newscasts on the hour. Gambling and Roberts began an unrehearsed repartee after one of these newscasts about a human interest story, and this soon became a regular routine every hour. The following is a sample of the dialogue: "Swords" was pronounced with a "w."

Roberts: An author in Britain wants to revive the art of dueling to defend a lady's honor.
Gambling: Good grief! You mean with swords, or pistols, or both?
Roberts: No, with swords, sir. Michael Thornton believes that the Duchess of Leominster has been insulted by three men, including her stepson, and so he's challenged these three people to combat.
Gambling: With swords?
Roberts: With swords. Dueling has been outlawed in Britain for over 100 years, says the dispatch, and it also notes that Mr. Thornton is the Duchess' accountant. He maintains that dueling is the only way to defend her honor.
Gambling: How about defending her against the tax man? Will a sword help there very much, or maybe a sharp pencil would be . . .
Roberts: I think maybe a pencil just thrown at the man. Anyway, when it came time to deliver his challenges, accountant Thornton used modern methods. He didn't walk up to them, and with a traditional slap on the face with a glove, issue the challenge.
Gambling: What, instead, did he do?
Roberts: He just posted letters to his opponents, and so far he hasn't had a reply.
Gambling: Maybe they weren't delivered. They have the same problems in Britain that we have here.
Roberts: Ha. Ha. Ha. Ha. (forced laughter)

Another of John A. Gambling's innovations was helicopter traffic reports, done initially in 1962 by Bob Schmidt, then for many years by Fred Feldman and, later, by George Meade.

The following outlines a typical hour of "Rambling with Gambling" in its heyday, when it was the most listened-to radio show in the United States:

7:00   News: Harry Hennessy
7:14   Song: "Everybody's Out of Town," B. J. Thomas

***Opposite:* "The World's Greatest Little Orchestra"**

7:17   John A. greets his audience and talks for a moment about the good visibility, gazing across the Hudson River to the Watchung Mountains; he reviews a light news item from the morning newspaper.

7:19   Commercial: Pan American Airlines

7:20   Helicopter traffic report: Fred Feldman

7:21   John A. talks about delays on the Central Railroad of New Jersey Main Line for the 6:08 and 6:30 a.m. trains originating at Hampton, New Jersey.

7:22   Commercial: John A. does a live commercial for Al Cooper's Restaurant, endorsing the prepared-to-order food and friendly service.

7:24   John A. reports on a water main break along Third Avenue, and announces additional commuter delays, this time on the New Haven Railroad.

7:25   Commercial: Trailways Bus System (John A. talks over the commercial for reduced fares to Framingham and Natick.)

7:27   Song: "Mr. Sandman," Bert Kampfaert Orchestra (John A. talks over the introduction portion of the song with a time check and a brief weather report.)

7:30   Commercial: John A. does a live commercial for the Walter B. Cook Funeral Home.

7:31   Helicopter traffic report: John A. announces a quick traffic check again with Fred Feldman to spot a problem on the Grand Central Parkway in Little Neck.

7:32   John A. introduces Peter Roberts with a belated 7:30 newscast.

7:32   News: Peter Roberts

7:36   Peter Roberts concludes the news and announces that John A. will now give the weather. There is silence. Roberts shouts in a louder voice for John A. to give the weathercast. John A. is then heard panting as he runs back to the microphone and delivers the weather.

7:37   John A. and Peter discuss the impending barbecue season. Peter recites "Hooray, hooray for the month of May, backyard picnics start today." The two discuss barbecuing methods and end up concluding that it is wise to keep a fire extinguisher nearby.

7:41   Commercial: Thomas' English Muffins

7:42   Helicopter traffic report: John A. announces Fred Feldman's traffic report.

7:43	John A. repeats the problems with the New Jersey Central Railroad and the New Haven Railroad announcing which trains will be delayed.
7:44	Commercial: John A. does a live commercial for Carey Limousine Service.
7:45	John A. introduces Don Criqui, who does a live sportscast.
7:49	Commercial: Lincoln-Mercury Dealers
7:50	John A. introduces weatherman Bill Korbel for a detailed look at the weather.
7:53	John A. discusses the weather with Bill Korbel.
7:54	Commercial: Carolina Rice
7:55	John A. gives another live transit report.
7:56	Commercial: John A. does a live commercial for Hillshire Farm Kielbasa.
7:57	Helicopter traffic report: John A. introduces Fred Feldman for another traffic report.
7:58	Song: "It's Impossible," Perry Como
8:00	John A. introduces Henry Gladstone with the news.

Please note that there were 13 commercials in the 60 minutes. One commercial was done by Peter Roberts during the 7:30 news, and one was done during Don Criqui's sportscast. Two additional commercials were done within Harry Hennessy's 7:00 news.

Service and dependability have been the hallmarks of "Rambling with Gambling's" success. I remember a "rock 'n' roll" classmate of mine in 1970 who nevertheless relied on the show in the mornings for traffic, transit, weather, and news delivered by capable professionals. And, when John A. Gambling endorsed a product, we had confidence that he truly believed in it.

By the early 1970s, John A. Gambling's salary averaged $300,000 a year. Actually Gambling's "salary" was mainly a commission, minus certain expenses, based on airtime sold. The hefty figure was testimony to his effectiveness in selling products.

Beginning around 1966, John A. seldom did his Saturday show live. Instead, he would prerecord about an hour of it each weekday after the regular show. Few listeners could discern that Gambling was not really at the station on Saturdays, because the production was done flawlessly. Gambling's producer, Bill McEvilly, showed me how the show was done when I toured the WOR studios back at that time.

Since Gambling knew the exact length of each song and commercial, he would set a Kodak darkroom timer for that number of seconds, turn it on, and resume talking. Since each program carried 15 minutes of news on the hour, 5 minutes on the half-hour, and 18 minutes of commercials, it literally would take Gambling only about 22 minutes to record an hour of the Saturday show, or about 2 hours to prerecord an entire 5-hour show.

McEvilly also showed me other ingenious production techniques he had concocted with Gambling. For example, if a flub was made on Saturday, they had a prerecorded cartridge of John Gambling apologizing for the error: "Everyone in the radio business knows the feeling: you push a button and nothing happens. Let's try again this time."

McEvilly introduced me to Dick Willard, one of WOR's distinguished staff announcers. Announcers, in the traditional sense, were not deejays. Willard's job was to keep the log, cue the deejay or host, read some of the commercials, and call the station breaks. John A. stopped using a live announcer in the 1960s, but WOR has continued to use them at other times of the day, a practice nearly extinct in the business. The particular announcers who worked with Gambling now are either retired or deceased.

If I had to name one trend-setting trait which set John A. Gambling apart from his contemporaries, it was his injecting personal and family information into his show. Even though I never met his wife Sally or children Anne, Sarah Jane, or John, or his dog named "Little Bear's Nana," they always were like part of an extended family for me. After all, I had cousins and uncles whom I did not hear from for months on end, whereas I heard something about the Gamblings every morning.

Even after John B. Gambling retired and no longer substituted for John A., he appeared as a frequent guest on the program until his death in 1974. I remember the first time John A.'s son John R. appeared as an adult guest. A communications major at Boston College, he sounded remarkably like his father, and it was obvious to me that he was being groomed as the heir to "Rambling with Gambling."

After working at small stations in Massachusetts, Florida, and upstate New York, grandson John R. got his own WOR weekend program in 1978. He took over the weekday afternoon drive-time slot in 1981, and in just a few years was cohosting "Rambling with Gambling." In 1989, John A. announced that he was becoming the "minor partner" in the show, and a year later, he retired, coming back only when John R. was sick or on vacation. By 1992, John A.'s retirement was complete, with substituting handled by newsman Rodger Skibenes or talk-show host Paul W. Smith.

John R. Gambling (*left*) and John A. Gambling

John R. brought a couple of further changes to "Rambling with Gambling." The music, which had become a bit too contemporary for the older fans, was dropped entirely. By the 1990s, "Rambling with Gambling" had more interviews and even some telephone call-ins.

A major difference between John A. and John R. is that John R. is more topical and is not afraid to take stands on controversial political issues. For example, when a gunman shot 17 commuters on the Long Island Railroad in December 1993, John R. spoke to witnesses and then proffered his views on gun control legislation. Surely the late John B. would have told his grandson that a breakfast show should be bland and lighthearted, but, in this high-tech era when there is a need for instant information, and few people sit down to a real breakfast, most listeners would probably dismiss John B.'s show (or even John

A.'s old repartee with Peter Roberts) as out of touch with the times.

At the end of 1993, the program hours were changed again, from 5:00 to 9:00 a.m. weekdays and 5:30 to 10:00 a.m. on Saturdays. Some of the Saturday shows are prerecorded, but during important breaking developments such as snowstorms, John R. comes in to broadcast them live.

John R. Gambling, although quite a different fellow from his grandfather, at least maintains the sincere style of his predecessors. While 'Rambling with Gambling" bears little resemblance to its original form, we at least should be thankful that some shreds of it have survived with its rightful heir. And, in this era of "shock jocks" and automated formats, that is an achievement in itself.

GENE RAYBURN

Gene Rayburn pioneered the "morning duo" format of a funny man and a straight man. It was old hat in vaudeville and films, but until World War II, no one had adapted the partnership to morning radio.

Rayburn actually began his career as a solo act. The Illinois native worked on WGNY in Newburgh, New York, on WITH in Baltimore, and on WFIL in Philadelphia, before becoming morning man in 1942 at WNEW in New York, which was experimenting with a recorded music format. After a stint in the U.S. Air Force as a bombardier-navigator in World War II, Rayburn returned to WNEW and teamed up with Jack Lescoulie to form the show "Scream and Dream with Jack and Gene," a takeoff on the name "Swing and Sway with Sammy Kaye." The program, which aired Monday through Saturday from 7:00 to 9:00 a.m., was soon renamed "Anything Goes."

"We were totally spontaneous, very irreverent," Rayburn recalled. In addition to witty dialogue, the program was the first to inject sound effects and pieces of records during other records. For example, a Spike Jones novelty sound would suddenly interrupt a wistful Peggy Lee tune. Or the sound of a gurgling water fountain would break in to a commercial for toothpaste. Rayburn did some of the sound effects live, and both Rayburn and Lescoulie controlled the turntables, although an engineer would open and close the "pots," i.e. input channels connected turntables, machines, or microphones.

In 1947, for a reason Rayburn could not recall, station manager

Bernice Judis fired Lescoulie "out of the blue" and asked Rayburn to recommend a replacement. Rayburn recommended staff announcer Dee Finch, whom he called "the perfect straight man." "We shook up New York!" Rayburn proclaimed. To prove their immense popularity and ability to promote songs, Rayburn asked a music publisher to give him the absolutely worst tunes he had in his files. The publisher presented him with two songs which Rayburn and Finch played five times a day. Before long, "Music Music Music" and "Hopscotch Polka" were near the top of the charts.

Rayburn's favorite part of the show was choosing a "Mother of the Week" and inviting her to be on the show and to have breakfast with the duo. It sounds trite today, but this was innovation in the late 1940s, compared to the stodgier, more predictable format of John B. Gambling's number one rated program "Rambling with Gambling." The Rayburn and Finch" show ran from 6:00 to 10:00 a.m. Monday through Saturday until 1953, when Gene Klavan replaced Rayburn. According to Rayburn, the split-up occurred because "Finch didn't want to work. Everybody wanted us, but he insisted on staying at WNEW." When Rayburn got a lucrative offer from NBC, Judis got wind of it and offered Finch a huge raise if he stayed at WNEW.

The split ended Rayburn's career as a morning man. But it was just the beginning of his path to national fame. First, NBC put him on a short-lived children's television show which copied "Beat the Clock." When his contract expired, Dick Pinkham, NBC vice president of programming, cast him as Steve Allen's sidekick on the original "Tonight Show," long before Ed McMahon had this role. In the late 1950s, Rayburn realized his dream to act. He starred both in television ("Robert Montgomery Presents") and on Broadway, in "Come Blow Your Horn" and, in 1961, in "Bye Bye Birdie."

Rayburn's most recognized role was as the original host of "Match Game," on NBC beginning in 1963. But during the seven-year run of the game show and another three years on "Dough Re Mi," he appeared in numerous other television shows and stock theater productions, some even with his wife Helen and daughter Lynn.

Beginning in 1962, Rayburn served as a Saturday morning host of "Monitor," an NBC network radio magazine format which ran from 1955 until the mid–1970s. While not a drive-time program ("Monitor" began at 9:00 a.m. eastern time), it gave Rayburn opportunity to perfect an interview format which has been copied by many talk-radio morning show hosts of today: witty, spontaneous and friendly.

Although in his mid-seventies at this writing, Rayburn still

Gene Rayburn (*left*) and Dee Finch

appears in stock productions of musicals. A health food and exercise enthusiast for decades, Rayburn is not the kind of man to give up a fight. When he broke his leg in 20 places while skiing back in the 1950s, he bounced back to a full routine in just six months. Rayburn could remember only one time he became truly nervous on the air: when he interviewed Julie Andrews. "I worshipped her," he laughs. "I saw her on stage in 'My Fair Lady' seven times."

BOB ELLIOTT
and RAY GOULDING

Dry Yankee humor with sophistication, that was the recipe that made Robert Brackett Elliott and Raymond Walter Goulding successful in radio, television, commercials, books, and theater. Erudite and witty, Bob and Ray first gained widespread recognition as morning men at WINS in New York, many years before it became an all-news station.

Bob (*right*) and Ray

The dozens of characters which Bob and Ray impersonated were parodies of world celebrities as well as everyday people, but unlike the shock jock routines of the 1990s, they were gentle, at times even reverent with their characters such as Wally Ballou, the bumbling reporter; Charles the Poet, who sounded much like everyone's poorest English teacher; and Mary McGoon, who dispensed recipes in the manner of Mary Margaret McBride.

Bob and Ray had a great deal of success parodying celebrities and shows that were no longer in the public eye. For example, the five-minute serial vignettes "Mary Backstage, Noble Wife" were based on a radio soap opera "Mary Noble, Backstage Wife," which ceased to exist in the 1950s, yet Bob and Ray continued this ever-evolving series until nearly 1980. As *The New Yorker* wrote in 1973, "Instead of falling by the wayside, since parody generally exists only as long as its original does, it has taken on a life of its own. It is an independent comic-surrealist world."

The following is a sample of Bob and Ray's show:

Bob: We came across a gentleman in Henderson, Vermont, recently. His name is Nelson Malamon, and his story struck us so much that we invited him to tell it himself.

Malamon (Ray): And I want to thank you and the generous Bob and Ray organization for underwriting my trip, too. It's a wonderful experience.

Bob: You deserve it — particularly with the run of bad luck you've had. Tell everyone what it is you do, Nelson.

Malamon: Well, I own a four leaf clover farm back in Henderson. I developed a breed of hybrid four leaf clovers some years ago.

Bob: And you found a market for them?

Malamon: Right. Anyway, I thought this was going to be a banner year for my business until last June.

Bob: That's when your troubles started.

Malamon: It was Friday the thirteenth — that's the funny part — and my assistant, Neil, was taking my entire first crop by truck to Bellows Falls. From there it goes to my biggest customer in New York.

Bob: What happened?

Malamon: The truck went over a cliff and we lost the entire crop. Neil was unscathed, however.

Bob: He was unlucky, anyway.

Malamon: My second crop came out rather badly. It takes about six weeks for a crop to be ready for harvest.

Bob: I was going to ask you that.

Malamon: I couldn't tend it properly because I was laid up. I got hit on the head with a horsehead that was hanging over the door of my greenhouse.

Bob: Yes, I can still see the lump there.

Malamon: No. That's the way it always was!

Bob: Well, go ahead.

Malamon: Besides me being laid up, the crop-dusting plane crashed, so a lot of the clovers ended up with leaves eaten away, and there's nothing more worthless than a four leaf clover with only two or three leaves!

Bob: I agree. Looks like this whole year past will have to be written off as a disaster.

Malamon: You know the rest. The day you visited me back in Henderson was the day the telephone pole fell on my greenhouse, destroying the entire third crop.

Bob: And that bit of misfortune involved your neighbor, if I remember correctly.

Malamon: Yes. He raises hares for rabbits' feet. Well, he had his truck laden with rabbits' feet and was headed for Bellows Falls when he swerved to avoid hitting a black cat...

Bob: ...and hit the pole, knocking it onto the greenhouse.

Malamon: Hardly any wonder you thought my story worthy of telling on Friday the thirteenth!

Bob: Right, and you certainly have had a tough time this year.

Malamon: Well things are looking up, though. I recently met a glass blower,

and we're going into business. He's made up some beautiful crystal glass
four leaf clovers that'll be surefire sellers. Would you like to see them?
Bob: Sure would.
Malamon: I'll get them.
Bob: And so I guess you'd say there is a silver lining behind every dark cloud.
Mr. Malamon's story of incredible bad luck apparently has a happy ending
after all . . . (loud crash of glass backstage)
Bob: On second thought . . .

An original verse the duo composed and often sang, with full
orchestral accompaniment, began the following way:

> I've got a rose between my toes from walking barefoot
> through the hothouse to you, pretty baby.
> I got it torn right near my corn from walking barefoot
> through the hothouse to you.

The evolution of Bob and Ray began in 1946 in Boston at WHDH,
where Elliott was morning man from 6:00 to 9:00 a.m. and Goulding
was newscaster. Born in 1923, Elliott had gone to drama school before
working for WHDH before and after the war. Goulding, a year older,
had been raised in nearby Lowell, Massachusetts, where his brother
worked for WLLH and gave him a job at the tender age of 17. He went
to WEEI in Boston and switched to WHDH after the war.

Bob and Ray worked many different shifts during their radio
careers. In 1953, they took an evening shift on the ABC network, then
in 1954 went back to 6:00 to 10:00 a.m. on WINS, with baritone newsman Peter Roberts, whom they always called "Bob Peters." When
WINS switched to a rock 'n' roll format later in the 1950s, Bob and Ray
did not fit in, and concentrated more on writing scripts and screen-
plays, and on being the cartoon voices for "Bert and Harry" for Piel's
beer.

Then, in the early 1970s, when WOR was experimenting with
different formats for its evening drive-time show "Radio N.Y.," Bob
and Ray were chosen as permanent hosts after several other tem-
porary hosts like Soupy Sales and Sandy Baron had filled in. The show
was almost a carbon copy of their WINS morning show, and lasted for
several years.

Goulding is no longer alive, so I am glad I had the opportunity to
meet both men in person back in the 1960s backstage during the brief
Broadway run of "Bob & Ray: The 2 and Only." Elliott and Goulding
were gracious in person, and as lovable as the characters they portrayed.

JACK LESCOULIE

Perhaps better known in television than radio because of his role as an original cohost of NBC's "Today" show, Jack Lescoulie went center stage in 1924 at age seven in a family vaudeville act, singing and dancing alongside a sister and brother. That was not too unusual, considering that Lescoulie was born into show business. His father was a technician in silent movie studios; his mother was an actress in the old Morosco stock company. By the time Lescoulie was a student at Fremont High School in Los Angeles in the early 1930s, he was performing in school plays. Lescoulie studied drama at several colleges in California and worked with a theater group. After winning a scholarship to the Pasadena Playhouse, he landed a role in the movie *Lottery Lover*, and did a brief stint as a disc jockey on KGFJ. He lost the radio job when he asked for a raise.

Lescoulie moved east to New York City when he was offered the part of an elephant in the Broadway production *Achilles Had a Heel*. He performed offstage, creating elephant calls—a talent he perfected by hanging out at a zoo and listening to elephants trumpet. Although the play had a successful trial run in Pasadena, it closed after only seven days on Broadway, leaving Lescoulie broke and forcing him to find work as a soda jerk and a delivery man for a dry-cleaning business. After a year, he made his way back home to California, where he returned to radio and took bit parts in low-budget movies. Professionally unsatisfied, he wanted a radio show of his own, and eventually created "The Grouch Club" with writer Nat Hiken. The show was picked up by NBC's Pacific Coast network and Lescoulie reaped the financial rewards until the show was dropped by its sponsors. Lescoulie then got a job spinning records at KFWB, but his earnings had dropped from $750 a week to $35 a week. He took "The Grouch Club" to WEAF in New York, but it was eventually dropped there also.

Lescoulie went on to serve in World War II as a combat reporter in the Army Air Force. He headed back to New York after the war, teaming up with Gene Rayburn to do a local early-morning radio show. He later joined WOR as an all-night disc jockey, tapping Jackie Gleason, then an unknown, as a guest. Finally, through a camp job in the Poconos, Lescoulie made the connections that would bring him stability and television success. He was hired as a production assistant at CBS, then became program director. In 1952, he was plucked away

Jack Lescoulie *(left)* **awarding a prize to a Bergen Co., N.J., paper boy for meritorious service.**

by NBC, helping to launch its "Today" show. (Lescoulie stayed for 15 years, with a brief absence in 1961.) Lescoulie was first teamed with Dave Garroway for more than nine years, displaying a wit and managing to enliven dull interviews. He later cohosted with Hugh Downs. On "Today," Lescoulie wrestled a walrus, had an apple shot off his head, and interviewed a penguin.

Despite his long run with "Today," Lescoulie was almost fired by NBC in the 1950s when Gleason, landing his own television show on CBS, offered an additional job to his old friend. Lescoulie took it, becoming the show's announcer. Although NBC was initially rattled, Lescoulie was asked to stay on until a replacement could be found. One was not. Eventually, Lescoulie also made commercials for Milton Berle's show and hosted NBC's sports-interview series called "Meet the Champions." In the early 1960s, he hosted an educational series for children on NBC. The show lasted one season. Lescoulie died in 1987.

ARTHUR GODFREY

Arthur Godrey literally burst onto radio in 1929 via an amateur show on Baltimore's WFBR. The "ole Redhead" had questionable talent as a single and banjo and ukulele player, but he eventually managed to build a remarkable rapport with radio listeners with his relaxed delivery. By the mid–1940s, he had built an estimated nation-wide audience of 40 million listeners and had to put sponsors on a waiting list. And, just as his career had been launched on an amateur hour, Godfrey at one point helped new talent by featuring them on his radio, and later, television shows.

Godfrey gained prominence in the 1930s and 1940s by poking fun at advertising copy, often ad-libbing and tossing away prepared scripts — sometimes to the chagrin of his bosses and his sponsors. In a more famous on-air episode, he grew embarrassed as he read the copy for a lingerie sale. "As I read it," Godfrey once told an inter-viewer, "my face got red and I said to myself, "Somebody's played a lousy trick on me."" But rather than turn off listeners, Godfrey, with his honest and spontaneous response to the copy, had piqued custo-mers' interest. The following day, women flocked to the department store to buy the lingerie.

Godfrey bounced from job to job prior to finding huge success on radio. Raised in Hasbrouck Heights, New Jersey, he was one of five children born to Kathryn Morton Godfrey and Arthur Hanbury God-frey. His father was a newspaperman and magazine writer. When family fortunes took a downturn, the young Godfrey quit high school and at the age of 15, ran away from home. He found a $10-a-week job in an architect's office in New York City. Robbed of his first week's pay, he washed dishes in exchange for a meal and slept nights between rolls of newsprint in the plant of the former *New York Tribune*.

Godfrey drifted into other jobs, trying his hand as an Army typist, a coal miner and a lumberjack. By 16, he made his way to Ohio, where he befriended an Irish police sergeant who helped him get a job as a finisher at a tire plant. Eventually a Catholic priest persuaded Godfrey to join the Navy and continue his education. Godfrey studied hard, taking radio training courses. Although he later passed the entrance exam for the Naval Academy in Annapolis, he volunteered for duty as a radio operator on a destroyer in the Mediterranean Sea during the Greek-Turkish War.

Arthur Godfrey

In 1924, following his hitch with the Navy, Godfrey resumed his nomadic ways, taking jobs that took him from New Jersey to Detroit, Michigan. He wrote advertising copy. He helped build Ford cars. He washed dishes, flipped hamburgers and managed a cheap hotel. In Detroit, he made a lot of money selling cemetery lots door to door, then sunk his savings into a traveling vaudeville show. In 1926 the show went broke in California, and Godfrey pawned his banjo and headed to Chicago. He worked for a while as a cab driver; then the following year, he enlisted in the Coast Guard.

One fateful night in 1929, Godfrey was with some buddies in a Baltimore, Maryland, speakeasy, listening to a radio station's amateur show. Spurred on by his friends, Godfrey went to WFBR with his banjo and was put on the air as "Red Godfrey, the Warbling Banjoist."

The station hired him, and Godfrey eventually became an announcer for the National Broadcasting Company's station in Washington, D.C. Though exuding personality on radio and using good diction, Godfrey had not yet hit upon the style that would bring him national fame. An automobile accident in 1931 changed all that.

While recuperating from severe injuries suffered in a head-on crash, Godfrey listened to the radio. And over the four to five months recovery period, he did not like what he heard. Finding that announcers spoke with too much formality, he decided that he would be much more informal on the air and speak to his listeners as if he were face-to-face with each. When he went back to work at NBC radio in Washington, he tried his new approach. His bosses thought he was still ill, but Godfrey had struck upon a style that charmed his listeners and sold products. By 1933, he was dismissed from NBC, but was quickly picked up by rival CBS station WJSV (later WTOP) in Washington, hosting "The Sundial" from 6:30 to 8:30 a.m. Like many other deejays who would copy his style in the 1940s, he hit a gong to announce the time. Godfrey became so popular that once when he wished aloud for coffee, some 8,000 early morning listeners showed up at the station with coffee in hand. In a typical show, Godfrey would chat about boating on the Potomac, the latest Joan Crawford film, or a poorly executed sound effect on a record he played. By 1941, his show was being carried in New York. But Godfrey's big break did not come until four years later when CBS radio gave him a half-hour morning show that featured live talent instead of records.

Godfrey grabbed the nation's attention in 1945 with his moving commentary of President Franklin D. Roosevelt's funeral procession. His voice cracked with emotion as he described what he saw, and when Roosevelt's vice president and successor approached, he wept. "God bless President Truman," Godfrey blurted to listeners. There were plenty of other memorable radio moments with Godfrey at the microphone. During one early morning show in his career, he announced that his station's decision to have him play the "William Tell Overture" was silly, considering that listeners were just waking up and probably wanted "a little peace and quiet." He broke the record midway through its play and gave his boss a Bronx cheer. "Those guys don't listen," he told his radio audience. "If they do, I won't be here tomorrow morning." But Godfrey was not fired. His success was growing.

By 1948, Godfrey was on radio day and night spinning records, telling jokes, and making fun of advertising copy. His "Girl Friday" was

Mug Richardson, an ex–beauty queen whom he had first hired as a secretary. Godfrey was on New York's WCBS from 6:00 to 7:45 a.m., then repeated the daily show by long-distance wire for Washington's WTOP. He also had a daily half-hour show on the CBS network, and a weekly Monday night show that showcased amateur talent. His long list of sponsors included Lipton Tea and Chesterfield cigarettes. While the early morning hours at times proved draining, Godfrey was well aware of the financial benefits. "That's $200,000 a year before the average fellow even gets to the audience," he once told a *Newsweek* interviewer.

Godfrey delighted in poking fun at advertising copy, much to the enjoyment of his listeners. "Aw, who wrote this stuff?" he would say. "Everybody knows Lipton's the best tea you can buy. So why get fancy about it? Getcha some Lipton's. Hot the pot with plain hot water for a few minutes, then put hot water on the tea and let it just sit there." Sponsors learned to give Godfrey free reign, especially since his wit, spontaneity and folksy manner often translated into sales of their product. In Godfrey, listeners had apparently found someone they felt they could trust.

Godfrey moved into television in December 1948, with "Arthur Godfrey's Talent Scouts," and later hosted "Arthur Godfrey and His Friends" and "The Arthur Godfrey Show." He continued in radio as well, helping to launch the careers of such entertainers as Julius La Rosa and Rosemary Clooney. Later chagrined when La Rosa got an agent and formed a recording company, Godfrey stunned his audience by dismissing La Rosa on the air. "That was his swan song," Godfrey announced after La Rosa had finished singing "I'll Take Manhattan."

Godfrey made a tearful farewell to this radio audience in 1959, when he discovered he had lung cancer. After his recovery, he attempted a comeback in television, but the medium had changed. His live network radio show continued until the CBS network began recording the broadcasts to be aired at the discretion of affiliates. Miffed that so many stations relegated the program to "dead of night" time slots, Godfrey quit CBS in 1972 and never had a regular show again. He was 79 when he died in 1983.

Part II
The Golden Age

Hundreds of articles and essays have been written about the "golden age of radio," discussing some aspect of network programs before the advent of television: "The Jack Benny Show," "The Shadow," "Charlie McCarthy," "Gangbusters." Virtually all of these programs were broadcast in the evening, or "prime time," as it has come to be called. But the golden age was not limited to nationally renowned persons, nor to the nighttime hours. Long before stations developed specialized formats to cultivate a stable audience, the value of a popular early morning host as a "hook" to keep listeners tuned later in the day became apparent.*

There is no time of day more important to local radio stations than early morning. Before television, early morning programs were the only way for listeners to immediately learn about the day's weather, travel conditions, local news, school closings, and other vital information. By the time television had caught up to offer comparable information, most people had automobiles and needed local information while driving to work, school, or recreation.

The morning man was, and is, a reflection of the culture and social mores outside the radio studio. It was no coincidence that the most popular morning deejays in virtually every American city in the 1940s were gracious, articulate, and reserved. After all, that was the way people were expected to behave in public. In fact, the morning man could reinforce this behavior by inspiring listeners with flawless diction and impeccable manners, just as Clark Gable or Ronald Colman did with movie-goers. It would probably astonish a lot of youngsters to learn that many morning men dressed for work in suits and ties, even though no one could see them. It behooved a station to seek out a warm, well-known individual to open the broadcast day to build an audience not only for the day, but in some cases for decades.

This device is still practiced today by television network executives who place a very popular show in a new lineup prior to one for which they wish to build ratings.

Format radio was the primary cause of the decline of the golden age. Like the fall of the Roman Empire, it has been a slow and almost imperceptible death which still is not consummated. Some remnants of the golden age survive in the form of aged morning men left over from that era, or successors who have bucked the trend by following an earlier style. They are testament to the fact that not everyone is indifferent to the demise of warm, homespun radio personalities.

JACK STERLING

In an interview with *Tropic* magazine, the inimitable Steve Allen quipped that television talk-show hosts are like radio deejays: very few have or need any talent. But Allen himself was a deejay in an era when he and his contemporaries had some combination of wit, class, musical knowledge, a theatrical background, and personal warmth.

Jack Sterling had all of the above. From the late 1940s to the early 1960s, his morning show on New York's WCBS offered a blend of live entertainment unparalleled in originality. A live five-piece orchestra comprised of top jazz musicians supplemented the recorded music and provided a background for Sterling's limitless supply of skits, monologues, and anecdotes.

It all came naturally for the seasoned performer, who literally grew up in the theater. Sterling's father had a stock company in Saskatchewan, and little Jack (né Jack Sexton) traveled all over with his parents and sister, staying in boardinghouses and appearing in child parts. At the age of seven, he improvised a vaudeville act when a scheduled performer failed to show up. He sang, told jokes, and did a monologue. The audience was ecstatic, and his father beamed with pride. But the road show was no place for school-aged children, so his parents gave up the theater and opened a restaurant. The theater was in Sterling's blood, though, and at the age of 15 he signed up with a stock company. When the Depression cut into theater attendance, he emceed on a Mississippi riverboat and at various nightclubs.

It was at a club in Peoria, Illinois, that Sterling was discovered by WMBP radio, and asked to do a 12-minute routine of songs and gags on the air for the then magnanimous sum of $5. He became a regular there, then moved to WTAD in Quincy, Illinois, and then to KMOX in St. Louis, where he became program director. He then became program director at WBBM in Chicago, one of the largest CBS affiliates.

Sterling's big break came in 1947, when the ubiquitous Arthur Godfrey decided to give up his stint as morning man at WCBS. Sterling made an audition record, sent it to New York, and did not give the job a second thought until WCBS telephoned him to come in for a meeting with Godfrey. After several interviews, Sterling was hired with the mandate that he change his name from Sexton to Sterling.

Taking over a show from a celebrity as popular as Godfrey was both a curse and a blessing. A curse because the Godfrey followers missed him and used him as the standard by which Sterling was measured. A blessing because Sterling automatically captured most of the ratings from those accustomed to turning to WCBS. To retain that audience, though, Sterling would have to be talented in his own right. Sterling's ratings did slip a bit, but that can be attributed to WNBC's bringing in "Buffalo" Bob Smith as morning man. Prior to WNBC's entry into the early morning competition with a heavy hitter, the only serious competition to Godfrey was WOR's John Gambling.

Back in the late 1940s, when most New York area people commuted to work by train or bus, the concept of a "morning drive-time" show had not been born. By 8:00 a.m. at the latest, the breadwinner was presumed to be at or en route to work, and there were no portable radios to be carried along. For that reason, most morning shows ran from 6:00 to 8:00 a.m. Sterling's show was no exception. By the mid–1950s, program directors realized that they could boost ratings and sell more prime-rate commercial time by lengthening the duration of the morning show. Sterling's show was expanded to 5:30 and 9:00 a.m. in order to reach early commuters who had long distances to drive, as well as farmers in exurban areas like Hackettstown, New Jersey, and Monroe, New York. Much of the 5:30 to 6:00 a.m. portion was devoted to agricultural news and egg and vegetable prices, prepared with Sterling's whimsical commentary and up-tempo music (never rock 'n' roll, however).

After 6:00 a.m., the whimsies grew into longer routines, coming into full bloom after 6:30 a.m., when the live band came on duty. Tyree Glenn played vibes, trombone, valve trombone, banjo, and player piano. The regular pianist was Tony Aless. Andy Fitzgerald was on clarinet. Buddy Jones was on bass, and Mary Osborne on guitar rounded out the band. An LP record, now extremely rare, was issued.

Along with lively banter with the musicians, Sterling had a number of regular entertainment features, some quite brief (akin to today's faster pace) and others more labored. Brief interludes included Sterling's "Anti-Collegiate Dictionary," which defined "adverse" as a commercial jingle and "explain" as eggs without ham. Another feature, "Yuck for a Buck," offered a dollar for a listener's joke if used on the air. "Where could I get a writer for a buck a day?" laughed Sterling. The longer features gave Sterling the actor a chance to really shine. The following was one of Sterling's "Feeble Fables," "The Mouse Who Learned Self-Confidence":

> Once upon a time there was a mouse named Elroy. Elroy was a timid little fellow. He always ran away from human beings and cats. And when he saw a mousetrap, he gave it a wide berth.
>
> Then one day he met a mouse whose name was Dale Vincent Overstreet. Dale was a great believer in the doctrine that self-confidence is the key to success, which he had proved by writing several books on the subject, all of which were book club selections. "Elroy," he said, fixing our hero with a glittering eye, "just keep repeating to yourself, 'You never know what you can do till you try.'" Elroy spent the whole night repeating, "You never know what you can do till you try." The next day he marched out of the mousehole, bold as brass. And the first time he saw a human being, he reared up on his hind legs and squeaked. The human being in question happened to be female, and nervous, and she jumped up on a chair and screamed. Elroy was drunk with power!
>
> He went right up to a mousetrap and stole a piece of cheese. The trap had been improperly set, so he got away with that, too. From then on, Elroy was insufferable. He went around to all the other mice telling them, "You never know what you can do till you try." "Sure, sure," they said. So to prove his point, Elroy went looking for a cat. The cat was sleeping in front of the fire, and Elroy went right up and punched him in the nose. The cat opened one eye, reached out with one paw, and knocked Elroy flat.
>
> Moral, you never know what you can't do till you try, either!

Better yet was the array of zany characters which Sterling voiced: the old philosopher from Juniper Jct., Maine; Colonel Basil Rumphingham returning from "Injiah"; news analyst John Commerabund Sneezy; and know-it-all scientist Dr. Hiawatha Hackenschmidt.

According to retired broadcaster David Moore, one of Sterling's best friends for decades, Sterling was brimming with an endless supply of anecdotes and impersonations off the air too. Moore stated that many of the characters Sterling portrayed "were the kind your maiden aunt would pretend she didn't like." A loving, caring family man, Sterling raised his daughters Patty, Beth, and Cathie in Connecticut during the WCBS years. He would rise at 3:30 a.m., shower and shave, and drive to the Stamford Railroad Station to catch the 4:20 a.m. into Grand Central. Producer Bob Vanderheyden recalled that "if that train was late, one half of New York's favorite broadcasters would be missing, including much of the 'Today' show crew."

At the 9:00 a.m. end of the show, Sterling's day was far from finished. There were meetings with producers and sponsors, supermarket dedications (which were popular in postwar suburbia), rehearsals for the next day's show, and prerecording sessions for the Saturday show. On Saturdays, Sterling was ringmaster on CBS's "The Big Top."

Daily client luncheons were a key ingredient in Sterling's success formula. Because Sterling appreciated good food and drink and possessed impeccable social graces, he cultivated a stable of loyal advertisers and paid them back with his personal product endorsements on the air. In the 1960s, the show was extended to 10:00 a.m., and "by then, all the WCBS bills were paid," Vanderheyden declared. Unfortunately, by 1966, the old ways of doing business were fading along with fedoras and wing-tip shoes. Arbitron ratings, not swanky luncheons or even personality, were all that most advertisers cared about. Sterling saw WINS succeed with an all-news format, and, perhaps sensing the future direction of WCBS, resigned. The station replaced him with Pat Summerall, a former New York Giants place-kicker with no radio experience outside of sports. Summerall was soon dropped when WCBS went all-news.

Sterling resurfaced within a few months as morning man on New York's WHN, with 15-minute newscasts on the hour delivered by suave, sophisticated Dean Lewis. The station, however, was no WCBS, in either wattage or tradition. While the show at WHN retained occasional quips and comments, it provided little showcase for Sterling's theatrical talent. Following the national trend, chatter at WHN took a back seat to bland recorded music by innocuous groups such as the Midas Touch and the Ray Conniff Singers. To say that Sterling had passed his peak would be unfair; demand for Sterling's type of show was disappearing. In 1969, Sterling withdrew to Connecticut, where he became morning man for a while on WEZN in Bridgeport before hanging up his microphone.

Sterling had been blessed with fame and fortune, all of which he modestly took in stride. But for the last 20 years of his life, his luck went somewhat awry. He divorced twice, and although his third marriage to Trish was a good one, during that time Sterling developed lung cancer. Unable to bear the Connecticut winters, he and his wife tearfully bade farewell to their circle of friends and relocated to Stuart, Florida. It was a lush, beautiful place to live, but Sterling's health continued to decline. Sterling's savings also declined, due partly to a disastrous investment in a Westchester County, N.Y., restaurant, as well as ownership in four out-of-town radio stations. Sterling's talents lay in entertainment, not business.

One day in 1991, Sterling called his wife to his bedside and told her he was going to die. There were no tears or regrets, but no jokes either. He thanked her for being there for him during the more difficult years. "He grasped my hand, said 'good-bye,' and he was gone," Mrs. Sterling tearfully recounted. A touching ending to be sure, but I prefer Sterling's closing scroll from WCBS, a parody of television variety shows of that time:

> The dramatic portion of this program was spontaneous and unrehearsed. It's just that Buddy's belt broke.
> Mr. Aless' piano decorated by Mr. Aless' cigarette butts.
> Miss Osborne's guitar dusted by Miss Osborne's sleeve.
> Tyree Glenn's goatee by Monty Woolley.
> Mr. Fitzgerald's performance of Bartók's Concerto was not heard because Mr. Fitzgerald never heard of Bartók's Concerto.
> Jokes on this program were uncalled for.
> Mr. Sterling's wardrobe by Mrs. Sterling.
> So long, folks—see you tomorrow morning.

"BUFFALO" BOB SMITH

Just about every "baby boomer" knows that "Buffalo" Bob Smith created "The Howdy Doody Show," but few of them know that Smith also had an illustrious radio career years before that. In fact, the moniker "Buffalo Bob" had nothing to do with the western theme from "Howdy Doody." Smith got the name from his hometown of Buffalo, New York, where, as an 11-year-old, at his father's behest, he auditioned for "The Boys' Club of the Air" at WGR. For no pay, he was chosen to play piano, sing, and announce spelling bee words. It was "the sort of experience I could never have bought at any price," Smith reflected.

As a senior in high school in 1933, Smith and two classmates were a smashing success in the school's Gilbert & Sullivan operetta. The three boys formed a trio and auditioned for the "Simon Supper Club of the Air" at WGR's chief competitor, WBEN. They were hired to sing three nights a week as "The Hi-Hatters," for the then large sum of $25 per boy per week. When the immensely popular Kate Smith

"Buffalo" Bob Smith

came to town, nearly 1,000 acts tried out for her CBS network show. The Hi-Hatters were one of just two acts selected. But after a few months of living in a hotel room, Smith and one of his classmates felt homesick. So, when WGR offered Smith a job as a staff pianist and as a partner in a singing duo with his classmate Johnny Eisenberger, he jumped at the chance and returned to Buffalo.

A big break came for Smith in 1942, when Corning Glass Works offered him $250 to prepare and present a Sunday afternoon live remote talent show over WENY in Elmira and WHCU in Ithaca. Smith would board a train on Friday night, rehearse and audition Saturday, and broadcast on Sunday before riding home. Meanwhile,

Smith's duties during the week were increasing. He did a quiz show with Foster Brooks on WGR called "Stump Bob Smith." He also emceed, produced, directed, and wrote "The Cheer Up Gang," a daily variety show which WGR fed to the Mutual Network.

At that time, Buffalo's number one rated morning man, Clint Buehlman, was lured away from WGR to WBEN. Buehlman's new show ran from 6:00 to 9:00 a.m., followed by 15 minutes of news. Then, most listeners would switch over to ABC's "Breakfast Club" with Don MacNeil. To hold on to some of the audience, WBEN's promotional director, Julian Trivers, decided to team up the station's heavy-hitter, Buehlman, with Smith for a show similar to MacNeil's, but all locally based. Called "Early Date at Hengerer's," in just six months, the show turned the ratings around from 3 percent of the Buffalo market share to over three times the "Breakfast Club's," which had been 17 percent. Smith was a sensation with his piano playing, singing, stunts, and contests. Such a sensation, in fact, that in 1946 WBEN offered to double Smith's salary if he would leave the Corning job and do a Sunday afternoon quiz show, and an hour-long lunchtime show on weekdays.

The general manager at WBEN was so excited about the success of "Early Date at Hengerer's" that he tried to convince the NBC network to air the program. The network liked what it heard, but the local tie-in was not appropriate for a national audience. Instead, NBC offered Smith a job as the first morning man at WEAF, which later became WNBC. So Smith moved his wife Mil and children to Westchester County in August 1946, and began his six-day-a-week commute to midtown Manhattan.

The "Bob Smith Show" ran from 7:00 to 8:30 a.m. initially, then from 6:30 to 8:30 a.m., and later from 6:00 to 8:30 a.m., and was followed by "Tex & Jinks," a husband-and-wife talk show. Smith was witty and clever on the air, but one of his best talents was his ability to accurately segue into and out of records using his piano. He would ask the engineer (usually Jack Petry) to cue the record, and he would then imitate the artist or make some funny remark while playing the piano. For example, if he had a commercial to do before a Vaughn Monroe record, Smith would pretend to interview Monroe in person (which was really Smith himself), and have "Monroe" sing the commercial as a segue into the real record. This required a precise rehearsal which few modern deejays bother to do any more.

By now, Smith was earning $600 per week plus commissions on commercial sales, an incredible sum for 1947. This enabled Smith to hire his own writers, one of whom was Bob Keeshan, who went on to become Clarabell the Clown and Captain Kangaroo. Station executives then asked Smith to host a children's show on Saturdays at 9:30 a.m., the "Triple-B Ranch," which was renamed "The Howdy Doody Show" and evolved into television the next year.

The "Howdy Doody" radio and television shows, along with other television work for NBC, strained Smith's schedule. He gave up the morning deejay position in 1952, but in 1954, he had a 10:00 to 11:00 a.m. national variety show on NBC radio.

Preparing for and performing in all these positions took its toll that year. Smith suffered a heart attack and was unable to work for several months. On doctor's orders, he gave up all of his radio and television work except for "The Howdy Doody Show."

While most of Smith's old competitors are now gone, "Buffalo Bob," who came close to death in 1954, is still active, lecturing across the country about "The Howdy Doody Show" and the early days of television. His brief time as a morning man is overshadowed by his pioneering work in television. But "Buffalo Bob" was one of the trailblazers who set the pace and style for other pre–rock 'n' roll deejays like his successors at WNBC, Johnny Andrews and, later, "Big" Wilson.

FRANK HARDEN
and JACK WEAVER

One of the longest running morning duos in radio, Frank Harden and Jack Weaver bantered on WMAL in Washington, D.C. for 32 years until 1992, when Weaver died from complications of diabetes.

For most of its years, the show was a blend of music and talk, until music was eliminated entirely in the 1990s. During the 1980s, the music format alternated between contemporary songs and traditional 1930s and 1940s standard songs.

Harden and Weaver's magic revolved around Weaver's ability to impersonate people, including women, and Harden's ability to play the straight man. The gentlemen were also noted for their longwinded anecdotes and topical comments.

The following are examples of news items covered in a typical program.

Frank Harden and Jack Weaver

- "Due to the drought in Australia for several years, officials may have to cancel the wild boar races. There aren't enough 50-pound boars that are ideal for racing. Some of the boars are too large, with tusks too dangerous to race."
- "A wedding had to be canceled because the judge never showed up. By the time a minister could be summoned, most of the guests had left in disgust. The couple is suing the judge for $2,200. The judge's comment when he finally was reached was, 'I plumb forgot.'"
- "On this day in 1977, a man got out of his straitjacket in 21 seconds. Maybe that doesn't amaze you, but he did it while suspended from a helicopter!" Harden: "'What do you hold onto?'"

Although there was nothing spectacular about these topics, they provided a comfortable and friendly ambience for the Washington area wake-up crowd. On the negative side, the show had become so cluttered with commercials, traffic reports, and other housekeeping chores, that little time was left for the creative dialogues. One radio critic also felt that Harden and Weaver had aged and had lost some of their dazzle from decades past. Nevertheless, the program remained creative and full-service, with superb newscaster Bud Steele backing up Harden and Weaver.

In the early 1990s, the Saturday shows were discontinued.

Gene Klavan 35

In October, 1992, 72-year-old Jackson Weaver died. Tim Brandt and Andy Parks have joined Frank Harden, while Jack's son Mark Weaver, who has his own show, occasionally makes an appearance. The talk format, while not as corny and folksy as it used to be, still retains much of the original flavor of the program.

GENE KLAVAN

In musical taste, I may have been my father's son, but when it came to radio personalities, I was more like my grandfather. While my grandfather and I were unswerving John Gambling fans, at our family breakfast table, Klavan and Finch reigned supreme. My father loved the zany characters they portrayed, Klavan's hilarious guitar compositions, and the comedy records they played, especially by Stan Freberg and Larry Verne.

Actually, my father's listening to WNEW began prior to Klavan joining the team. Before "Klavan and Finch" in 1952 there was "Rayburn and Finch," with Gene Rayburn as cohost. And before 1947, there was "Jack and Gene," with Jack Lescoulie as the straight man.

New York's WNEW was the first radio station in the United States to develop a 24-hour deejay format. Before television, when radio was expected to provide a variety of programming, the morning man was often a station's only deejay; drama, comedy, quiz shows, soaps, and variety shows comprised the rest of the day. But WNEW's station manager Bernice Judis decided to gamble on a new format which set the standard for the next three decades: pop music 24 hours a day hosted by deejays on four- to six-hour shifts.

Judis sensed what every station manager knows today: a morning man (or team) which "hooks" listeners will help ratings later in the day. People will tend to keep the dial set at the position they choose when they awake.

By 1952, when Gene Rayburn announced his departure for the NBC network, other stations were changing over to deejay formats. It was the golden era of personalities, and WNEW executives knew they needed a heavy-hitter to hold Rayburn's place.

Baltimore native Eugene Klavan had always loved radio, and got his first job with Baltimore's WCBM in 1947. He quickly ascended to morning man at $63 a week. One day, Klavan got a call from Al Ross, morning man at the city's largest and oldest station, WBAL. Ross wanted to steal Klavan away as afternoon man. The deal was to be kept quiet. Unfortunately, Klavan fell on the steps at WBAL, broke his ankle, and attracted attention. Suspecting hanky-panky, WCBM demoted Klavan, who then quit. Klavan briefly worked for WITH and for WAAM-TV in Baltimore before getting a late-night show on clear-channel WTOP in Washington, where he was discovered by a friend of Durwood "Dee" Finch. He successfully auditioned for Rayburn's vacant position at WNEW and started on November 17, 1952.

Witty Gene Rayburn, with his unlimited supply of gags, like a bubbling faucet and sound bites from "St. George and the Dragon-Net," would be a tough act to follow, but Klavan had his own bag of tricks to draw from: an assortment of fictitious characters he could impersonate. Dr. Sy Cology, who offered outrageous advice to everyone, was the most enduring, if not endearing, character. Victor Verse, poet "lariat," was perhaps the most well-known of Klavan's coterie. He would make up little ditties to go with commercials and news items. For example, when in the late 1950s, Alaska and Hawaii were admitted as states, Victor proclaimed:

> Who let Alaska and Hawaii in
> To join our sacred union?
> Who let Alaskans and Hawaiians
> Enlarge the old communion?
> When we had only 48
> For poets, what proclivity
> To rhyme with 8 with state and great?
> But what will rhyme with fivity?

The poetry burst into full song when Klavan, in the early 1960s, got a guitar and accompanied himself off-key. Even weather forecasts were often given in a sing-song dialect with the twanging guitar.

Some of Klavan's characters were parodies of WNEW executives and the media bureaucracy. "Mr. Nat, coordinator of interrelations" was supposed to be producer Nat Asch, but only insiders and hard-core radio afficionados knew this.

Klavan also dared to spoof his sponsors, sometimes going beyond the limits of that time. For example, when Piel's beer produced a pretentious commercial with a voice resembling a Jewish cantor singing "Piels did it, Piels did it, put draft beer in a can," Klavan exclaimed, "why doesn't somebody shut him up!" And when Di-Gel was first introduced with the new miracle ingredient simethecone, Klavan averred

Gene Klavan

it was really part of a person, Seymour Methicone, known as "Sy" for short. Klavan would even mock some of the claims made by his advertisers. For example, if a lawn conditioner supposedly made grass easier to cut, Klavan would say, "Sure, after your lawn is burned out, cutting it will be no effort at all." Such quips seem tame compared to those uttered by the shock jocks of the 1990s, but it was radical for the 1950s to poke fun at a sponsor. Klavan was often called on the carpet about it, but most of the time it worked. After thirty years, I still remember some of Klavan's remarks about products.

Klavan and Finch also constantly mocked the records they played, often interspersing straight songs with incongruous pieces of other songs. For example, when they were playing Bobby Darin's "Beyond the Sea," they would have the engineer cue a phrase from an old Sir Harry Lauter record, "sailing on the good ship Kangaroo, yes I do, ho ho!" when Darin sang "never again I'll go sailing." This practice was in the tradition of Rayburn and Finch, but Klavan was just as skilled in making the selections. Sometimes, Klavan himself would inject a phrase in the middle of a song. It all provided a delicious, unexpected, spontaneous quality for the program.

With the advent of rock 'n' roll, Klavan and Finch steered a middle course between the deejays like Harry Harrison on New York's WMCA, who played only top 40 songs, and John Gambling, who initially played no rock 'n' roll at all. The format was heavily vocal "middle of the road" (M.O.R.) with a sprinkling of rock and big band. Such a format would not have worked a few decades later because it would have deterred more listeners than it would have attracted. But in 1960, a Nancy Wilson–Frankie Avalon–Oscar Peterson– Elvis Presley–Frank Sinatra lineup was satisfactory to most people. A Frank Chacksfield fan would probably listen to John Gambling anyway.

With the departure of the ailing Dee Finch in 1968, WNEW could have named another successor to be the straight man, but by this time the straight man in a morning radio duo was becoming an anachronism. Instead, WNEW let Klavan go solo, retitling the show "Klavan & Friends."

Now, instead of directing his trick voices at Finch, Klavan would answer them himself in his real voice, just as he had done whenever Finch was sick or away. It was double the work, but the $200,000 compensation, plus the uncontested fame, made it worthwhile. Despite the exclusive fame, Klavan really did miss Finch, who died in 1983. "He was absolutely fantastic," Klavan recalled, crediting Finch with many of the ad-libs that appeared to be initiated by Klavan.

It was about this time that I met Klavan purely by accident. To earn some money as a college student, I was working as a clerk in a camera shop in Great Neck, Long Island. A thin, bespectacled man dropped off film for developing under the name Klavan. I asked him if he was Gene Klavan, and he replied negatively and walked out.

After my boss laughed and assured me that the gentleman was indeed Gene Klavan, I persisted when he returned for his photos. He admitted he had lied. When I explained to him my passion for radio, Klavan warmed up to me. I have forgotten the rest of our conversation, except for one important part: Klavan warned me about a disturbing trend in the industry to depersonalize and to limit the artistic freedom of the deejay. He said he was constantly battling WNEW executives over their "more music, less talk" policy. Only Klavan's high ratings enabled him to defy 13 different general managers in his final 12 years and continue with his lengthy funny dialogues and skits. He was deeply concerned about how younger aspiring talented people would find an outlet for their talents. What I learned privately from Klavan in 1968 spread publicly a couple of years later. The *New York Times* reported that Klavan was embroiled in disputes over which kinds of music to play and over the use of the verbal routines. In November 1977, Klavan announced he would not renew his contract with WNEW. "I became persona non grata at WNEW," Klavan bitterly recalled. "In radio, they're used to firing people and then feeling sorry for you. I just quit so they resented me. I wasn't even invited to participate in their gala anniversary reunion."

For New Year 1978, Klavan resurfaced on WOR in the afternoon drive-time slot of 3:00 to 7:00 p.m. "Having him at WOR," boasted general manager Rick Devlin, "means we've gotten rid of a chief competitor in the morning." But the temperamental Klavan, whose afternoon show on WOR closely resembled his previous morning show, got into a dispute. When Devlin told Klavan in 1981 that his show was being shortened from 4:00 to 7:00 p.m., Klavan refused to lose the hour, so WOR silenced him; the station continued to honor his contract, paying Klavan to remain idle. A noncompete clause prevented Klavan from broadcasting elsewhere for the next two years. Klavan then was hired as a host for ARTS, the predecessor to the A&E cable TV channel. This was followed by a brief stint as a satirist for WCBS-TV News in New York.

In 1986, WNEW, which had replaced Klavan with Ted Brown Monday through Friday, rehired him for Saturdays only from 8:00 a.m. to 12:00 noon. While this could have been a transition back to full-time morning radio, times had changed, and FM radio had already stolen away millions of listeners from AM stations. The station sadly could no longer afford to pay for a top talent like Klavan, not even if he did work only on Saturdays. Within a year, Klavan's radio career was over.

But Klavan's overall story ends happily. After announcing for a revived NBC-TV "House Party," an audience participation show formerly starring Art Linkletter, which bombed, Klavan got a job from 1991 to 1994 taping intros and "outros" for television's American Movie Channel. "It's a lot easier than doing live radio, and the pay is great!" Klavan concluded. Klavan now is writing a play and a third book; in the 1960s he wrote an autobiography called *We Die at Dawn* and in the 1970s, a critique of the radio industry called *Turn That Damned Thing Off*. He currently resides in New York City.

BOB STEELE

In the volatile broadcasting business, where deejays often are "here today, gone tomorrow," Bob Steele is a phenomenon. For an incredible 48 years he reigned as morning man at WTIC, remaining the most popular drive-time deejay in the Hartford, Connecticut, market for virtually that entire period.

Born in 1911 in Kansas City, Missouri, Steele spent most of his childhood helping his divorced mother make ends meet. Although he was a good student, his teachers called him a "natural reader," Steele dropped out of school several times to take odd jobs. At age 8, he delivered prescriptions for a drug store. As a teenager, he was a Western Union messenger and a candy butcher on trains. In the early 1930s he tried his hand at prizefighting and went out to Hollywood where he got parts in early sound movies as a stuntman on a motorcycle. But life was still a struggle and Steele ended up on the WPA payroll as a timekeeper on a farm.

"One day a guy came running across the field and he had a telegram," Steele recounted. "I couldn't imagine anybody bringing a telegram to me in the middle of a carrot field. It said 'Come to Hartford as soon as you can. You've got a job, $30 a week.'" The job required Steele to announce motorcycle races over a public address system. The money was a good deal more than Steele was making with the WPA, so he began hitchhiking to Hartford. Steele's ride let him off in downtown Hartford at 2:00 a.m. on May 10, 1936, right across from the railroad station. Steele felt homesick and frightened. He noticed the statue of Indians raising their tomahawks by the Corning fountain in Bushnell Park, and in the eerie moonlight, he actually thought for a moment that they were alive.

At least in those days one did not have to worry about getting mugged. "It wasn't the style then," Steele commented. Not that it would have mattered much; Steele had only two dimes in his pocket. All of his clothes were in two broken-down cardboard suitcases. He had no coat, it was 40 degrees, and he was freezing.

Steele trudged over to the YMCA, but even in the depths of the Depression, 20 cents was not enough for a room. Steele promised to pay the remaining 80 cents the next day, but the clerk refused to admit him. "I thought this was the Young Men's Christian Association," Steele protested. "I'm a Christian, and I have no place to stay." The clerk claimed he had no more rooms, so Steele walked down to the Garde Hotel, at the time the most elegant lodging in Hartford. Too proud to ask for payment in advance, they gave Steele a room. The next day Steele called the race promoter, George Lannom, who advanced him five dollars. Steele paid his $1.50 room bill and went to work.

When the race season ended in September, Steele was left unemployed. One of the motorcyclists from the West Coast offered Steele a ride back. He was leaving the next day, so Steele had one day to kill. Steele passed by the Princess Theater, which, like the Garde Hotel and Bulkely Stadium, is no longer standing. In those days, most movie theaters had an outside cage with a ticket seller inside. The girl told Steele, "There's a mystery on. Come back in about 25 minutes and you'll see the beginning of the thing. Go in now and you'll ruin it."

With nothing in particular to do, Steele crossed the green and went into the Travelers Building. Travelers Insurance at that time owned WTIC. One of Steele's lifelong ambitions was to be a radio announcer, but in those days of polish and precision, announcers were usually required to have college degrees—which few persons did— and to speak three languages. So it took quite a bit of nerve for a racecaster with no real credentials to just walk into a premier network station and ask for a job.

As luck would have it, the station was conducting auditions that very day. He tried out with 13 other men and impressed chief announcer Fred Wade with his baritone voice and warm personality. Wade hired him on a trial basis at $35 a week.

Steele's background in boxing and motorcycling, coupled with

Bob Steele

his keen interest in baseball, quickly earned him a regular program, "Strictly Sports," at 6:15 p.m. When he correctly predicted that the St. Louis Browns would win the American League baseball pennant, folks started relying on Steele's sports predictions, which actually turned out wrong more often than right.

In 1943, when morning man Ben Hawthorne enlisted in the army, Steele was offered the job, replacing Hawthorne's wife, who had temporarily been assigned the 7:00 to 8:00 a.m. slot. At the time, the show was named "The G. Fox Morning Watch Program," after the large Hartford department store which sponsored the hour.

Gradually, through the years, the program was expanded back to

6:45 a.m., forward to 9:00 and 10:00 a.m., then expanded again to run 6:00 to 10:00 a.m., and finally 5:30 to 10:00 a.m., Monday through Saturday.

Unlike most other morning men who changed their style of broadcasting and music to cater to changing popular tastes, Steele maintained a remarkably similar style throughout the six decades in which he broadcasted. Steele tapped a xylophone for time checks, while a live staff announcer like Ed Anderson or Floyd Richards would read commercial copy and introduce weather reports and news. Steele's rambling discourses would cover every topic imaginable, from sports figures to fashion. His slow, articulate manner was anachronistic by the late 1960s, but Steele steadfastly refused to change. In fact, until the mid–1970s, no record that smacked of a rock beat would be aired during the morning hours. Instead, Steele continued to play records by artists such as Frankie Carle, Russ Morgan, and Claus Ogerman, who were immensely popular before the advent of rock 'n' roll. Sometimes Steele would whistle or sing along with the record. Eventually, the music policy gave way to more contemporary artists such as Air Supply and Dr. Hook, as older listeners died off and the show needed to appeal to listeners born after 1955 to hold its ratings.

Nevertheless, most of the nonmusical features of the program remained unchanged. A "word for the day" would give listeners a lesson in pronunciation; these features would be summed up on the Saturday show with a review of words for the week. The birthday list noted everyone 80 years old or older. Another section of the program, "Teletype Tiddlywinks," provided the lighter side of the news. And Steele had so many jokes, poems, and humorous anecdotes that he repeated year after year, they were eventually compiled in a now out-of-print book, *Bob Steele: A Man and His Humor*. Until the 1980s, he would play a recorded story just for children at 7:45 a.m. each day. These stories were often a series of sides from old 78 RPM albums, such as *Rusty in Orchestraville* or Hugh Brannum's *Little Orly*.

The following is a good example of Steele's inoffensive but informative humor: "Why do so many persons insist on saying 'irregardless,'" Steele rebuked. "Regardless is sufficient, unless you mean that the entire security force on Lake Erie went on strike and left Erie guardless." Other Steele routines were more drawn out and became centerpieces of the program, such as "The Lion and Albert," told in a cockney accent. (English comedian Stanley Holloway also has used this verse.)

There's a famous seaside place called Blackpool,
  That's noted for fresh air and fun,
And Mr. and Mrs. Ramsbottom
  Went there with young Albert, their son.

A grand little lad was young Albert,
  All dressed in his best; quite a swell
With a stick with an 'orse's 'head 'andle,
  The finest that Woolworth's could sell.

They didn't think much to the Ocean;
  The waves, they was fiddlin' and small,
There was no wrecks and nobody drownded,
  Fact, nothing to laugh at at all.

So, seeking for further amusement,
  They paid and went into the Zoo,
Where they'd Lions and Tigers and Camels,
  An old ale and sandwiches too.

There were one great big Lion called Wallace;
  His nose were all covered with scars—
He lay in a somnolent posture.
  With the side of a face on the bars.

Now Albert had heard about Lions,
  How they were ferocious and wild—
To see Wallace lying so peaceful,
  Well, it didn't seem right to the child.

So straightway the brave little feller,
  Not showing a morsel of fear,
Took his stick with its 'orse's 'ead 'andle
  And pushed it in Wallace's ear.

You could see that the Lion didn't like it,
  For giving a kind of a roll,
He pulled Albert inside the cage with 'im,
  And swallowed the little lad 'ole.

Then Pa, who had seen the occurrence,
  And didn't know what to do next,
Said, "Mother! Yon Lion's 'et Albert,"
  And Mother said, "Well, I am vexed!"

Then Mr. and Mrs. Ramsbottom—
  Quite rightly, when all's said and done—
Complained to the Animal keeper,
  That the Lion had eaten their son.

The keeper was quite nice about it;
  He said, "What a nasty mishap.
Are you sure that it's your boy he's eaten?"
  Pa said, "Am I sure? There's his cap!"

The manager had to be sent for.
    He came and he said "What's to do?"
Pa said, "Yon Lion's 'et Albert,
    And 'im in his Sunday clothes, too."

Then Mother said, "Right's right, young feller;
    I think it's a shame and a sin,
For a lion to go and eat Albert,
    And after we've paid to come in."

The manager wanted no trouble,
    He took out his purse right away,
Saying, "How much to settle the matter?"
    And Pa said, "What do you usually pay?"

But Mother had turned a bit awkward
    When she thought where Albert had gone,
She said "No! someone's got to be summonsed" —
    So that was decided upon.

Then off they went to the P'lice Station,
    In front of the Magistrate chap
They told 'im what happened to Albert,
    And proved it by showing his cap.

The Magistrate gave his opinion
    That no one was really to blame
And he said that he hoped the Ramsbottoms
    Would have further sons to their name.

At that Mother got proper blazing,
    "And thank you, sir, kindly," said she.
"What waste all our lives raising children
    To feed ruddy Lions? Not me!"

Steele first saw his wife-to-be, Shirley, in an elevator on his way up to the WTIC studios. He found out where she worked from the elevator operator, and sent her a note asking for a date. Shirley assumed the note was from a WTIC executive who owned a 1930 Cadillac touring car parked outside. Little did she know that Steele could not even afford a bicycle at the time; he rode the trolley to work. Nevertheless, the romance blossomed, and the Steeles ended up raising four sons in their Wethersfield home. One, Robert Hampton Steele, went on to become a U.S. Congressman. Incidentally, for the trivia collector, Bob Steele's middle name is Lee, but originally was Jesse, a name he never liked.

In his heyday, Steele captured over one-third of the market share in greater Hartford, a percentage unheard of in the fragmented radio industry. But when WTIC-FM broke away with an entirely different format in 1977, Steele's ratings fell in the same way that virtually every AM station's did at that time. The problem was that younger listeners were seeking out contemporary music formats with less talk. Nevertheless, Steele continued to command an impressive following right to the end.

In the late 1980s, Steele cut back his schedule from 9:00 to 10:00 a.m. Monday through Friday and 5:30 to 10:00 a.m. on Saturdays. It was a harbinger of his retirement, which came on September 30, 1991. Steele does return to the microphone on the fourth Saturday of each month and plays pre–rock 'n' roll music.

Steele attributed his successful career to his "steady, consistent presence" through turbulent times. As author Alvin Toffler points out in his book *Future Shock*, people in the late twentieth century psychologically need zones of security to hold onto during vast changes in technology and lifestyle. Steele provided that warmth and security for over a half million listeners every day.

CHUCK WHITTIER

Chuck Whittier never talked about anything personal on the air, other than calling himself "chief spoonerizer," "curator of hyperbole," and "curator of essential luxuries." Whittier was a linguist who migrated to Wilkes-Barre, Pennsylvania, from Missouri. Like Connecticut's Bob Steele, Whittier remained in the business until old age. Unlike Steele, however, who started his career at $35 a week and ended it making well over $100,000 a year, Whittier was still making less than one dollar an hour over minimum wage after 40 years in broadcasting.

Following several assignments at WILK, Whittier became the first morning man at WYZZ, a new FM station in Wilkes-Barre in the late 1950s. The station was using an experimental format similar to one being tried by WOR in New York. John A. Gambling's "Music from Studio X," a beautiful music, minimal talk format, was syndicated to several markets including WYZZ between 8:15 p.m. and 1:00 a.m. six days a week, and 1:00 to 5:00 p.m. on Sundays. The show featured lush string arrangements by such full orchestras as Frank Chacksfield, Percy Faith, and Paul Weston.

The station's founder, Richard Evans, Sr., was a visionary. He adapted Gambling's experiment to an around-the-clock format. He even called the show after 1:00 a.m. "Music from Studio Z." Evans' idea was simple: take the nonpersonality format of WPAT in Paterson, New Jersey, add a dash of personalities, a heavy dose of commercials, and a huge record library with some jazzier arrangements. Music would always reign supreme, but not 100 percent. With 50,000 watts, WYZZ penetrated huge areas of northeastern Pennsylvania. By the early 1970s, most other FM stations had copied some of WYZZ's format (today none do), but WYZZ retained a unique flavor.

Whittier was given what seems like an important shift, 6:00 to 12 noon, and his banter sounded like this:

Twenty-nine after six, by the "WHIZ" smoldering rope. That brings in Spike, our veriably veridical vaticinator, from his most recent weather reconnaissance. Spike has been out sniffing the breeze, and brings the intelligence that it will be mostly sunny today, with a high in the mid-to-upper seventies. Tonight, partly cloudy, a chance of occasional showers overnight, lows in the mid-fifties. Tomorrow, chance of rain early, then hazy and hot, a high near ninety.

Spike is wearing his tattersall vest, grey billycock tipped over one eye, smoking a trichinopoli cigar. Spike's making book: he'll give you three to one odds against any rain today.

Some of Whittier's remarks became familiar to regulars to the program. For example, after the commercials for La Piñata Gift Shop in the Poconos, Whittier would usually quip, "ask for Sasha the Borzoi or Peppy the Poodle. Tell 'em Spike sent you."

Spike, who actually existed as a real cat owned by Dick Evans, clearly was Whittier's alter ego. It was no doubt easier to role-play than to discuss reality; Whittier lived alone in a spartan apartment over stores on Academy Street. I sometimes pictured in my mind the gaunt, wizened old gentleman walking to work on the predawn deserted streets, dressed in a tie and jacket for a job where no one could see him.

In 1978, the 68-year-old Whittier became very ill and was frequently in and out of the hospital. When he finally returned, to an abbreviated 9:00 a.m. to noon shift, his voice and spirit seemed broken. Cracked and raspy, his delivery was devoid of word play or reference to Spike. Whittier passed away shortly thereafter, and his obituary in the local newspaper on December 16, 1978, was only about three inches long. The real cat Spike also died shortly thereafter. A few years later Evans sold WYZZ for $1 million to Susquehanna Broadcasting, which promptly fired everyone and turned the powerhouse into MAGIC-93 soft rock. The new listeners do not know or care about what happened before, any more than the new owners. "Essential luxuries" is no longer applicable oxymoron to the clone-like FM stations of the 1990s.

JOHNNY ANDREWS

Johnny Andrews was more than a typical radio morning man of the 1940s. Not only did he play the grand piano on the air at WNBC, segueing into and out of the recorded music, but off air, Andrews actually socialized with the leader songwriters of the time, even the reclusive Irving Berlin.

"In my 25 years with NBC, I got to interview hall of famers, movie stars, and controversial politicians, but I really wanted to meet the songwriters," Andrews once reminisced. When he took over the morning slot on WNBC from "Buffalo" Bob Smith in the early 1950s, Andrews got his chance. Music was the focus of the program, yet playing records was only a minor part. It was Andrews' intensive knowledge of and love for standard American popular music that made the show really special. Every record was handpicked, and Andrews knew all about them and could play his own arrangements of them.

Prior to his association with WNBC, Andrews hosted the "Morning Bandwagon Program" on WTAM in Cleveland. When he came to NBC, Andrews often substituted for Smith when Smith was ill or on vacation. Andrews actually was a better singer and pianist than Smith and was also more knowledgeable.

In addition to his radio work, Andrews continued the live patter for several decades at the Monkey Bar of the Hotel Elysée on East 54th Street in New York. Between the hours of 5:30 and 7:30 p.m., Andrews would play the grand piano in the bar, which was frequented by people who worked with celebrities more than by the celebrities themselves. Andrews continued to play at the bar until the early 1990s, and he died in early 1993.

Other hallmarks of Andrews' career included his serving as accompanist to the great young singer Buddy Clark in the 1940s, and his hosting of a short-lived children's television show in the mid–1950s on Channel 9, WOR-TV.

The television show, which was structured along lines similar to the radio show with the exception of the showing of cartoons rather

Johnny Andrews (left) and the author

than the playing of records, opened with an obscure David Carroll
record called "Blue Scarecrow." (Ironically Andrews himself could not
remember the name or artist of this record many years later.) Andrews
then typically would segue out of the record, singing over it, "Well,
good morning, it's the time to be happy; are you wearing a smile? Good
morning, it's the time to be happy, so come on in and stay awhile."

The beloved Andrews was in his element as pianist at posh
celebrity parties on 5th Avenue, and frequently traveled around the
country lecturing about the great songwriters of the past. His idols
were not only "household names" like Gershwin and Kern, but also the
lesser known composers like Dubin and Warren, and Dietz and
Schwartz. His encyclopedic knowledge of their works enabled him to
respond quickly to audience requests.

Andrews' show on WNBC aired from 6:00 to 9:00 a.m. Monday
through Saturday. The show lasted only a few years, and then Andrews
faded from the scene. He remarked to me in 1991 that "Forty years ago,
I would walk into the studios at Radio City and everyone knew me.
Today, I would walk in and nobody would know who I was."

JIM BRANDO

For over 30 years, Jim Brando has served as a deejay on WCDL in Carbondale, Pennsylvania, most recently as morning man. Brando's resonant voice, smooth as silk, upholds the standards of an earlier era which no longer apply for most local programming. Considering its prime time slot, Brando's show has shockingly little talk and commercials. In a typical segment, three songs are played in a row, followed by talk, one commercial, and a 1960s-style station identification jingle such as this one:

> We're swinging,
> WCDL, and we're glad you're listening.

Much of the recorded music is as outdated and obscure as the jingles, a refreshing change from the tried but tired "Music of Your Life" and similar canned formats. Brando's playlist includes, for example, Jimmy Durante's "Start Off Each Day with a Song," Janice Harper's "Forever, Forever," and Jerry Shard's "Washington & Lee Swing."

The following are a couple of examples of Brando's jokes:

- "Well, friends, today is Presidents' Day, when we especially honor George Washington. Now we all know that Washington had wooden teeth, but that didn't stop him from practicing a regular program of oral hygiene. Every night, he'd leave his teeth in the birdbath for the woodpeckers to clean."
- "You know, the world series this year is being played in Canada, and with the temperatures up there, they're changing a rule. You can use a dogsled now to round the third base."

While Brando will probably never make it on the comedy circuit, he provides a more palatable breakfast diet than many shock jocks.

Brando's show airs from 6:00 to 9:00 a.m. and 11:00 a.m. to noon, Monday through Friday, and from 6:00 to 10:00 a.m. on Saturday.

GEORGE EDWARDS

Suave, sophisticated George Edwards reigned for many years as morning man on WQXR in New York, playing light classics along

George Edwards

with helpful information to start the day. His show aired from 6:00 to 9:00 a.m., Monday through Friday.

When it began in the 1930s, WQXR was the first radio station with a classical format, and did not go on the air until 5:00 p.m. In the 1940s, the station expanded its hours from 6:00 to 1:00 a.m.

In the 1960s, when the FCC required stations in cities with populations under 100,000 to discontinue simulcasting both AM and FM formats more than 60 percent of the time, WQXR responded by offering two different classical choices at various hours. However, the early morning was not one of the times they chose to separate, thus giving Edwards a stronger presence. In the 1980s, WQXR entirely separated the AM and FM formats, and Edwards changed his shift. With the demise of WNEW as a traditional pre–rock 'n' roll hit station in 1993, WQXR-AM became the new 1940s jazz format station, relegating the classical format to FM only.

DON RUSSELL

To people outside Stamford, Connecticut, the name Don Russell probably meant nothing, but Russell's voice was well known nationally and still survives in reruns of the "Honeymooners," since he served as Jackie Gleason's announcer, along with the more famous Jack Lescoulie. Russell's perfect cadence and distinct nasal resonance made him a pleasure to listen to, even though coworkers described him as cantankerous and egotistical. In the 1950s, Russell was a staff announcer at WABD-TV, Channel 5 in New York, which later became WNEW-TV before it was bought out by FOX. In those early days of television, most stations had "booth men" similar to the old radio stations to provide station identification, read commercials live, and keep the program logs. Russell served in this capacity and was easily distinguished by voice alone, as were Fred Scott and Tom Gregory.

When new FM stations sprung up to provide a "beautiful music" alternative to the contemporary format AM stations, Don Russell was part of the original team at WTFM in Queens, New York. Executives at the station sought out disc jockeys with distinctive voices, such as Frenchman Charles Duval, and they snapped up Russell as the morning man.

Desiring to be closer to home as he aged, Russell became morning man Monday through Friday on venerable WSTC in Stamford, Connecticut, on its "Old Commuter" program. Later, he moved to WGCH in neighboring Greenwich, where he continued the same format on a six-day-a-week basis from 6:00 to 10:00 a.m.

Russell's musical tastes could be termed traditional American standards. He had great appreciation and fondness for the music of Johnny Mercer, Jerome Kern, and Lerner and Loewe. He often would talk about the compositions that he played and about his personal association with these great songwriters.

After a year or two at WGCH, Russell teamed up on Saturday mornings with Bill Codair horsing around on the guitar. Codair committed suicide when his career could not advance in New York radio after he had worked on WHN. Russell continued the show alone into the 1980s, and then retired to work as a columnist at the *Stamford Advocate* newspaper.

J. P. McCARTHY

Detroit's "WJR was one of the sole radio holdouts against the burgeoning television phenomenon," states a marketing piece issued by the station many years ago. Live variety shows continued on WJR decades after they had disappeared from most other stations.

J. P. McCarthy joined WJR in 1956 as a staff announcer, and became morning man in 1958. The New York City native was just 20 years old when he began, and, planning to move ahead, he soon accepted a better job at KGO in San Francisco. But McCarthy, his wife

J. P. McCarthy

Judith Ann, and his six children, were homesick for Detroit. McCarthy returned for good on December 7, 1964.

Fans in Detroit welcomed the return of their 27-year-old, top-rated, gracious morning host, and demanded more of him. For several years, he did both the morning and evening drive-time shows, then switched to a morning and a noontime show. He was appointed program director in 1971 and was chosen as *Billboard* magazine's national radio personality of the year four different times. McCarthy also had some talk shows on WJBK-TV, Channel 2.

Here is how the morning lineup looked back in 1972, in the waning years of AM radio's dominance over FM. Monday through Saturday from 5:05 to 6:00 a.m., Marshall Wells' "Town and Country Show" was broadcast and geared for farmers. Monday through Friday from 6:10 to 9:00 a.m. was McCarthy's slot, entitled, "Music Hall: The Sounds of the Morning." From 9:15 to 10:00 a.m., Jack Harris hosted a breakfast club show called "Open House."

On August 16, 1995, the 62-year-old McCarthy succumbed to a blood ailment which had forced him to take sick leave from his 6:15 to 10:00 a.m. shift a couple of weeks earlier. His 200,000 listeners were stunned.

McCarthy's shoes will be hard to fill, since he could not be toppled from the number one position in the Detroit market during his decades of service. Detroit Mayor Dennis Archer summed up McCarthy's success formula this way: "He made you feel like you were in his living room, and he genuinely cared what you had to say."

Part III

The Top 40 Era

New York's WNEW pioneered the 24-hour-a-day, all pop music and news format which would influence hundreds of other stations for the next several decades. A major change the format brought was that commercial copy was not read straight, but was ad-libbed from rough notes. This had been tried before to some extent by very strong personalities like John Gambling and Arthur Godfrey, but most personalities in the 1940s had commercials read verbatim by staff announcers on duty.

The second major change was the deejays' talking over the record at beginning and end. This had previously been regarded as impolite.

The third change the format brought was that time and weather were announced almost constantly, because they were the two most important things that listeners wanted to know.

The fourth change required deejays to include live talk between all changes and not to segue from a recorded commercial to recorded music.

There were many complicated rules about song rotation which most listeners would not know, but would recognize. The frequency of airplay of a song was in direct correlation to its position on the chart. According to Bill Stewart, a midwesterner who developed the top 40 format after WNEW showed promise, personality was still important, but now the formula was 40 percent music, and 20 percent promotion. That prescription began to change in the mid–1960s, when Atlanta's Bill Drake set a faster-paced format, allowing only seven seconds of talk at a time.

Besides the music itself, the biggest change in the way radio sounded could be summarized this way: no dead air. Everything had to move, and the tempo was noticeably faster than it had ever been before in broadcasting. Not only were the deejays speaking faster, they were trying to cover more ground by doing less.

The popularity of the top 40 format also quickly buried other types of music in many areas much to the chagrin of the typical World War II era veterans, and those folks even older, who disliked much of the contemporary music of the late 1950s. Some stations like WTIC in Hartford, Connecticut, hung on to the old Eddie Fisher and Jo Stafford records, refusing to accept top 40 as the new wave, but they were in the minority, and it took an extremely strong personality to prevent listener attrition to the new music. Some of the best deejays, however, were in their glory as top 40 personalities.

WOLFMAN JACK

Wolfman Jack a morning man? Yes indeed, the very same Wolfman Jack who howled his way through many a night from a "tower of power" across the Mexican border was also known as "Big Smith with the records" on KCIJ, an obscure 250-watt daylight country and western station out of Shreveport, Louisiana. The show began at sunrise from 1961 to 1963 with the clanging of a cowbell and the guitars of Lester Flatt and Earl Scruggs.

While the name "Big Smith" was stolen from a popular brand of overalls at that time, Smith was actually the Wolfman's real name. Wolfman Jack was born Robert Smith in New York City in 1938. From early childhood he was mesmerized by rhythm and blues music, dialing in black-oriented programs from distant cities on his large radio set. Smith was a teenager when this type of music evolved into rock 'n' roll and enveloped the mainstream culture thanks to promoters like Alan Freed and Murray the K.

Smith idolized the new breed of deejays, but they did not go far enough for him. The black dialects, mannerisms, and "soul" spirit became an obsession for young Smith. When he should have been on a school bus riding to high school, Smith would sneak off to a different bus stop and board the city bus to the Newark, New Jersey, studios of WNJR, where the personnel "adopted" him as an office boy. Smith absorbed every aspect of the operation like a sponge, proving that his poor school grades were not due to a lack of intelligence.

One day, as Smith was setting out to fetch doughnuts for the staff, an engineer called in sick. No one was available to fill in. In desperation, the deejay, "Mr. Blues," a white man who sounded black, let Smith run the board. It is important to remember that in the 1950s,

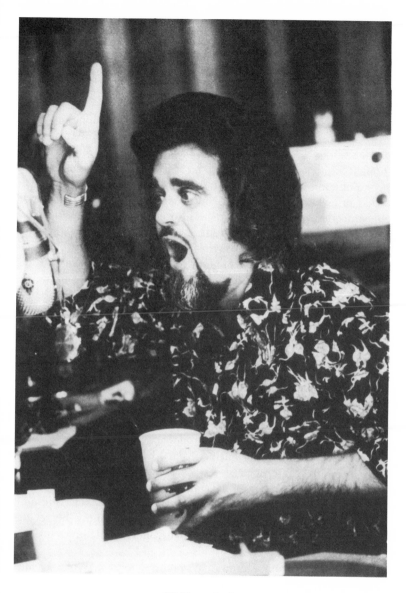

Wolfman Jack

the vast majority of deejays, even at small stations like WNJR, had strong personalities and were stars in their own right, not technicians; Mr. Blues did not belong in the control room. Smith did a sterling job. Although he did not break into radio that day, the incident gave the near high school dropout the incentive to pursue his dream.

Smith arrived home so late that night that he was severely pun-
ished. It was the beginning of a series of unfortunate incidents which
led to his being evicted by his own family. But through the kind inter-
vention of his sister, Smith's father agreed to spend $3,000 to enroll
him in the National Academy of Broadcasting in Washington.

The Academy was a high-brow place where the pupils aspired to
classy stations, which at that time meant non–rock 'n' roll. Everyone
thought Smith as weird to want to be a "jive-talking" character. But a
stroke of good fortune hit Smith at the time of his graduation. The
owner of a station in Newport News, Virginia, aimed at black audiences needed a white deejay who also could sell airtime to white
advertisers in the then-segregated city. Smith gladly accepted the job
and worked long hours at WYOU.

In Virginia, Smith met his future wife, Lou Lamb, and a radio
entrepreneur named Mo Burton who bought the Shreveport station
which was home to Smith for three years.

In Shreveport, "Big Smith" privately began developing the persona of Wolfman Jack. The "Wolfman" part derived from Smith's love
of horror flicks and his shenanigans as a "wolfman" with his two young
nephews. The "Jack" was added as a part of the "hipster" lingo of the
1950s, as in "take a page from my book, Jack," or the more popular,
"hit the road, Jack."

As the result of an impetuous journey across the Mexican border
to find the 250,000 watt XERF, Smith finally attained his goal to be
a wild, but knowledgeable, rock 'n' roll deejay with the same fervor of
the preachers who bought airtime from XERF. The "Wolfman Jack
Show" ran from midnight to 4 a.m. A night person, Smith never
worked early mornings again. His immense popularity brought him to
Los Angeles radio, and later to television. As host of "Midnight
Special," the first mainstream hard-rock television show, he set the
stage for MTV. The television show "Live from Planet Hollywood" was
his last regular endeavor before his death in 1995.

Although far from a traditional middle American, Wolfman Jack
shared with the traditional "white collar" deejays a lament for the days
when talent, rather than "continuous music," sold a station. For a
popular music station in the 1950s and 1960s, "the trip was to be more
of a master of ceremonies," he recalled. "The first priority was to create
a party mood."

In the early days of rock 'n' roll, as well as the earlier days of standard music, a listener could tell who was broadcasting just from the
playlist. Formats were much less rigid. Wolfman ran into the problems

of a changing industry when he joined WNBC in New York as an evening deejay in the 1970s and was forced to play only top 40 music. The frustrated Wolfman could not touch the thousands of rare R and B records he had accumulated for decades by Louis Jordan, Bo Diddley, Fenton Robinson, and several hundred other artists.

For a time, Wolfman Jack maintained a profligate lifestyle, but in his final years, he gave up his vices to settle down as a loyal family man. Wolfman did accomplish his prime goal, an even more important goal than emulating the soul singers and deejays: to make people happy.

JOHN LESLIE

John Leslie worked for a dozen different radio stations as morning man, but his longest and most significant contribution was at WNBF, Binghamton, New York, the oldest and most powerful AM station in that city. A West Virginia native, he had the morning slot at WNBF in the early 1970s, and then returned in the 1980s after working in many other stations and markets. Leslie switched to afternoon drive time in early 1993, returning in August 1993 to mornings.

At WNBF, Leslie carried the morning slot from a rather commonplace, informational format to a program loaded with contests, call-ins, unusual gimmicks, and extensive talk. Perhaps the most bizarre of Leslie's achievements resulted from a challenge from news director Bernard Fionti to organize an expedition to Kathmandu, Nepal. Initially a running joke, Leslie managed to raise funds for the trip and did climb the Himalayas, even feeding some remote broadcasts during his journey.

Staples of the program included extensive repartee with Fionti over human interest stories and with sports director Roger Neel about local and national teams. Another regular feature of the program in its later years was "Stump the Geniuses," which would air on Friday mornings between 8:35 and 9:00 a.m. Listeners would call Leslie, Fionti and Neel, and try to stump them with trivia questions for prizes. Much of the show as done tongue-in-cheek, with some listeners getting unmercifully teased.

Leslie always kept his show clean and free of taboo innuendo. However, some of the topics would have made the earlier breed of deejays uncomfortable. When Leslie received death threats from a

listener by fax, he read them on the air and then announced what he
would do to that person when he tracked him down.

Music played a decidedly secondary role in the program, basically
following a top 40 and oldies format. In 1993, when WNBF management decided to go to an all-talk format, Leslie took the afternoon
call-in show from 3:00 to 5:00 p.m., and the morning slot was given
to afternoon man Kerry Donovan. Donovan's show ran from 5:30 to
9:00 a.m., Monday through Friday. Leslie's show ran from 6:00 to
10:00 a.m., and when Leslie came back to the morning shift, from 5:00
to 9:00 a.m. There were also rare Saturdays when Leslie filled in for
weekend part-timers. Leslie's last year as a morning man was 1994. At
this writing he is pursuing independent productions.

JACK MIHALL

"Have no fear, Jackson's here; you've got the Breakfast Club."

While it bears the same name as the old variety show hosted by
Don MacNeil on the ABC network decades ago, the "Breakfast Club"
on WKII, 1070 AM, Port Charlotte, Florida, is a standard disc jockey
program in the fine tradition of the 1940s garrulous style, but with an
unimaginative playlist of mostly banal top 40 tunes of the past.

Jack Mihall, who hosts the program five days a week, talks between
approximately every two records. Most of the chatter consists of pithy
sayings, witticisms, and satire, such as "man's best friend is the hot dog.
It feeds the hand that bites it."

The Iowa native came to WKII in 1987, shortly after the birth of
his daughter Chelsea, who is a frequent guest on the program. He provided a local touch — everything is done live — to an otherwise canned
"Music of Your Life" format. The Breakfast Club ran from 7:00 a.m.
to 9:00 a.m. Monday throught Saturday. When Mihall was promoted
to sales manager in July 1994, the Saturday shows were dropped.

The gimmicks and clowning around are a throwback to the Rayburn and Finch type of morning show which was popular in the top
40 era. For example, Mihall will inject a recording of Tarzan after discussing a new vitamin supplement, or imitate Jack Nicholson after
playing a love song. "Elvis" and "Rocky" also make frequent appearances. At 7:15 each morning, Maurice the bugleman, one of Mihall's
fictitious characters, enters the studio bedraggled and hung over, and
blows reveille after muttering a phrase like "slip me a few shillings."

After each newscast with news director Bill Noel, Mihall and Noelle discuss a light news item in a manner reminiscent of John Gambling and Peter Roberts, but even more insipid; most of their jokes fall flat. "This is Smilin' Jack in my tumbledown shack with my flat friends, the records," Mihall often quips. The super salesman convincingly plugs many of his sponsors with ad-lib personal experiences. My mouth waters whenever Mihall describes a restaurant at the Fisherman's Village complex in Punta Gorda, and we even went out and purchased hurricane shutters after hearing Mihall's claim that they were effective.

Following is a typical playlist from a "Breakfast Club" hour: "Green Door" — Jim Lowe, "Evergreen" — Barbra Streisand, "Winchester Cathedral" — The New Vaudeville Band, "It's Only a Paper Moon" — David Rose Orchestra, "The Coward of the County" — Kenny Rogers, "Winter in New England" — Barry Manilow, "Cotton Candy" — Al Hirt.

BOB WOODY

The "Woody Guy," a Northeast Pennsylvania teen idol from 1972 to 1976 on WARM in Avoca, 3:00 to 7:00 p.m., occupied many time slots at different stations, including stints in morning drive time on WILK, Wilkes-Barre, Pennsylvania, and WSCR, Scranton, Pennsylvania. Besides his kazoo-tone time checks, Woody was known for introducing radio trivia contests to the area.

A multimedia personality, Woody now owns one of the largest advertising agencies in Northeastern Pennsylvania, and has succeeded in doing commercial voice-overs, and "Comedy Classics" on WNEP-TV 16. As in his radio show, he is a high-energy, gregarious, fun-loving fellow in real life. Woody also owns a major interest in KQV-FM 96, the "Imus in the Morning Classic Rock All Day" radio station.

Woody was first to offer "Airplane Traffic Reports" on WILK, 980, and KQV, and brought Larry King's talk show to Northeastern Pennsylvania on WILK in 1978, an action that was unheard of at the time on a music radio station. Presumably Woody's most important feat was the introduction of transformational business training, along with teaching advertising skills at his agency, named "The Ad Agency."

TOMMY GRUNWALL

A Floridian with no broadcasting experience, Grunwall was offered a disc jockey job by his father-in-law, Jim Gibbons, so he and his wife could move to Frederick, Maryland. Gibbons, now considered a giant in the industry, purchased WFMD-AM and WFRE-FM in 1967 and took a big chance on Grunwall by placing him in the prime-time slot on the AM bands. "Happy Johnny" Zufall, by far the number one morning man in Frederick, wished to retire gradually, so he reduced his shift to just one hour at 5:00 a.m., leaving the next four hours for Grunwall. Eventually, Grunwall took over the entire shift.

Grunwall did not disappoint his boss. His more sophisticated personality and updated record choices were perfect for the increasingly suburban audience. Unlike Zufall, Grunwall was not afraid to air his conservative political views. While many listeners did not agree with him, most of them respected the ex–Marine for his sincerity. As one friend stated, "There is no deception about Tommy Grunwall. His on-air personality is the same as his off-air personality. Humor is another key element of Grunwall's personality and his show, which is sprinkled with practical jokes and repartee with his sportscaster, Pierce Michael, and newsman, Kevin McManus.

Like his predecessor, Grunwall has worked tirelessly for charitable causes. In early 1993, he was awarded the Service to Mankind Award by the Frederick Evening Sertoma Club.

Also in 1993, Gibbons made a major decision to move Grunwall from the AM to the FM station, requiring him to play country and western music. Formerly, WFRE-FM was a nonpersonality "beautiful music" station. Like so many other AM stations, WFMD is now no music, all talk. Its morning man, John Fieseler, had substituted for Grunwall when he was sick or on vacation. Gibbons is gambling that his stations will move into the number one and number two positions in morning drive time.

WALLY PHILLIPS

Wally Phillips was the 5:30 to 10:00 a.m. morning man on WGN in Chicago from 1965 to 1986, and deserves credit for being one of the

Wally Phillips

pioneers who moved drive-time radio from a music-based format to a topical-talk format. Listener call-ins and trivia contests soon became a regular part of the show.

One friend aptly described Phillips as being three-dimensional: the "slick Wally of the dais," "the folksy Wally of radio land," and "a relaxed and debonair Wally who is a sophisticated, easy, and a thoroughly amiable luncheon companion." In short, Phillips had it all, which explained why his audience topped one million.

Born in Ohio, Phillips attended a drama school after a stint in the Air Force and then became a deejay at WJEF in Grand Rapids, Michigan, in 1947. In 1948, he moved to WSAI in Cincinnati, then on to WCPO in Cincinnati in 1950.

64

The Top 40 Era

A common early 1950s trick was to prerecord a famous person's responses to questions and then have the live deejay ask the questions, giving the illusion that the star was there in the studio. Phillips would alter the script to poke fun at the whole process. Conversely, he would record words and sounds to interrupt himself.

In 1952, Phillips moved to WLW in Cincinnati and started an hour long television show. He left Cincinnati for WGN in 1956. In 1986, Phillips exercised a contract option which gave him the right to refuse to work before 7:00 a.m. or after 7:00 p.m. Phillips was tired of rising at 3:00 a.m. in his suburban home. Since that time, he has occupied other slots, and now works live only on Saturday mornings from 9:00 a.m. to 1:00 p.m.

EV RUBENDALL

Williamsport, Pennsylvania's, WRAK was one of the last radio stations in the United States to hold out with a 1940s type program schedule. In the days before television, most radio stations switched to their network at approximately 8:00 a.m., with an extended newscast followed by a day of network programming. As an NBC affiliate, WRAK was no exception. However, when the NBC network stopped feeding network programs, WRAK retained Ev Rubendall as the morning man from 6:00 to 8:00 a.m., Monday through Friday, with the raspy-voiced but sanguine Bud Berndt stepping in at 8:15.

Rubendall's voice was nothing to brag about; in fact, it had a wishy-washy tone. However, the show had a very pleasing, relaxing sound for the early morning hour, with no rock 'n' roll music. Rubendall also worked as a newsman after 8:00 a.m. In the early 1980s, the sale of WRAK by owner J. Wright Mackey resulted in the hiring of George Gilbert and the dismissal of all the deejays at the station, ending Rubendall's career.

JOE ROBERTS

Long before Rush Limbaugh, there was Joe Roberts. Roberts took the typical 1940s style chatty deejay format and added his own

Joe Roberts

conservative political philosophies and commentaries, a phenomenon considered risky for the 1960s. For many years, Roberts was morning man at WBIC in Islip, New York, which later changed its call letters to WLIX. When, in the late 1960s, the station went to a nonpersonality, automated format, Roberts soon moved to nearby WBAB in Babylon and continued the exact format he had developed at WBIC.

Actually, there was much more to Roberts' immense success than his political views. The show was a full-service morning program in every sense of the word, and Roberts worked very hard to put together an interesting and talkative agenda six days a week. Jokes, stories, and advice abounded. Even those who disagreed with Roberts' right-wing views had to admit that he was always a polite and cordial host. Musically speaking, there was nothing remarkable about Roberts' choices. He basically followed the station's format, which evolved from a top 40 format in the early to mid–1960s to a blander format which included songs by such groups as the Ray Charles Singers and the Gunter Kallman Chorus. The station followed an adult contemporary format.

The hours for Roberts' show on WBIC and WLIX varied because it was a daylight only station. Therefore, the program could start as early as 5:00 a.m. in the summertime or as late as 7:15 a.m. in the dead of winter. The show ended at 10:00 a.m., after which time Roberts hosted the "Party Line," an early telephone call-in program, which gave Roberts additional time to expound his conservative views. When Roberts moved to WBAB, the "Party Line" moved with him, airing at 9:00 a.m., shortening the length of the morning program. The "Party Line" did not air on Saturdays, when WBAB presented "Adventuring," an old-style children's show.

A dispute with management at WBAB in the early 1970s led to Roberts' departure. Roberts became morning man at the now defunct WRFM in Queens, New York. It was a soft-music, easy-listening station that gave Roberts no opportunity to project his personality. He next worked at WGSM in Huntington, Long Island.

Roberts now syndicates a 4-hour weekly radio program featuring pop standards and conversations with celebrities, as well as a feature carried over from his old morning show, "The Joe Roberts Service Deptartment," featuring tips on gardening and homemaking.

PAUL HEMMER

Paul Hemmer has been the morning man at WDBQ in Dubuque, Iowa, since 1967. He began his career at the station when he was a sophomore at Wahlert High School. In 1958, he had begun hanging out in the observation booth at the station, which had beautiful old-time studios above the First National Bank Building in Dubuque. Hemmer was fascinated by local deejays, but his real hero was Wally Phillips of WGN. In 1959, Hemmer purchased a tape recorder at the then hefty price of $189 and practiced doing a deejay show with his record changer. After hundreds of hours of practice, he finally sent a tape to the station's general manager, lied about his age, and was called in for an interview. Since Hemmer looked and sounded older than 15, no one ever asked his age. Over the next seven years, Hemmer worked odd shifts at the station before attending the University of Wisconsin at Platteville as a music major. On August 15, 1967, Hemmer started as a morning man in the tradition of Wally Phillips, with lots of "drop-in visitors," comedy, character voices, telephone contests, and chatter with newsmen Tom Berryman and others. Hemmer and Berryman sounded something like the old Bob and Ray team, and they continued from 1969 to 1991, when Berryman left the radio business. In 1969, Hemmer became program director of WDBQ-AM and FM. The full-service nature of Hemmer's program extends well beyond the confines of the control room. His achievements include the development of the first community awareness program in the area, the production of 22 original radio dramas produced and acted by local people, the writing and direction of original musical comedies, and crowd coordination work for the movie *Field of Dreams* which was filmed near Dubuque. Both of Hemmer's children are now actively involved in broadcasting. Michelle Hemmer is programming coordinator for Sega Communications, which owns more than 24 radio stations; she lives in Stamford, Connecticut. Steve Hemmer, whose air name is Steve Stevens, also began at age 15 at WDBQ and now is a midday personality on KGMO-FM in Cape Girardeau, Missouri. Hemmer intends to retire in 1998, but not to become a condo dweller or beach bum. His plan is to open his own FM radio station, which, at the time of this writing, is in the early phases of construction.

Part IV
The Post–Top 40 Era

More than just the old-style John Gambling types are in trouble. The top 40 deejays, once the idols of trendy youths, are in "dire circumstances," to quote a 1991 *New York Times* article. They must compete with oldies, hip-hop, and hard rock formats. "The fragmentation and segregation has done wonders for advertisers," the article concludes.

Advertisers can target highly specific age, income, and ethnic groups. But as advertising dollars get spread thinner, stations must charge less or have fewer advertisers; either way there is less revenue available to pay truly talented personnel. Once that point is reached, we are trapped in a vicious circle. If there is no real talent, listeners choose their morning program based on music, not personality. Ratings do not drop, so advertisers stay happy, and there is no incentive for the stations to improve.

"Conventional wisdom says when you do a great job, you get rewarded. Not anymore in New York radio," lamented the *New York Post* on September 3, 1991, when WNEW refused to renew the contacts for the morning team of Bob Fitzsimmons and Al Rosenberg. The wise-cracking duo, successors to the Klavan and Finch brand of humor, was just too expensive to support on a declining budget. Less than a year and a half later, WNEW, the original pop music station in the United States, vanished forever, replaced by a business news format with no special morning personality; however, there are still some strong personalities in most markets, and even some of the "shock jocks" are gifted performers in their own way.

DON IMUS

Don Imus could be labeled the original shock jock, although his routines are tame compared to Howard Stern and some of the other bizarre deejays of the 1990s. Nevertheless, Imus still enjoys a large following. As recently as 1991, his morning show on WFAN ranked number three with men aged 25–54, and he generated $14 million in advertising revenue that year, or seven times his salary.

If you tune into Imus, expect to hear scorching impersonations of celebrities, derision of the Catholic Church and "born-again" Christians, and plenty of references to the female anatomy. Like the infamous Howard Stern, Imus developed much of this pattern while still in school. But there, the similarity ends. Unlike Stern, a New Yorker who grew up Jewish and middle-class, Imus came from a wealthy Protestant cattle raising family in California and seriously misbehaved in school. Things went from bad to worse. Imus' parents divorced, then his father died, and much of his parents' legacy went to pay taxes. The silver spoon was badly tarnished. Moving to Hollywood, Imus tried to break into the rock 'n' roll scene, and ended up homeless in the streets.

Eventually, Imus got a radio job in Palmdale, California. He got married and had four children. Things began to brighten, as he then found a better job in Stockton. He was eventually fired from his job for sponsoring an Eldridge Cleaver look-alike contest; first prize was a $5,000 fine plus ten years in jail. Stockton was not ready for such humor, not so soon after the Watts riots.

Imus found another radio job in Sacramento, where his routines became bolder as industry standards liberalized. His next move was to WGAR in Cleveland, and in 1971 he landed at WNBC in the same slot where, 20 years earlier, Bob Smith and Johnny Andrews had regaled New Yorkers with piano segues and Gershwin tales. New York was a very different place by the time Imus arrived, but not entirely different; not everyone was ready for Imus' irreverence. The station lost the Irish Airlines account after Imus quipped, "Protestants have to ride coach."

As troublesome to management as Imus' knocking sponsors was, more troubling were his work habits. On his second day on the job at WNBC, Imus overslept and missed the show. Imus' heavy drinking did not help his punctuality. In 1973, he missed work 100 days, a record

Don Imus

which must have appeared incredible to assiduous competitors like John A. Gambling who were rarely even a minute late for work. By 1977, station executives had had enough of Imus' sloppy attendance and truculent attitude toward them. Fired, Imus retreated to WHY in Cleveland.

Ironically, WNBC's advertising sales stagnated, and their station's general manager Bob Sherman (son of WINS newsman Paul Sherman, a former deejay himself) ended up inviting Imus back. One might think that Imus would have been on top of the world, but his cocaine habit was destroying him. Even after he stopped, his drinking continued. Imus finally checked into a detoxification center after Howard Stern, who had occupied the late afternoon slot at WNBC, was fired and joined a different station to compete with him in the morning. When station owners sold the 660 AM frequency to Infinity Broadcasting, WNBC was replaced by WFAN, a sports station. Imus was permitted to continue with his nonsports gags and routines; Infinity realized it could syndicate Imus just as K-Rock was doing with Howard Stern. Today, Imus exercises regularly and no longer drinks.

Imus' sidekicks on his show have made names for themselves: newsman Charles McCord; writer Al Rosenberg, who went on to his own morning show on WNEW; and Carl C. Watkins, a former bond trader who used to call in to the show on a regular basis.

HOWARD STERN

Few morning men enjoy national recognition simply because the nature of their work is localized. But Howard Stern is an exception. Not only is his New York morning show on WXRK-FM simulcast in Philadelphia and other cities, it is rebroadcast, much like the old radio dramas and comedies, at wake-up time on the West Coast.

There is another reason people out of range of his program know about Howard Stern. In late 1991, the Federal Communications Commission fined a Los Angeles station $105,000 for indecent broadcasting as a result of a complaint by a station employee. Previously, three other stations that had aired a "lewd and vulgar" 1988 Christmas broadcast had paid a $2,000 fine.

Stern's entire career history is strewn with management battles and firings over the limits of good taste, despite his ability to boost ratings significantly. The "schoolyard wise guy" deejay, as he was deemed by one writer, literally began developing his routines in his Long Island school yard around 1967, at age 13, using marionettes performing sex acts. At Boston University, Stern got involved on the campus radio station, where he was frequently reprimanded for his brash style. He graduated in 1976 and worked for WRNW in Westchester County, New York; WCCC in Hartford, Connecticut, WWWW-FM in Detroit; and WNDC in Washington, D.C. Along this path, he encountered his present fellow humorists, Fred Norris and Robin Quivers.

Stern's big break came in 1982 when WNBC in New York offered him $200,000 per year to take over the sagging afternoon drive-time slot. Stern brought the always laughing Quivers and witty Norris with him, along with his panoply of ethnic, sex, and toilet related jokes and routines.

While ratings climbed immediately, so did protest letters, especially from black, gay, women's, Jewish, and Catholic groups. In less than a month's time, WNBC suspended Stern for disobeying management by airing outrageous skits involving the Virgin Mary. Numerous staff meetings followed to impose guidelines and restraints on Stern, which he seldom followed. Station executives even tried to limit his talking periods to three, two and one half minute "schticks" per hour. But Stern defied them, even violating one of the most sacrosanct rules of radio: he talked over the network news.

By 1985, Stern had taken WNBC's ratings in the evening drive time from number eleven to number one. But Stern's shocking on-air routines, such as force-feeding an anorexic woman and itemizing Nazi doctor Joseph Mengele's appalling torture methods, finally backfired. "Though Stern had indeed delivered the ratings he was hired for," explained writer Jan Hoffman in *New York Magazine*, "his show was not sought by many blue chip advertisers. . . . Despite ratings, a radio station still had to consider its public image." On September 30, 1985, WNBC fired Stern.

Fortunately for Stern, the few remnants of moral standards from the Johnny Andrews days at WNBC were virtually absent from newer stations with no established traditions. Within two months, Stern was working again, this time at "K-Rock" WXRK-FM in New York. In early 1986, WXRK moved Stern to the morning slot. Within one year, the station's ratings surpassed WNBC, which was dying a slow death. By 1991, venerable old WNBC had disappeared forever, and Stern was number one in New York morning radio, with 9.5 percent of the market share. Less outrageous but more established Don Imus was in ninth place with 3.6 percent at WFAN, ironically at the same dial position WNBC had occupied.

By 1991, the *New York Post* reported that Stern was earning $1.6 million per year. A *New York Times* article noted that "the difference in advertising rates between first place . . . in the morning and 21st place is considerable." However, according to *The Daily News*, in

Howard Stern

October 1991, Stern was actually number two to all-news WINS. All-news WCBS was number three, followed by John Gambling at WOR, Harry Harrison at WCBS-FM, and Don Imus at WFAN.

In addition to his morning radio show, Stern was also "doing his thing" on television with a Saturday night program originating at WWOR-TV. It was an expensive show to produce, with its entourage of bikini-clad models and guests. Several stations in more conservative areas of the United States dropped the program after barrages of viewer and advertiser complaints. There are no serious threats to Stern's longevity as a New York morning man.

Of course, shock comics are nothing new; Lenny Bruce, for

example, talked about taboo subjects over 50 years ago, but not on the radio. The FCC feels that explicit references to sex or excretory functions are taboo. Mel Karmazin, WXRK's station manager, retorts that if Stern should be silenced, then so should Oprah, Geraldo, and Phil Donahue. The only difference, Karmazin asserts, is Stern's humor.

It has been suggested that the nation's best known morning man should be forced to clean up his act. In a 1978 Supreme Court discussion, Justice John Paul Stevens wrote, "In the home, the individual's right to be left alone plainly outweighs the First Amendment rights of an intruder. One may hang up on an indecent phone call, but that option does not give the caller a constitutional immunity."

Whether or not one agrees with the court, one fact remains clear: there is a tremendous public demand for the sophomoric antics of Howard Stern and his kind.

DAN GEIGER

One of the best examples of a station that is targeting a specific market is radio AAHS. This satellite network, originating in Minneapolis, is aimed directly at young children. In the early morning, "The All American Alarm Clock" show, hosted by Dan Geiger and Angie Mannella, brings to radio what some of the early children's shows on television did 40 years ago. Magic, practical jokes, stories, poems, and weird sound effects are included. Approximately half the program is music, which is a mixture of inoffensive contemporary sounds and an occasional traditional children's song,

Dan Geiger

such as "A Spoonful of Sugar." Geiger plays a number of characters besides himself, such as Mandrake the Magician and a bumbling postman who delivers letters from the children. Breakaway periods allow the insertion of weather forecasts, other vital information, and, of course, local commercials. The "All American Alarm Clock" show is heard Monday through Saturday mornings.

JAY DANIELS
and JOHN WEBSTER

Jay Daniels and John Webster became the morning team on Rock 107, WEZX, in Scranton, Pennsylvania, beginning in 1985. Although not as outrageous as some of their bigger city counterparts, they discuss taboo subjects and poke fun at well-known people in northeastern Pennsylvania. They create skits, spicy songs, and fake commercials, and give raunchy advice to "callers."

At the very beginning, Daniels did the show by himself. He had been working at WRKZ-AM and FM in northeastern Pennsylvania. Webster would drop in on the show as the character "Swami." The duo hit it off so well that the station management decided to make Webster a permanent part of the team.

Following the station's format, most of the music aired on the "Daniels and Webster Show" would be classified as hard rock, although Daniels occasionally likes to sneak in unexpected music, such as an obscure jazz record by the Dave Pell Octet from the early 1960s. Daniels and Webster were the first strong personalities on the FM band in northeastern Pennsylvania.

Part V

Other Prominent Morning Personalities

Adams, Bob   Featured country and western music for his late 1960s Fresno, California, audience. He was heard from 5:00 to 10:00 a.m. on KEAP.

Adams, Jeff   At WTTR in Westminster, Maryland, Adams runs the morning show from 5:30 to 10:00 a.m. playing popular adult music and featuring trivia contests.

Adams, Mike   Combined the popular-contemporary music of the late 1960s with listener call-in features. The features included "Columbus Speaks," which dealt with the topics of the day, and "Homemaker SOS," where listeners called in household problems, and others called in solutions. Adams aired from 6:00 to 10:00 a.m. on WCOL, in Columbus, Ohio.

Adams, Timothy (G.)   Aimed for the Grand Rapids, Michigan, adult market (ages 18 to 34) with a selected of adult contemporary music. He aired on WLAV from 6:00 to 10:00 a.m. during the late 1970s.

Aderhold, Vic   Was Atlanta's laid-back alternative to the fast paced pop stations of the mid–1970s. From 6:00 to 10:00 a.m. he played a carefully blended mix of Golden Oldies and current hits. He was heard on WPLO-FM.

Ahrens, Larry   On Albuquerque's KKOB-AM from 5:30 to 10:00 a.m. Ahrens provides a full-service morning show with hits from the 1960s to the present.

Alcorn, Don   Used the hours from 6:00 to 10:00 a.m. to bring Pontiac, Michigan, features of local interest and the best hits. Heard on WPON during the mid–1970s.

Alexander, Frank   Used his energetic show of the mid–1970s to entertain the teen and young adult market. He played a combination of contemporary Hits and rhythm and blues from 6:00 to 10:00 a.m. on WMPP, out of East Chicago Heights, Illinois.

Alexander, Les   Used his charm and warmth, plus top 40 music, to fill the hours between 6:00 and 10:00 a.m. on WCAO beginning in the early 1950s; he left the Baltimore market for a brief interlude.

Alexander, Marvin   Provided listeners with farm news, NBC News and weather. His show aired from 5:00 to 10:00 a.m. on country and western station WNAD during the 1970s in Norman, Oklahoma.

Alexander, Oscar   Was known as "Daddy-Oh on the Patio" to his Baltimore listeners. A 10-year broadcasting veteran by the late 1960s he filled the hours between 6:00 and 10:00 a.m. at WEBB with humor and rhythm and blues.

Allen, Gary   Took over the 6:00 to 9:00 a.m. slot at WCUZ, Grand Rapids, Michigan, in the late 1970s. He brought his listeners the best of modern country music along with news and local information. Allen also served as the station's program manager.

Allen, Pat   Occupied the 5:30 to 10:00 a.m. slot on KMGA in Albuquerque. Allen's light rock show is best known for his "Listen While You Work" contest, where an entire office can win.

Allen, Perry   The morning man at WKBW in Buffalo, New York, in the 1950s, Perry Allen joined KRLA of Los Angeles in 1959 and broadcast from 6:00 to 9:00 a.m. Allen quickly grew unhappy with the top 40 format, and, in a move common to baseball but rare in broadcasting, was traded to KHJ in Los Angeles for Wink Martindale.

Allen, Robert, III (C.)   Better known as "RCA," Allen took the 6:00 to 10:00 a.m. stint at WCAO, Baltimore, Maryland, during the mid–1970s. His improvisational skills and constant updates on local information made him a Baltimore favorite.

Alley, Pat   Brought Atlanta a selection of rhythm and blues from 6:00 to 9:00 a.m. on WXAP during the mid–1970s.

Allison, Ron   A well-known morning man, Allison seduced listeners on WINW in Canton, Ohio, with his quick wit and smooth delivery in the early 1970s. Popular standards were the format of his 6:00 to 11:00 a.m. show.

Anderson, Mark   Included progressive country music, along with traffic reports and local news on his show. He occupied the 6:00 to 10:00 a.m. slot in the 1970s on station WTMT in Louisville, Kentucky.

Andres, Bill *see* **Giese, John**

Andrews, Perry   Used interesting talk and top hits of the late 1960s plus oldies to entertain the Baltimore area. Joining Andrews from 6:00 to 10:00 a.m. on WBAL was Galen Fromme with the news.

Andrews, Scotty   Sophisticated rhythm and blues plus top 35 hits comprised Andrews' 6:00 to 10:00 a.m. program on WIGO in Atlanta, Georgia, in the early 1970s.

Anthony, Bill   Used humor, public service announcements and a music combination of standards and big band sounds to entertain his mid–1970s audience mornings from 6:00 to 8:00 a.m. Anthony was also the program and operations manager for WLYN and WLYN-FM, Lynn, Massachusetts.

Anthony, Dale   Brought his "Wake Up with Dale" show to his Chattanooga listeners in the late 1960s on WFLI. From 6:00 to 9:00 a.m. he played the top popular hits of the day.

Anthony, Gene   Was the early morning dee jay for Southington, Connecticut station WNTY in the 1970s. Anthony was known for his great sense of humor and his captivating charm. His morning show was central Connecticut's most popular. His 20 years' experience in the broadcasting field led him to being one of the best known performers in Connecticut.

Anthony, Len   Kept Atlanta hopping during the late 1970s with News-watch Quizzes, traffic reports, "Teacher of the Day" salutes, phone contests, and modern country music hits. He was heard from 6:00 to 10:00 a.m. on WPLO.

Anthony, Nick   Hosted a controversial and thought provoking call-in show during the late 1970s on WHLO, Akron. He could be heard mornings from 9:00 a.m. to 12:00 p.m. Anthony was also the station's program manager.

Antrim, J. (Parker)   Pulled no punches as he attacked everyone with his special brand of humor. Laughter and the contemporary music of the late 1970s filled his 6:00 to 10:00 a.m. show on WCOL, Columbus, Ohio.

Armstrong, Tom   Did mornings from 5:30 to 10:00 a.m. on WGAR, Cleveland, beginning in the late 1950s. His show included a mix of popular music and standards along with his "Word for Today." Armstrong was an AFTRA award winner for "Best Popular Radio Show."

Arnie and Amos   Were heard in the 1970s from 5:00 to 10:00 a.m. on WGBS in Miami, Florida. Arnie provided service information and patter with his alter ego, weatherman Amos Rutledge. Total Information News, sports and traffic reports also were heard.

Arquette, Joe   Had delivered a combination of news, local information and beautiful music to the Waterloo, Iowa, area for 16 years by the late 1970s. Arquette was on the air at KFMW between the hours of 6:00 and 8:30 a.m. He was also the station's program manager.

Artis, Fairlie   Played Disco music during the late 1970s from 6:00 to 10:00 a.m. on KNOK and KNOK-FM, Fort Worth, Texas.

Ashberry, Jim   Gave his Binghamton, New York, listeners the current hits of the late 1960s plus their favorite oldies along with the local news and information. He was heard from 5:00 to 10:00 a.m. on WINR.

Avery, Marc   Played a careful selection of up-tempo contemporary music of the late 1960s along with news and traffic reports. He aired from 6:00 to 10:00 a.m. on WJBK, Detroit. Van Patrick did the sports.

B. Larry   Used modern country music, a quick wit, enjoyable stories and a knack for getting his listeners involved to keep Cincinnati laughing during the late 1970s. He was heard from 6:00 to 9:00 a.m. on WUBE and WUBE-FM.

B. Peter   Teamed with Bob Lee in the late 1970s to bring modern country music to Denver each day from 6:00 to 10:00 a.m. on KLAK.

Bacon, Bob   Greeted his Albany, New York, listeners during the late 1960s with his "Early Bird Roundup" show. Bacon combined country and western music with telephone interviews, temperature guessing contests and requests. He was heard from 5:30 to 10:00 a.m. on WEEE.

Badger, Bob   Moving from a competing area station, Badger became the morning man on WABY, Albany, New York, in the early 1970s, playing pop standards from 6:00 to 9:00 a.m. (Badger also served as general manager of WMID, Atlantic City, New Jersey, from approximately 1968 to 1970.)

Baer, Ted   Residing in the Washington, D.C., area, at this writing and no longer working in radio, Ted Baer worked in several different markets, most notably Binghamton, New York, where he served as morning man at WNBF in the 1960s and early 1970s and later at WENE. Humor pervaded the entire broadcast, which was laden with gags and funny characters created by Baer.

Bailey, Bill   Used telephone gag calls, psychic Irene Hughes, current hits and golden oldies to entertain Detroit each day from 6:00 to 10:00 a.m. at WDRQ. Bailey doubled as the station's program manager during the mid–1970s.

Bailey, Bill   Got things moving during the 1970s at Houston's KENR from 5:30 to 9:00 a.m. This humorous deejay continuously played country music. Bailey was well-known for his pledge to his community and to country music.

Bailey, Chuck   Combined popular 45's and albums with news and information his teenage audience wanted. The late 1970s found him at WGRD and WGRD-FM, Grand Rapids, Michigan, during the hours of 6:00 to 10:00 a.m.

Bain, Paul   Used his 18 years of experience to create an entertaining blend of news and music. He was heard from 5:00 to 9:00 a.m. on KROD, El Paso, during the mid–1970s. His pal Charlie joined him every day at 7:00 a.m. In the late 1960s Bain did afternoons for KROD.

Baldwin, Ben   Station KTRH in Houston featured "Talk of Houston" with Ben Baldwin from 8:30 to 10:00 a.m. Baldwin talked with the station's audience and with newsmakers. The station also aired CBS and local news on the hour, with morning business news on the half hour. Baldwin was also the station's news director.

Ballard, Gary   Worked for oldies station WCZN, Flint, Michigan, during the mid–1970s. From 6:00 to 9:00 a.m. Ballard combined music, news, and humor. He doubled as the station's program director.

Banks, Ricky   Played rock music's greatest hits along with the day's top 20 during the late 1970s. His show was on from 6:00 to 11:00 a.m. on WNIA, Buffalo.

Barrett, Art   Kept his late 1970s talk show listeners informed and entertained. He held court from 6:00 to 10:00 a.m. on WAVI, Dayton, Ohio.

Barrett, Ronnie   Used the hours between 5:00 and 10:00 a.m. to bring Cleveland the "Grin and Barrett" show during the late 1960s. His show on WERE featured sports commentary, business reviews, stock market reports, local news, popular music and oldies.

Barry, Ron   Combined standards, popular hits and show tunes for his listeners in the Allentown, Pennsylvania, area. Barry's energetic show could be heard during the late 1960s from 6:30 to 10:00 a.m. on WCRV, Washington, New Jersey.

Bartley, Bruce   Anchored "WRNG All News in the Morning" along with co-host Mitch Leonard. During the late 1970s they conversed with their audience and kept Atlanta informed from 6:00 to 9:00 a.m. daily.

Bauer, Dave   Bauer's cheerful personality made it easy to wake up to contemporary music, news, sports and traffic. His show aired during the 1970s from 6:00 to 10:00 a.m. in Oklahoma City, Oklahoma.

Baumer, Ed   Used a cozy down-home style and uptown country music, plus lots of location information, to entertain and inform his listeners on WHOL, Allentown, Pennsylvania. In the late 1970s he could be heard from 6:00 a.m. to 10:00 a.m.

Baxley, Ron   Brought Atlanta popular-contemporary music from 6:00 to 9:00 a.m. on WKLS during the mid–1970s. There was news every half hour and traffic reports every 15 minutes. After leaving WKLS, Baxley hosted a big band format from 5:00 to 9:00 a.m. on WAPI in Birmingham, Alabama, Baxley loads his program with informational features from news services.

Baxter, Gordon   Baxter's easy style made him well-known in the Beaumont, Texas, area. During the late 1960s he could be heard from 5:00 to 9:00 a.m. on KTRM. By the mid-1970s he had moved over to KLVI and aired from 6:00 to 10:00 a.m.

Bea, Chuck   Gave a bright, up-tempo good morning to listeners of WCRV in Washington, New Jersey, in the early 1970s on his 6:00 to 10:00 a.m. program featuring contemporary music, news, weather, time checks and road conditions.

Beaman, Frank   Teamed up with Dale McCarren in the late 1970s to bring news and information to Chicago from 6:00 to 10:00 a.m. on WBBM. Also included were sports with Brad Palmer and politics with John Madigan.

Beattie, Jay   Took over the 5:00 to 10:00 a.m. slot at WXAP, Atlanta, when the station switched over to country music format in the late 1970s.

Beaulieu, Dave   Beaulieu's show had an adult rock format that also contained live news, weather and national sports. Each day Beaulieu featured an artist. From his personal collection, he delighted listeners with some classic oldies. The show aired from 6:00 to 9:00 a.m. on KGOU during the 1970s in Norman, Oklahoma.

Beedle, Jim   Established a large audience in his long tenure in the Chicago market. During the mid–1970s he played country and western music from 6:00 to 10:00 a.m. on WJJD and WJJD-FM. Beedle's personal appearances always drew large crowds.

Benjamin, Paul   Played beautiful music in the late 1970s from 6:00 a.m. to 12:00 p.m. on WHSH, Latham, New York.

Benny, Frank   Used a combination of charm, wit, popular hit music and comprehensive news coverage to entertain Buffalo during the late 1960s. He was heard from 5:00 to 10:00 a.m. on WGR.

Benson, Buck   "Up to 5 a.m.?" Benson's one-hour morning show blended popular standards with news, weather, commodity prices and award-winning local news on WORK in York, Pennsylvania, in the late 1960s.

Benson, Buzz   Benson's program "The Buzz Benson Big Band Show," from 5:00 to 10:00 a.m. on WAMB in Nashville, consisted of easy listening music and original recordings of the swing era. The show, which aired in the 1970s, also furnished listeners with weather and one-liners.

Berlak, Mike   Had been a 10-year radio vet when he found his way to KFYE, Fresno, in the late 1970s. Playing the best music, his show aired from 6:00 to 10:00 a.m.

Berlin, Bill   Berlin's disco program also provided traffic reports. It aired during the late 1970s from 6:00 to 10:00 a.m. on WMAK, Nashville, Tennessee.

Berndt, Bud   A broadcasting teacher at the Williamsport Area Community College, Berndt was widely known in the Williamsport, Pennsylvania, area for his raspy, basso profundo voice, flawless pronunciation, and enthusiastic delivery. He served as the morning man on WRAK AM & FM from 8:00 to 11:00 a.m. Monday through Friday, with "The Coffee Break" program which followed the Ed Rubendall program. Berndt also worked the Saturday night shift, which was extremely unusual for a morning man. On Saturday nights, Berndt would play soft music and an hour of an original cast Broadway show album, offering commentary between the songs. Berndt passed away in the late 1980s.

Berns, Don   Played top 40 music and broadcast news every hour on WHB in Kansas City, Missouri, from 6:00 to 10:00 a.m. in the winter of 1978.

Besesparis, Ted   Along with David Gould, hosted "Radio Reveille" from

5:30 to 9:00 a.m. during the late 1970s. Their show on WPBR, Palm Beach, consisted of talk, call-ins, news, sports, weather and consumer reports.

Bethman, Gene   Was with WEST, Easton, Pennsylvania, for almost 40 years. During the 1970s his "Yawn Patrol" delivered humor, local information and golden oldies daily from 5:00 to 9:00 a.m.

Beuret, Dave   Handled the 6:00 to 10:00 a.m. slot of KIXL's (Dallas, Texas), all-day middle-of-the-road format with an emphasis on show tunes and film favorites in the early 1970s.

Bickel, Andy   Bickel's "Andy Bickel in the Morning" program on WEBR in Buffalo, New York, greeted early risers with a bright, amusing show that appealed to all ages in the early 1970s. Bickel's program aired from 5:00 to 9:00 a.m. and included free-form news and sports and contemporary standards.

Bickins, Clyde   Delivered modern country top 50 plus oldies and requests, along with time and weather checks, to his listeners in the Utica, New York, area each morning from 6:00 to 10:00 a.m. "The Clyde Bickins World" program in the late 1970s moved to WADR, Remsen, New York.

Billota, Frank   Played beautiful music over WGLD's airwaves for High Point, North Carolina, audiences during the 1970s. Bellota's show was from 6:00 to 10:00 a.m.

Biondi, Joe   On Albuquerque's KKOB-FM from 5:30 to 9:00 a.m., Biondi and Phil Sisneros (nicknamed the "Bean") provide human interest stories and information.

Bishop, Jerry (G.)   Featured the contemporary music of the late 1960s, plus comedy and human interest stories, on his 5:00 to 9:00 a.m. show on WCFL, Chicago.

Black, Bill   Brought gospel sunshine to Atlanta in the late 1970s. Black and his guests could be heard from 6:00 to 11:00 a.m. on WXLL.

Blackmon, Carol *see* **Roberts, Mike**

Blagmond, Vernon   Used the soul-sounds of rhythm and blues to entertain his late 1960s Baltimore audience each morning from 5:00 to 8:30 a.m. His "Mr. V. Show" was heard on WSID.

Blair, Henry   A 30-year veteran of radio by the late 1970s, Blair began his career in Midland, Michigan, and Fort Wayne, Indiana. Blair then worked as a morning man in the Chicago area for over 13 years. In the late 1970s he could be heard playing the top hits of the past and present from 6:00 a.m. to 12:00 p.m. on WFVR, Aurora, Illinois.

Blake, Cliff   Brought Worcester, Massachusetts, the contemporary music of the late 1970s from 6:00 to 9:00 a.m. News director Steve D'Agostino joined him twice each hour. Blake was also WFTQ's program manager.

Blakley, Doug   Combined the top 40 hits of the late 1970s with soul music, news, weather and sports. Each hour there was also the "Say It and Win" contest. He was heard from 6:00 to 10:00 a.m. on WUFO, Buffalo.

Blythe, Teresa *see* **Marcum, Dave**

Bo, Bobby   Humor, information and the hits of the day: Bo blended them all during his 6:00 to 10:00 a.m. show on WQEO, Albuquerque, New Mexico, in the 1970s. Catering to housewives, Bo slowed down the music tempo for his show's last hour.

Boggs, Otis   Since the 1950s, "The O.J. Show" has aired on WLUS, Gainesville, Florida, from 6:30 to 8:30 a.m. Monday through Friday. The show is almost exactly as it was 40 years ago, with anecdotes and community service interviews. Boggs' sidekick Jim Finch constantly barters with him. Each morning, Boggs and Finch award a prize for the lucky youngster who calls in and correctly answers a quiz question. "The Music of Your Life" standards are played.

Bohmann, Brent Albert and Joanie Bohmann   Albert Bohmann played popular album selections and Joanie Bohmann provided local, state and national news. The show occupied the airwaves in the 1970s from 6:00 to 10:00 a.m. on WPLX in Milwaukee, Wisconsin.

Bolland, Chuck   Used his caustic humor to enhance partner Stan Matlock's stories on their 6:00 to 10:00 a.m. "Daybreak Show" during the mid–1970s. Heard on Cincinnati's WKRC, their show featured Lieutenant Heinlein with traffic, Paul Sommercamp with sports, Doug Anthony with news, and new and old music hits. Bolland was also the news director.

Bond, Lou   Brought an energy-filled show to Grand Rapids, Michigan, in the late 1960s mornings from 6:00 to 10:00 a.m. He filled the time with contemporary and popular music, news and audience participation at least once an hour. Bond aired on WGRD.

Boone, Dave   Presented "Country Time," four hours of country and western music starting at 6:00 a.m. during the mid–1970s. Boone was also the news director of WCLU, Cincinnati.

Boortz, Neal   Took over the 7:30 to 10:00 a.m. slot on WRNG, Atlanta's exclusive all-talk station. Boortz's show interspersed news bits with guests like George Wallace, Timothy Leary and Cale Yarborough in the 1970s.

Borders, Johnny   Used his warm voice and charm to put his late 1960s Detroit listeners at ease while he delivered news, special features and Easy Listening music. He was heard from 5:30 a.m. to 9 a.m. on WWJ.

Borrero, Jerry   Played Spanish music on his "Wake Up" show for South Jersey's Hispanic community. During the late 1970s he was on from 6:00 to 9:00 a.m. on WDVL, Vineland, New Jersey.

Bowe, Mike   Played contemporary-popular hits of the late 1970s for his listeners on WMVB and WMVB-FM, South Vineland, New Jersey. Bowe's time slot was from 6:00 to 10:00 a.m. He also doubled as the music manager.

Box, Bob   Played contemporary music of the late 1970s for Cleveland from 5:00 to 9:00 a.m. on WZZP.

Box, Bobby   Greeted Albuquerque during the mid–1970s with a pleasing mix of hit music and local information. On the air from 6:00 to 10:00 a.m. on KQEO, he softened the music in the last hour of his show for the listening housewives.

Boyd, Ty   Used a combination of popular music and standards, along with his own enthusiasm for life, to entertain Charlotte, North Carolina, from 6:30 to 10:30 a.m. on WBT. He started in the early 1960s and continued through the 1970s, at which time the hours were changed to 6 to 10 a.m.

Bradford, Joe   Started his career in afternoon drive-time on WHTG in Eatontown, New Jersey. He could be found in the late 1970s from 6:00 to 10:00 a.m. on WRLB, Long Branch, New Jersey, where he supplied the North Jersey Shore with news, weather, sports and contemporary music. Occasionally, Bradford would poke fun at his own weight saying, "I can barely squeeze behind this console!"

Bradley, Mike   Moved from his mid–1960s 10:00 a.m. to 2:00 p.m. time slot to do mornings from 6:30 to 10:00 a.m. during the late 1960s on KBUY, Ft. Worth, Texas. His morning show featured swinging country music along with news, sports, time and weather.

Brady, Jim   Lit up Fort Wayne mornings in the mid–1970s with his wit and with country music. "Diamond Jim" was on WLYV from 6:00 to 10:00 a.m. daily. He was also the operations and program manager.

Branch, Charles   Manned the 7:00 to 11:00 a.m. time slot spinning contemporary music for teenagers and young adults in the early 1970s on WMPP in East Chicago Heights. Branch was also the station's program director.

Breedlove, Jim   Went from Texas to Yakima, Washington, in the 1970s to be heard from 6:00 to 11:00 a.m. on KUTI. His personality brightened the morning while he played modern country music.

Brennan, Jim   Gave Albany both rock and disco during the late 1970s from 6:00 a.m. to 12:00 p.m. on WWOM.

Brennan, Larry   Delivered the current hits along with much-needed morning information plus birthdays and anniversaries on his show, the "Alarm Clock Club." In the mid–1970s he was on WJLK and WJLK-FM,

Asbury Park, New Jersey, from 6:00 to 10:00 a.m. The "Morning Chapel" was at 9:15 a.m.

Briggs, David   Combined country and western music with jokes and weather checks mornings from 6:00 to 10:00 a.m. He was heard during the late 1970s on KICT, Wichita, Kansas.

Bright, Brad   Provided an easy listening format during the 1970s with an emphasis on northern suburban events. This mainly instrumental show had a get-you-up pace, which included major newscasts. It aired from 5:00 a.m. to 1:00 p.m. on KTWN in Anoka, Minnesota.

Brisbane, Al   Brought rhythm and blues to the Buffalo area during the late 1960s. He was heard from 7:00 to 11:00 a.m. on WUFO, Amherst, New York.

Britain, Ron   Played late 1970s adult contemporary music for his Chicago audience from 5:30 to 10:00 a.m. on WCFL.

Brooke, Jerry   Did an afternoon program for housewives on WIXY, Cleveland before moving to Cincinnati in the late 1960s. There he aired on WSAI, playing contemporary music from 6:00 to 10:00 a.m. Brooke was originally from California where he worked at a number of stations.

Brooks, Rod   Runs a telephone talk show from 6:00 to 9:00 a.m. on KHBU in Anderson, Indiana.

Brother, Louie   Mixed jokes and rock music to please his audience of young listeners. In the mid–1970s he could be found from 6:00 to 10:00 a.m. on WCUE-FM, Akron.

Brown, Bruce   Kept the hours of 6:00 to 10:00 a.m. filled with contemporary music in the 1960s and 1970s. Brown was also the program manager of KELP, El Paso.

Brown, Bud   With a mellow and resonant voice, Brown was morning man for many years at WBRE-AM and FM in Wilkes-Barre. In 1992 Brown became a full-time newsman, moving to WILK-AM in Wilkes-Barre as news director. He currently hosts an all-news program in the early morning, Monday through Friday, until 9:00 a.m.

Brown, Charlie   Combined popular hits with a quick wit and entertaining characters to amuse his listeners. He was heard from 6:00 to 10:00 a.m. on WPTR, Albany, New York, beginning in the mid–1960s.

Brown, Ed   Played the top rock music along with the best sounds of yesteryear. Big Ed could be found during the late 1970s at WTAC, Flint, Michigan. His show aired from 5:00 to 10:00 a.m.

Brown, George *see* **Wayne and Wally**

Brown, Greg   Could be heard in the mid–1970s from 6:00 to 10:00 a.m. on Chicago's WBBM-FM. He featured top hits and presented a showcase for both lesser known and local artists. In the late 1970s he played rock for Chicago from 6:00 to 10:00 a.m. on WMET.

Brown, Jack   This dynamic personality on WINN in Louisville, Kentucky, helped liven up the airwaves during the 1970s. Jack "Bucks" Brown got listeners up and going, while adding humor to his program by taking potshots at local officials and TV personalities.

Brown, Les   Had an upbeat show with a wide appeal during the mid-1970s. He played a mix of hits, rhythm and blues and jazz, from 6:00 to 10:00 a.m. daily on WVKO Columbus. Brown was also operations manager and a member of WVKO's Community Leadership Program.

Bruce, J.   Played a carefully selected program of great standards and the current hits, intermixed with his humor and satire. From 5:00 to 10:00 a.m. during the late 1970s, Worcester, Massachusetts, listed to Bruce on WTAG. Joining him were Rich Kirkland with the news and Brian Leary with sports.

Bruton, Bob   Played the contemporary music of the late 1960s mornings from 5:00 to 9:00 a.m. for his listeners on KXOL, Ft. Worth, Texas.

Bryant, Ron   Played country and western music from 5:00 to 9:00 a.m. while giving his listeners all the local information, including safety driving tips. He aired in Charlotte, North Carolina, during the late 1960s on WKTC.

Buchanan, Buck   *see* **Hudson, Bob**

Buehlman, Clint   Appealed to all ages playing an abundance of peppy music with lots of local news and information mixed in. His show began in the early 1940s and ran through the 1970s, first on WGR, then on WBEN (both stations were in Buffalo), from 6:00 to 10:00 a.m. He had many popular routines and corny gags, such as weather consultant "Arthur Mometer."

Burbank, Gary   Played popular-contemporary music from 6:00 to 9:00 a.m. for CKLW, Windsor, Ontario, during the mid-1970s.

Burns, Don   Took over as morning man at KRLA, Los Angeles, in late 1971 for just a few months.

Burns, Joe   Delivered top 40 music to Cleveland during the late 1970s from 6:00 to 10:00 a.m. on WGCL.

Burns, Zak   Played late 1970s progressive rock for Detroit from 6:00 to 10:00 a.m. on WABX.

Butler, Bob   Gave El Paso, Texas, the best country and western music plus all the local and regional news, mornings from 6:00 to 10:00 a.m. His late 1960s show on KHEY also featured a "Poem of the Day."

Butler, Steve   Combined a little bit of everything in his show: sports, weather, news, and adult contemporary music. His show aired in the 1970s on WREC in Memphis, Tennessee.

Butts, Mike   Set Denver on its ear with his off-the-wall "Butts in the Morning" show. His career took him from the mailroom to *Billboard's*

1970-71 "Personality of the Year." Heard from 5:00 to 9:00 a.m. on KIMN and KIMN-FM during the mid–1970s.

Cafaro, Al   Used his New York acting experience to entertain mid–1970s Charlotte, North Carolina, during its first progressive music morning show. Heard from 5:00 to 10:00 a.m. on WRPL.

Cage, James   Brought late 1970s Detroit to life while playing the Motown sounds. He was heard from 7:00 to 11:00 a.m. on WGPR.

Cain, Jess   Could be heard from 6:00 to 10:00 a.m. on WHDH, Boston, from the late 1960s to the late 1970s. He wove a mix of current hits around his daily supply of humor, news, weather, traffic reports and sports. In the mid–1970s columnist Tim Horgan of the *Boston Herald American* joined him for a look at sports. By the late 1970s it was Nick Mills and Joe Clementi with the news and sports. A true professional with legitimate theater background, Cain played pop standards while entertaining Bostonians with character voices from 6:00 to 10:00 a.m. on WHCH for decades.

Caldwell, Al   Used his 11 years at KAYC to develop a perfect cast of characters for the Beaumont, Texas, area. He played 1970s contemporary music interspersed with local information and one-liners. Caldwell also served as operations manager. Full of local humor, Caldwell's morning show reflected his warm and outrageous personality. Known for crazy stunts and inserting his own lyrics into songs, Caldwell's reputation spread all over Texas. His show ran from 6:00 to 10:00 a.m.

Callahan, Bob   Was a personality in the Baltimore area during the 1970s. Besides playing contemporary music from 6:00 to 10:00 a.m. for WVOB, Bel Air, Maryland, he also hosted a weekly TV show on the Maryland Public Broadcasting System.

Calton, Debbi   Became the only morning woman disc jockey in Charlotte, North Carolina, during the late 1970s. She played progressive rock from 6:00 to 10:00 a.m. on WRPL. Calton was also the program manager.

Cann, Charles   Cann was heard on his 1970s easy listening show that aired in the 6:00 to 10:00 a.m. time slot on KDAN in Newport, Minnesota. Delightful tidbits were heard, along with sports, weather, and a giveaway.

Cantreel, Steve   Spent five years greeting his native Ohio from 5:00 to 9:00 a.m. on WMNI, Columbus. Features included farm news, modern country music and "Day-By-Day with Jesus." Martin Petree did the news. Then in the late 1970s he moved up to the 1:45 to 6:00 p.m. afternoon slot. The station's farm director in the mid–1970s, Cantreel had added program manager to his list of titles by 1978.

Capps, Chet   Mixed gospel music with religious programs from 6:00 a.m. to 12:00 p.m. on WRIP and WOWE, Chattanooga, Tennessee. He aired during the mid–1970s.

Capron, George   Aired from 6:00 to 9:15 a.m. during the late 1970s on

WBRV, Boonville, New York. His "Morning Show" featured music, farm news, news and swap shops.

Captain John and Ludlo   Provided a contemporary disco program that was South Florida's most popular morning show during the 1970s. Dave Ryder and Officer Jim provided news and traffic reports on WQAM, Miami.

Carl, George   Began each "Good Morning Show" in the late 1960s at 5:30 a.m. with 15 minutes of news. Carl then proceeded to give his Napa, California, listeners a pleasing mix of contemporary music, humor, and phone calls until 8:30 a.m. News director Pat Stanley joined him at 7:00 a.m. and 8:00 a.m. Carl was also general manager at KVON.

Carlson, Morrie   Delivered the news to mid–1970s Detroit from 5:30 to 9:30 a.m. on WWJ. During the late 1960s Carlson did afternoons for WWJ.

Carns, Susanne   Spent the late 1970s with her partner Bill Coffey bringing modern country music and all the local information to Akron from 6:00 to 10:00 a.m. on WSLR. She was known for her entertaining tidbits of information.

Carroll, Brothers   Brought a large cast of characters and popular music to his mid–1970s show on WGAS, Gastonia, North Carolina. By the late 1970s the station's and Brothers' format changed over to Christian music, Bible readings, and personal witnessing. He could be heard from 6:00 to 10:00 a.m.

Carroll, Michael   Offered late 1970s Detroit a selection of popular singles and oldies on WXYZ, Southfield, Michigan daily from 6:00 to 10:00 a.m.

Carroll, Ray   Was morning man on WMCA in New York after it became a top 40 radio station in the mid–1950s. Carroll then went on to become morning man at WNAB in Bridgeport, Connecticut. Carroll had a fast wit and liked to poke fun at celebrities. For example, he would introduce a record by Peggy Lee calling her "Peggala."

Carroll, Tom   In the 1980s, WENE in Endicott, New York, which is now WMRV, tried to topple John Leslie's strong ratings by bringing in some heavy hitters. After trying several deejays, the station hired Tom Carroll, a personable, talkative fellow who emphasized call-ins from listeners. But Carroll lacked Leslie's fast wit and incisive commentary, and his relative dullness failed to draw much audience from Leslie.

Caruso, Dan   Played contemporary pop music for Lansing, Michigan, station WVIC from 6:00 to 10:00 a.m. during the winter months of 1978. Caruso's show included the "Star Trekin' Morning Patrol." He presented news twice an hour, and Paul Harvey at 8:55 a.m.

Caruso, Mickey   Was on from 6:30 to 9:00 a.m. on WRLB, Asbury Park, New Jersey, during the mid–1970s. He brought his audience the best standard-popular music along with traffic, news, morning fishing and Coast Guard boating reports.

Carver, Dwayne   From 5:30 to 10:00 a.m. on WSDA in Ann Arbor, Michigan, Carver plays country music and presents a full-service program.

Case, Lee   Was Baltimore's "Morning Mayor" from 5:00 to 10:00 a.m. on WCBM for decades, beginning in the late 1950s. He played a mix of popular music and award winning local news. Neal Eskridge and Tom Davis did the sports.

Cassidy, Scott   Was the "Sweet Child of Inner Truth and Beauty" on Buffalo's WEBR from 6:00 to 10:00 a.m. during the late 1970s. His twisted humor and a combination of hits and oldies mixed nicely with Mike Dewey's newscasts.

Castleberry, Eddie   Started in radio in the mid–1950s and moved to Columbus, Ohio, in the late 1960s. There the "Mayor of the Morning" combined rhythm and blues with jazz and popular music, mornings from 6:00 to 9:00 a.m. on WVKO. Before moving to Columbus, "Reveille Eddie" worked at WCIN, Cincinnati, and WBAQ, Cleveland.

Castrodale, Dave   Was morning man on WDBQ in Dubuque, Iowa, between 1956 and 1958.

Cavanaugh, Paul   Entertained Buffalo, New York, with his own compositions, contests, citizen salutes, horoscopes and traffic reports. He also played the contemporary music of the mid–1970s from 6:00 to 10:00 a.m. on WYSL, Buffalo.

Cavanaugh, Pete   Was on the air during the mid–1970s from 5:00 to 10:00 a.m. on WTAC, Flint, Michigan. His show aimed at the entire family with lively hit music, news and sports, and included four farm reports in the first hour. Previously he had done evenings for the station during the late 1960s. By the late 1970s he was off the air serving as WTAC's general manager.

Cavanaugh, Pete   Played contemporary music for his late 1960s listeners on WTLB, Utica, New York, mornings from 6:00 to 10:00 a.m.

Chapman, Ron   Introduced contemporary pop favorites during the 6:00 to 10:00 a.m. time slot at KVIL, Dallas, Texas, through the 1970s. The station's 24-hour format also included national and local newsbreaks, weather and Howard Cosell on sports.

Charles, Bob   Brought the easy rock of the late 1970s plus comedy cuts and all the local information to Cleveland each morning from 6:00 to 10:00 a.m. Charles was also the production manager at WDMT.

Charles, Tommy   Teamed up with Doug Layton in the late 1960s to bring top 40 music to the Birmingham area. The "Layton and Charles Show" was heard from 6:30 to 9:00 a.m. on WAQY. Charles then moved to the 6:00 to 10:00 a.m. slot on WMPS, Memphis, Tennessee, with adult contemporary music. By the late 1970s Charles had joined with John Willoughby to bring contemporary music and wacky humor to Birmingham.

They could be heard from 6:00 to 10:00 a.m. on WSGN. Charles was also the sports director.

Charlie and Harrigan Were heard in the late 1960s from 5:30 to 9:00 a.m. on WKYC, Cleveland. Their show consisted of situational satires of topical events mixed with upbeat contemporary music. In the mid–1970s they moved to KLIF, Dallas, where from 6:00 to 10:00 a.m. each morning they supplied guests such as "The Lone Ranger," "Herman T. Werlitzer" and "Seymour Broomwad," among others. Andy McCollum did the news.

Chase, Barry Cohosts the "Fat Mattress" program with Scott Woodside. Chase plays traditional old rock 'n' roll from 6:00 to 10:00 a.m. on WZGC in Atlanta.

Childs, Leland Had already been in broadcasting for over 35 years by the late 1960s. At that time he was at WCRT, Birmingham, where his down-home philosophy, local information and popular music filled the hours between 5:00 and 9:00 a.m. By the mid–1970s Childs had moved his Southern charm to Bessemer, Alabama. There, at WYAM, he became general manager and could be heard mornings from 5:00 to 9:00 a.m. playing country and western music.

Childs, Paul From 7:00 to 10:00 a.m. during the 1970s on WNOV in Milwaukee, Paul Childs played a light jazz, disco and rhythm and blues contemporary format. This bright personality's show also included sports, news, and weather.

Childs, Paul Could be heard playing rhythm and blues to 6:00 to 10:00 a.m. on WIGO, Atlanta, during the late 1970s.

Choat, Morgan Let country and western music and his laid-back style entertain his later 1970s listeners from 7:00 to 11:00 a.m. on KJIM, Fort Worth. Choat was also the program manager.

Christy, Jill *see* **Stevens, Eric**

Christy, Jerry Would begin the day easy then pick up the pace to get his audience jumping by lunchtime. Heard on KCBC, Des Moines, during the mid–1970s. Joe Kelly did the news.

Clancy, Gary Used a combination of contemporary music, news, sports and trivia to entertain his late 1970s listeners on WNTN, Newton, Massachusetts. He was heard daily from 6:30 to 10:30 a.m. Virginia Tashjian joined him each morning with "Book Corner."

Clark, Jay Headed up the 6:00 to 10:00 a.m. slot in WTRY in Troy, New York, playing the station's contemporary sound throughout the 1970s.

Clark, Manny Worked an ever-expanding morning time slot from the late 1960s on through the 1970s. He could be heard on WGIV, the only black station in Charlotte, North Carolina. Clark had over 15 years of radio experience.

Clark, Mike   Got Manchester, Connecticut, station WINF off to a good start from 6:00 to 7:00 a.m. in the 1970s. Clark catered to the working class as he filled the airwaves with middle-of-the-road music (Frank Sinatra, Tony Bennett, Nat "King" Cole, Johnny Mathis, Barbra Streisand, etc.) and broadcast the news at 7:05 a.m. Jeff Jacobs, who was also the station's general and program manager, joined Clark until 7:30 a.m. with Frank Sinatra tunes. Clark continued his show until 10:00 a.m. with easy listening music.

Claveria, Moses   Began Hawaii's days with Filipino music and news from Waipahu's KAHU from 5:00 to 6:00 a.m. in the 1970s. Terry Slane followed Claveria with "The Coffee Hours" from 6:00 to 10:00 a.m. This native born deejay got the day started for the station's audience with country and western music, and with five minutes of news on the hour. The station appealed to the military population with its choice of music.

Clay, Tom   Played the top popular music of the mid–1970s each morning from 5:00 to 9:00 a.m. on WTRX, Flint, Michigan. There were news breaks every half hour.

Clayton, Buck   Presented "Carolina in the Morning" from 5:00 to 9:30 a.m. on WOKE, Charleston, S.C. He put his personal stamp on a mid–1970s show that was a mix of popular music and standards plus news and local information.

Clayton, Dan   Played the KBTR playlist of top 40 (plus 5 other records) while entertaining Denver, mornings from 6:00 to 10:00 a.m. during the late 1960s.

Cloer, Mike   Could be heard from 6:00 to 9:00 a.m. playing country and western music for his late 1960s listeners on WWOK, Charlotte. He also produced several national radio and TV shows for major agencies and had several songs published.

Clooney, Nick   Presented a combination of news and popular music, held together by his warm charm, from 6:00 to 10:00 a.m. on WCKY, Cincinnati. He was there during the mid–1970s.

Cobb, Joe   Came to WVON, Chicago, in 1965 after a stint on the radio in Arkansas. Also known as "Youngblood," Cobb played rhythm and blues first in the afternoons during the late 1960s before moving to the 6:00 to 9:00 a.m. slot in the mid–1970s.

Cobb, Larry   Got listeners moving with a contemporary Christian format, news and weather. His show occupied the 6:00 to 8:30 a.m. time slot during the 1970s on WPMH in Portsmouth, Virginia.

Coffey, Bill   Teamed up with Susanne Carns in the late 1970s to bring modern country music and all the local information to Akron from 6:00 to 10:00 a.m. Coffey was also WSLR's program manager.

Cole, Johnny   Did the "Wake Up Show" for WTAC, Flint, Michigan, during the late 1960s. From 5:00 to 6:00 a.m. there were four farm reports. Cole played a combination of popular hits and standards while delivering all the news, sports and weather until 10:00 a.m.

Cole, Lindy   During the 1970s, this personable morning woman awakened listeners to adult contemporary music and information. The format also included sports with Curt Gowdy, Mutual News, Jack Anderson commentary, Jerry Adams and traffic reports. The program occupied the time slot from 6:00 to 10:00 a.m. on KCFX, Edmond, Oklahoma.

Coleman, Townsend   Used offbeat humor and contemporary music to brighten mornings in Akron during the late 1970s. Joining him on WCUE from 5:00 to 10:00 a.m. were Clifford T. Bonzo and traffic reporter Lieutenant Biff Sterno.

Collins, Doug   Aired mornings from 7:00 to 9:00 a.m. on WOIO, Canton, Ohio, during the late 1960s. His "OIO Road Show" was a mixture of top 40 and oldies, plus talk, news, weather and sports with Hymie Williams.

Collins, Michael   Played the popular albums and singles of the late 1970s each day from 6:00 to 10:00 a.m. on WRIF, Southfield, Michigan.

Como, Hunter   Became the morning anchorman for KDAL, Duluth, Minnesota, in 1948 and was still there decades later. Besides playing popular music with no rock, he supplied news, weather and traffic. He aired from 6:00 to 9:00 a.m.

Condon, Joe   Program manager for WHRL, Condon could be heard during the late 1970s playing beautiful music for Albany from 6:00 a.m. to 12:00 p.m.

Conners, Bob   Supplied contemporary hits from 6:00 to 10:00 a.m. on WBNS, Columbus, Ohio, during the mid–1970s. By the late 1970s he was still in Columbus but on WTVN in the afternoon. During the late 1960s Conners had also been at WTVN where he did afternoons. Before this he worked at stations in Buffalo, New York, San Diego and Pittsburgh.

Conrad   Played a selection of modern country music for his listeners on WCUZ, Grand Rapids, Michigan. In the mid–1970s he aired from 6:00 to 10:00 a.m. Later in the decade he switched to the midnight to 6:00 a.m. slot. Conrad did not use his first name on air.

Cooke, Henry   Used his dry wit plus adult music and all the news and local information to prepare his Chicago listeners for the day ahead. He was heard during the late 1960s daily from 6:00 to 10:00 a.m. on WMAQ.

Cooper, Ray   Played black contemporary music for late 1970s Chicago from 6:00 to 10:00 a.m. on WBMX.

Corbitt, Jim   Aired from 6:00 a.m. to 12:00 p.m. on WMQM in Memphis, Tennessee, during the 1970s. His format included religious programs and music which made for delightful Christian listening.

Cordell, Lucky   The "Baron of Bounce" and program director of WVON, Chicago, aired each day from 6:00 to 9:00 a.m. during the late 1960s. His show included rhythm and blues music and "On the Scene with Bernadine."

Cordic, Rege   Cordic & Company, a staple during the 1950s and 60s on KDKA in Pittsburgh, PA, epitomized the golden age of early morning radio. With a wide range of inflections and intonations, Rege Cordic's resonant voice consistently set the proper mood and held listeners' attention no matter what the subject. Even a simple weathercast or traffic report were delivered with style and class. Cordic later moved on to KRLA in Los Angeles.

Corry, Gary   Played popular-contemporary music interspersed with doses of humor to entertain Cincinnati during the late 1960s. He aired on WUBE from 6:00 to 9:00 a.m.

Corse, Bob   Known as the "Early American," Corse bubbled onto the air in the 1960s keeping listeners wide awake with drive-time pop, standard music and fun, in addition to the regular menu of news, weather, sports and traffic reports. Corse's program aired 6:00 to 10:00 a.m. on WILM in Wilmington, Delaware.

Cory, Armand, Jr.   Provided lots of local information plus modern country music for WXRL in Buffalo from 6:00 to 10:00 a.m. during the mid–1970s. A long-time Buffalo radio personality, Cory was also the station's news director.

Couzens, Ed   Was on WGMA, Hollywood, Florida, from 6:00 to 10:00 a.m. during the 1970s. He played modern country music combined with news and local information. On Saturday he supplied the "Flying Fishing Reports."

Cox, Bill   Asheboro, North Carolina, station WZOO aired Bill Cox's antics from 6:00 to 10:00 a.m. during the 1970s winter months. Cox played contemporary music and kept information flowing with his "Zoo Morning Crew," which included such characters as the Chinese weatherman "Usually Wong" and the public service person "Hermit the Frog." Cox was also the station's program director.

Crawford, George   Presented his contemporary style for over 40 years. His many antics and quick wit made him the most popular morning man in the Tidewater area of Virginia. The show aired from 6:00 to 9:00 a.m. on WGH in Newport News, Virginia, during the 1970s.

Crook, Ken   Crook's format of pop contemporary appealed to the middle income and up listeners of WCSC in Charleston, South Carolina, in the early 1970s. His 5:00 to 9:30 a.m. program included farm reports, news, time checks, weather and sports.

Cross, Elwin   Aired his down-home country show from 6:00 to 8:00 a.m. on KEAP Fresno, California, during the 1970s. A radio veteran, Cross doubled as the station's music manager.

Csanyi, Zoltan   "Music Kalyente" is Csanyi's declared format for his 6:00 to 10:00 a.m. show on KALY in Albuquerque. While the emphasis is on Spanish songs, some of the show is done in English.

Cunningham, Joe   Mixed contemporary late 1960s music with his easygoing charm to entertain his listeners from 6:00 to 9:00 a.m. on WHLO, Akron.

Currier, Cosmo   Hosted a telephone talk show during the late 1970s from 6:00 to 8:00 a.m. on WJOB, Hammond, Indiana.

Curtis, Anderson   Greeted Baltimore's black audience during the mid–1970s with a selection of rhythm and blues. He aired each morning from 6:00 to 10:00 a.m. on WEBB.

Curtis, King   Entertained Cleveland with rhythm and blues while working from 7:00 to 10:00 a.m. at WABQ during the mid–1960s.

Dahl, Steve   Brought his humorous cast of characters to WDAI, Chicago, in the late 1970s. Joining Dahl on his 6:00 to 10:00 a.m. show was professional meteorologist Dr. Walt Lyons.

Dahlgren, Doug   Worked with Dick Sainte in the mid–1970s to bring Chicago "The Dick and Doug Show." They combined contemporary music with humor and relevant local information that kept their listeners informed. Heard from 6:00 to 10:00 a.m. on WCFL.

Dale, Dr.   A civically active morning personality, Dr. Dale was popular in the mid–South. "Wake Up with Dale" aired on WFLI, Chattanooga, Tennessee, from 6:00 to 9:00 a.m. in the early 1970s, featuring contemporary music.

Dale, Jeff   A morning show crowded with everything morning listeners needed to know was presented by Dale in the early 1970s on WFAA, Dallas, Texas. Pop standards, news, weather, traffic reports and community announcements were interspersed with Paul Harvey commentaries. The show aired from 6:00 to 9:00 a.m.

Dallas, Steve   Indianapolis' gospel station WNTS featured Dallas 6:00 to 7:30 a.m. during the 1970s. Dallas played a broad variety of Christian music during his airtime.

Dalrymple, Trent   Used a combination of modern country music and local news and information to entertain his listeners. In the late 1970s he aired from 6:00 to 10:00 a.m. on WKMF, Flint, Michigan.

Daniels, Jack   Modern country music with an all-request line was the mainstay of Daniels' 6:00 to 10:00 a.m. program on WWOL in Buffalo, New York, in the early 1970s.

Daniels, Mac   On country station WVAM in Altoona, Pennsylvania, from 5:00 to 10:00 a.m., Daniels provides a strong personality.

Darro, Tom   Spent six years doing the morning show on WJJL in Niagara Falls from 6:00 to 10:00 a.m. until the late 1970s. Then he began doing the "News of Niagara" each day from 8:00 to 9:00 a.m.

Dauro, Johnny   Entertained the Toledo, Ohio, area with modern country and western music and all the local news and information. He aired during the late 1960s from 5:00 to 10:00 on WMGS, Bowling Green, Kentucky.

Davala, Chris   Had a six-day-a-week morning program on WGCH in Greenwich, Connecticut, entitled "Breakfast Special." He was succeeded by Don Russell.

Davey, Harry   Used his call-in talk show to keep his Atlanta audience well informed through the mid–1970s. The knowledgeable conservative could be heard from 7:00 to 10:00 a.m. on WRNG.

Davis, Bill   Supplied Baltimore listeners with late 1970s top 40 rock and the day's news, weather, tide times and information. He was heard from 5:30 to 10:00 a.m. on WNAV.

Davis, Brad   Known by teenagers in the late 1950s for his toothy smile and Dick Clark style hosting of teenage dance hops, Davis worked for many years as a staff announcer for WTIC, in Hartford, Conn., often accompanying the legendary Bob Steele as the reader of commercials and station identifications. In the 1970s, Davis broke away and competed with his old morning show at nearby WDRC in Hartford. Davis captured some of the baby boomers who thought Steele too old-fashioned for their tastes.

Davis, Charlie   Led the "Early Risers Club" daily from 5:30 to 9:00 a.m. on WAPI, Birmingham. His late 1960s show mixed popular hits and standards with frequent news and information updates. In the 1970s his laid-back style could be heard from 5:00 to 9:00 a.m. on WCRT, Birmingham. There he presented a mix of news, sports and rock 'n' roll.

Davis, Don   Aired from 6:00 to 10:00 a.m. during the 1970s on WNOR in Norfolk, Virginia. With his contemporary format, Davis opened the day with lively music, news, information and traffic reports.

Davis, Frank   Played top 40 and oldies for Utica, New York, during the late 1960s from 6:00 to 10:00 a.m. on WIBX.

Davis, George (L.)   Gave his Albany, New York, listeners an energetic show full of country and western hits, popular music and standards and enjoyable humor. He started the business in the early 1940s but did not move to Albany until the 1950s. He spent years doing New York Yankees baseball with Mel Allenon WGY from 5 to 9 a.m.

Davis, Jim   Played the popular-contemporary music of the mid–1970s from 6:00 to 10:00 a.m. on KIOA and KIOA-FM, Des Moines.

Davis, Johnny   His "Wake Up Show" entertained Birmingham in the late 1960s and again in the late 1970s from 5:00 to 9:00 a.m. on WVOK. He featured the best in contemporary music and the "OK Farm Report." Ruth Victor added news and Ken Michaels traffic reports. Davis was also the station's sports and farm director.

Davis, Larry   Mixed popular contemporary hits of the late 1960s with news, weather and sports to entertain Davenport, Iowa. He was heard on KSTT mornings from 5:00 to 9:00 a.m.

Day, Bob   Brought contemporary music, news and local information, including traffic, to Buffalo each morning from 5:30 to 9:00 a.m. on WYSL.

Day, Carl   A veteran of radio, television and movies, Day put on the morning coffee at WHLO in Akron in the late 1960s and early 1970s. Known for his racing exploits (he won the first International Lobster Race in 1970), he played pop standards interspersed with topical and sincere comments from 6:00 to 9:00 a.m. for Akron, Ohio, residents.

Day, Deano   Could be heard from 6:00 to 10:00 a.m. during the mid–1970s on WDEE, Detroit. He combined interviews with local figures and modern country music to entertain his listeners. Day was constantly involved in community activities.

Dayton, Bob   Combined modern country music and telephone chats for his Chicago listeners in the late 1970s. He could be heard from 5:30 to 10:00 a.m. on WJJD.

Dean   Is the morning man on sports station WDCQ in Fort Myers, Florida. Dean is similar to his competitor in Port Charlotte, Jack Mihall, and has a running topical commentary on almost everything under the sun. However, Dean's routines are much more sardonic and actually border on the nasty. He mercilessly teases Pedro the engineer about losing his job. The music is quite different from Mihall's also. Virtually all of the songs are satires on popular songs or are just plain funny, such as "Burgers on the Grill." Dean's program airs Monday through Friday. (Dean never uses his last name.)

Dean, Peter   Gave his listeners adult contemporary music, humor, local news, sports and information. During the late 1970s he could be heard from 5:30 to 10:00 a.m. on WPON, Pontiac, Michigan.

Dee, Gary   Gave mid–1970s Cleveland "The Strange World of Gary Dee" from 6:00 to 10:00 a.m. on WERE. It was a call-in talk show that provided many humorous surprises as well as local information. Bob Neal did the sports. By the late 1970s Dee had switched over to WHK, Cleveland, where he added modern country music to his call-in format.

Dee, Steve   "Jamboree with Steve Dee" greeted country and western fans in Baltimore on WBMD in the 1970s. Dee provided "a new, young modern sound" to the country venue.

DeHaan, Gary   Played gospel music for his Grand Rapids, Michigan, listeners during the late 1970s. He could be heard from 6:00 to 10:00 a.m. on WYGR.

Dekle, Ben   Had spent ten years playing modern country music for WCAY, Cayce, South Carolina, by the mid–1970s. "Friendly Ben" worked into his 6:00 to 9:00 a.m. show topical discussions and features such as "Coffee Hour with Joe." Joe Morris was his sidekick.

DeLaney, Tony   Interspersed late 1960s rock 'n' roll with news, local information and a touch of country and western music. He aired from 6:00 to 9:00 a.m. on KQEO, Albuquerque.

DelGiorno, Bob   Combined contemporary music with the news team of Jim Gannon, Dick Elliot, Earl Finkle and Dave Baum. They kept Chicago entertained and informed in the mid–1970s from 6:00 to 10:00 on WIND.

Delgiorno, Bob   Was on the air during the 1970s from 6:00 to 9:00 a.m. with the "Morning Report" on WWL, New Orleans, Louisiana. This entertaining telephone talk show included CBS News, weather and sports.

Dennis, Allen   Used his improvisational skills and hit music to brighten up Chattanooga, Tennessee, between the hours of 6:00 and 10:00 a.m. during the mid–1970s. Jim Clark performed as his sidekick. Dennis was also WDXB's program manager.

Denson, Chuck   Debuted as a morning air personality in 1978 at WKDD, Akron. From 6:00 to 10:00 a.m. he gave the city bright music, guests and listener call-ins. He doubled as the station's public affairs director.

Desmond, Gerry   In the days when some soft-music, easy-listening stations also had personalities, Desmond was in his prime. He hosted the "Top of the Morning Show" on WLNA-AM and FM in Peekskill, New York, from 5:30 to 10:00 a.m. Monday through Saturday. Desmond had a strong and winsome personality, as did the other deejays at WLNA: George Birdas, Dick Nedin, and several others. The FM station later changed its call letters to WHUD, and although much of the music format has been retained, there are no longer any strong personalities.

DeSuze, Carl   A real Boston legend, DeSuze established himself as a WBZ fixture throughout the forties, fifties, sixties and seventies. Whimsical and charming, he featured contemporary music backed with news, weather, sports, traffic and ecology reports from 6:00 to 9:00 a.m. (later, from 5:30 to 9:00 a.m.)

Diamond, Jack   Brought the late 1970s top 40 hits plus golden oldies to Boston between 5:30 and 10:00 a.m. on WACQ.

Don, Solano   Don's show during the late 1970s was a combination of contemporary music and requests with provocative commentary and contests. There was an emphasis on local news and weather. Don was on from 6:00 to 10:00 a.m. on KUIC, Vacaville, California.

Doney, Jim   Doney's quiet warmth and popular music gave his 6:00 to 11:00 a.m. show a comfortable feel. The features on his mid–1970s show included bingo and the "Jim Doney Flea Mart." Gib Shanley did the sports. Before being on WSUM, Parma, Ohio, Doney spent time on television and as a world traveler.

Donovan, Joe   Along with Don Patrick, Donovan has supplied Detroit with a complete package of news, sports, traffic and features for decades. They could be heard from 5:00 to 10:00 a.m. on News Radio WWJ. Farm news was given each day at 5:55 a.m.

Dooley, Scott   "The Breakfast Flakes" is on from 6:00 to 10:00 a.m. on KPXR in Anchorage, Alaska.

Doremus, John   Beginning in 1965, Doremus joined WAIT in Chicago and was still going strong in the early 1970s on his morning show "Try a Little Tenderness." Honored by the Chicago Radio Industry as "Best Radio Personality," Doremus played album standards from 5:00 to 10:00 a.m. along with time and temperature checks, and weather and traffic reports from phone-equipped drivers.

Dorick, Tom   Was morning man on WJLK-AM and FM in Asbury Park, New Jersey, for many years. Dorick hosted the "Alarm Clock Club" Monday through Friday and on alternate Saturdays. Evening drive-time personality Jim Michaels stepped in on alternate Saturdays. Later in the day, Dorick also hosted the "Bird Watchers Society Program."

Dorman, Dale   Dorman's contemporary sound chased the morning grumpiness out of Bostonians in the 1970s on WRKO from 6:00 to 9:00 a.m.

Douglas, Art   Has hosted the "Morning Wake-Up Show" for WCOJ, Coatesville, Pennsylvania, for several decades. From 5:30 to 10:00 a.m. Monday through Friday, he sings along with standard music and offers lots of commentary.

Dow, Wally   Was morning man on WHTG-AM and FM Eatontown, New Jersey, in the 1960s and 1970s. He would play several songs in a row by the same artist, and then talk with a rich baritone voice. The type of music was easy listening. He also broadcast news twice an hour, and did the "Noon News Round-up" from 11:55 a.m. to 12:10 p.m.

Dowe, Ken   Brightened mornings with his partner Grandma Emma in

Dallas during the late 1960s and 1970s with plenty of humor. Contemporary music, news and local information were also part of the show. Dowe aired from 6:00 to 10:00 a.m. during the late 1960s on KLIF, and 7:00 to 9:00 a.m. through the 1970s on KNUS, where he was operations manager.

Doyle, Tom   Supplied the Worcester, Massachusetts area with "Superstar" album rock music during the late 1970s. He aired from 6:00 to 10:00 a.m. on WAAF.

Drake, Bill   Got Spartanburg, South Carolina, jumping as he played adult contemporary music on WSPA from 6:00 to 10:00 a.m. during the 1970s. The music was geared for listeners aged 25–49. Drake also covered local and national news and sports.

Drennan, Jay   Played modern country music while entertaining Akron with his personable style. The "Jaybird" began his career in 1944 and joined WSLR in 1966. In the late 1960s he was heard from 6:00 to 9:00 a.m. His show was expanded by an hour in the mid–1970s to 6:00 to 10:00 a.m. He then went to KRLA in Los Angeles.

Driver, Rick   Played country music for WBBR's early morning crowd from 5:00 to 9:30 a.m. during the summer of 1978. This Travelers Rest, South Carolina, gospel station appealed to its on-the-road audience with an upbeat sound.

DuCoty, Chuck   Used the late 1970s to combine popular rock music, sports, weather and traffic reports on WKTK, Baltimore, from 6:00 to 10:00 a.m.

Dunaway, Ray   Runs a full-service morning program on WTIC in Hartford, Connecticut.

Duncan, Dopey   Bounced his quick wit off straight man Paul Galgon to form "Two on the Sunnyside" during the late 1960s. Their humorous show aired from 6:00 to 9:00 on WKAP, Allentown, and included news, weather, features and popular music. By the mid–1970s Duncan moved to WEZV, Bethlehem, Pennsylvania.

Dunn, Dusty   From 6:00 to 10:00 a.m., WBIG's Dunn woke up his Greensboro, North Carolina, audience with contemporary and upbeat middle-of-the-road music and local news.

Dunn, Paul   Wove the best easy listening music, past and present, with humor and news and sports with Bruce Hamilton. They were heard during the late 1970s, mornings from 6:00 to 10:00 a.m. Dunn doubled as program manager for WDBF, Delray Beach, Florida.

Dunn, Tom   Began each day at 5:30 a.m. with a half-hour farm report. Easy-listening music then filled the morning until 9:30 a.m. He could be heard from the mid–1960s through the mid–1970s on KOB, Albuquerque.

Durant, Naomi   A black pastor, Durant is the morning host on WBGR in Baltimore between 5:00 and 10:00 a.m. The program is aimed at the black working person.

Early, Bobby   The "Bobby Early Show" aired during the 1970s from 6:00 to 10:00 a.m. on WBOK, New Orleans, Louisiana. This wild and crazy deejay supplied listeners with an "anything goes" soul music show, and was number one on the drive-time slot.

Edwards, Jay   Spent the late 1960s playing standards and popular music to his listeners on WEEX, Easton, Pennsylvania, mornings from 5:00 to 9:00 a.m. Dave Reynolds did the news.

Edwards, Willie   Woke up his WTOB audience with his unique style from 6:00 to 10:00 a.m. He played contemporary top 40 hits and local news during the 1970s. Edwards was a well-known deejay at this point, and had his share of fans. He had been WTOB deejay for eight years. He was also this Winston-Salem, North Carolina, station's operating and program manager.

Edwardsen, Bill   Is morning man on WABY in Albany, New York, from 6:00 to 10:00 a.m. playing music from the 1950s, 1960s, 1970s and 1980s. In the 1950s through the 1980s, Edwardsen's "The Grump Club" could be heard from 6:30 to 11:00 a.m. on WQBK, Albany. Joining the fun were Hank Kunze, the "Farm and Garden Advisor"; and Jim Kenealy, "QBK's Outdoor Editor." Edwardsen's irreverent wit brought him high ratings beginning in the 1950s.

Elena, Maria   Called the "Grand Lady" of Spanish-speaking radio, Elena was well-known to the Spanish speaking population of Bakersfield, California. By the early 1970s she had established herself as a local leader of the Mexican-American community with over 14 years on the air. Her program on KWAC (a 24-hour-a-day Spanish language station in Bakersfield) featured ethnic music and aired from 7:00 to 10:00 a.m. during the 1970s.

Ellery, Jack   Has been, with some interludes, morning man on WCTC in New Brunswick, New Jersey, for decades. His format was fastpaced for 1963, but was average for 1993. Ellery also worked at WNBC in New York. The music format grew more conservative as younger listeners deserted AM radio, and WCTC no longer simulcasts on FM.

Elliott, Mike   Was morning man for WGST in Atlanta, Georgia, playing contemporary favorites from 6:00 to 9:00 a.m. during the early 1970s.

Elwell, Roy   At many television and radio stations throughout his career, Elwell did a prerecorded morning show on KRLA, Los Angeles, in the early 1970s.

Emm, Lou   Had Dayton, Ohio, "Dialing Emm for Music" each day from 5:00 to 10:00 a.m. The show contained local news and Emm's own brand of humor along with the popular hits of the day. Emm was also program director at WHIO. By the late 1960s Emm had been on the air in Dayton for over 25 years. Winston Hoehner joined Emm in the late 1970s and added to the show with his quick wit.

England, Jack Brought beautiful music and news on the hour to the Napa Valley during the late 1970s. He aired from 6:00 a.m. to 12:00 p.m. on KVYN, Napa, California.

Engleman, Ron Played contemporary music with John London during the late 1970s for Denver each day from 6:00 to 9:00 a.m. on KTLK.

Enlow, Doug Kept his show rocking with contemporary hits and local information. He aired on WNOK, Columbus, South Carolina, from 6:30 to 10:00 a.m. during the mid–1970s.

Erickson, Rick Played the top 40 hits of the mid–1970s along with local information in Davenport, Iowa. His show was heard from 6:00 to 10:00 a.m. daily on KSTT.

Ervine, Jeff Airs from 6:00 to 10:00 a.m. on KWIZ-FM in Santa Ana, California. His cohost is John Kobik. Soft rock is the musical format.

Erwin, George Started in the 1930s as morning man on KFJZ in the Fort Worth area. His 5:00 to 10:00 a.m. show played contemporary music aimed at adults. Erwin doubled as the music manager at the station. In the late 1970s he moved over to KXOL where he played modern country music.

Ethridge, Joe P. An easygoing personality, Ethridge headed up the 6:00 to 9:00 a.m. time slot on KRYS in Corpus Christi, Texas. Ethridge began in 1965 and continued through the 1970s.

Eubanks, Bob A popular television game show host, Eubanks got his start at KRLA in Los Angeles, first as the all-night man, then as morning man in 1962 when his predecessor, Wink Martindale, asked listeners to vote for the next morning man. Eubanks opened several night clubs in the Los Angeles area, and later became a concert promoter. He switched shifts in 1963, and was succeeded by Bob Hudson.

Evans, Dan An audience of affluent adult listeners flocked to Evans' cheery patter and topical comments on KDEF in Albuquerque, New Mexico, in the 1970s. Evans' program, which featured pop standards, ran from 6:00 to 9:00 a.m.

Evans, Don Brought contemporary Christian music, news and information to Dallas in the late 1970s. The show aired mornings from 6:00 to 10:00 a.m. on KPBC.

Evans, Garry Beginning in 1963, Evans headed up the 5:00 to 9:00 a.m. time slot on KEYS, Corpus Christi, Texas, playing pop-contemporary music. Doubling as farm editor at the station, he dispensed advice on everything from "making a sack lunch" to "cotton-growing" problems.

Evans, Jack   With partner Dick Zipf, Evans entertained Columbus, Ohio, listeners in the late 1970s. They also added adult contemporary music and local information to their 5:30 to 10:00 a.m. show on WBNS.

Evans, John   Aired his "Wake Up Show" during the late 1970s from 6:00 to 8:00 a.m. on WNSR and WLYN, Lynn, Massachusetts. He spent the time playing a mix of standard-popular music along with the Big Band sound.

Everhart, Bill   Captivated local people with his amiable voice as he played golden hit music for Lexington, North Carolina's, WBUY during the 1970s. This warm-hearted 17-year veteran was proficient with local news and was an exceptional ad-libber.

Fanady, Nick   Teamed up with Bob Vernon to lighten up late 1970s Detroit with a special brand of humor. Their cast of characters included, among others, "Buzz and Jugs," "Uncle Lenny's Wake-Up Stories for Grownups" and "The Graffiti Lady." They performed from 6:00 to 10:00 a.m. on WCAR.

Farrell, Jim   Gave Boston a "Commuters Concert" each morning from 6:00 to 9:00 a.m. on WCRB. The music of his late 1960s show consisted of marches, waltzes and light concert favorites.

Fat Daddy   A legend in Baltimore since his show began in 1960, Fat Daddy gave morning listeners something to talk about at work with his unusual delivery. Billed as the "hottest and fastest radio program ever," Fat Daddy spun rhythm and blues music for morning listeners on WWIN in the 1960s and 1970s.

Faye, Marty   Jazz music was the feature of Faye's 6:00 to 9:00 a.m. program on WBEE in Chicago in the early 1970s. The show appealed to the black audience. In the late 1970s, the airtime changed to 7:00 to 11:00 a.m.

Felder, Dave   Opened the airwaves for Houston, Texas, station KCOH from 6:00 to 9:00 a.m. during the 1970s. This deejay really got things rolling with his exhilarating vitality as he played rhythm and blues, including oldies four times an hour.

Fennoy, Dave   Presents jazz from 6:00 to 10:00 a.m. on KBJZ in Santa Monica, California. His sophisticated pattern is aimed at an upscale audience.

Field, Allan   Follows a "Music-of-Your-Life" format between 6:00 and 10:00 a.m. on WITH in Baltimore.

Finan, Joe   Was very knowledgeable, a trait that helped him as he discussed a wide variety of topics with his call-in listeners. He aired from

6:00 to 11:00 a.m. during the late 1960s on KTLN, Denver. Finan returned to Cleveland in the 1970s to be on the air from 6:00 to 10:00 a.m. on WHK. He provided Cleveland with country hits and his own special brand of quick chats with his listeners. By the late 1970s his show had moved up to the 10:00 a.m. to 1:00 p.m. slot.

Finch, L. Durwood ("Dee")   Got his start in radio over 50 years ago at Binghamton's oldest station, WNBF. He became famous when he joined Gene Rayburn and later Gene Klavan at WNEW in New York.

Finch, Jim *see* **Boggs, Otis**

Fisher, Ed   Used a combination of piano playing, old and new hit music, and lively interviews and discussions on the "Grouch Club" to entertain and enlighten Cleveland from the late 1960s through the 1970s. His 5:30 to 10:00 a.m. show on WJW also featured in-depth news, traffic, sports and business reports.

Fisher, Joe   A former entertainer and professional model, Fisher was playing rhythm and blues music for WRBD during the late 1960s. Staying in Fort Lauderdale, he moved over to WCKO and 13 years later, was still there in the late 1970s. His 7:00 to 11:00 a.m. show on WCKO included an interesting mix of disco, jazz and music for lovers. Fisher was also the station's director of operations and program director.

Fisher, Kelson   Has worked in his hometown of Baltimore since 1954. During the mid–1970s he could be heard playing rhythm and blues from 6:00 to 10:00 a.m. on WWIN each morning. Better known as "Chop-Chop," he also worked with the Baltimore Urban League and other civic organizations.

Fiske, Fred   Began in the late 1940s on the radio in the Washington, D.C., area and continued for decades. Fiske's combination of in-depth news, sports, popular music and standards could be heard from 6:00 to 10:00 a.m. on WWDC.

Fitzgerald, Bob   Plied his listenable personality from 5:00 to 10:00 a.m. on WHBF in Rock Island, Illinois, during the early 1970s. His format included pop standards dotted with time checks, temperature readings, weather reports and general information.

Fitzsimmons, Bob   A master raconteur and interviewer with a smooth delivery, New York native Fitzsimmons was best known on now defunct WNEW-AM, where he worked sporadically beginning in 1962. At that time, Fitzsimmons played "Trevor Traffic," providing road reports to the Klavan and Finch team. Fitzsimmons ran the afternoon drive-time show on WNEW from 1973 to 1979, and from 1989 to 1991, he was half of WNEW's morning team, along with Al Rosenberg. When Rosenberg left in 1991, Fitzsimmons ran the show alone for over a year. Between these stints at WNEW, Fitzsimmons worked for WRKL in New City, New York; WFMJ in Youngstown, Ohio; WPEN in Philadelphia, Pennsylvania;

and WHN and WABC in New York. Fitzsimmons was only 53 when, on June 2, 1993, he collapsed and died at a Manhattan restaurant.

Flagg, Paul (W.)   Transformed on the air into "Sir Raggedy Flagg of WIGO" each day from 6:00 to 9:00 a.m. Arriving at WIGO, Atlanta, from Columbus, Georgia, in the mid–1960s, he filled his show with rhythm and blues, popular music and local information. By the late 1960s he had moved over to WERD, Atlanta, where he aired from 5:00 to 9:00 a.m.

Flying Dutchman   With sports reporter Charles Eckman and the WFBR "trafficopter," the "Flying Dutchman" got Baltimore listeners to work with his refreshing, appealing commentary on popular standards from 5:30 to 9:00 a.m. in the 1970s.

Ford, Mike *see* **Robbins, Jim**

Foreman, Jim   Could be found during the mid–1970s waking Baton Rouge listeners each morning from 6:00 to 10:00 a.m. with rhythm and blues hits. Big Jim was also WXOK's operational manager.

Forrest, Tal   Was heard from 6:00 to 10:00 a.m. on WEBB during the late 1960s. He played a combination of popular hits and rhythm and blues for his Baltimore audience.

Forte, Bud   Gave Wheeling, West Virginia, the best of modern country music in the late 1970s. He aired from 6:00 to 9:00 a.m. on WWVA. Jerry Kelanic did the news.

Foster, Rebel *see* **Hudson, Bob**

Fox, Bill   Worked from 6:00 to 9:00 a.m. on WPOC, Baltimore, where he delivered a mix of country music during the mid–1970s.

Fox, Charlie   Played contemporary late 1970s album rock for his Denver listeners from 6:00 to 10:00 a.m. on KXKX.

Fox, John   Ran a tight show from 6:00 to 9:00 a.m. on WPLO, Atlanta. From the late 1960s through the mid–1970s he played a carefully balanced blend of country western music with regularly scheduled breaks for weather, traffic and local news. Before this his on-air jobs ranged from reporting news and playing symphony music.

Fraim, John   Began hosting WTVN's 5:30 to 10:00 a.m. slot in 1965 and was still at it in the late 1970s. He used a combination of offbeat stories, current hits and local news and information to keep Columbus, Ohio, entertained. Fraim also did a stint as the station's news director.

France, John   Mixed topical humor with news and country music to get mid–1970s Des Moines going in the morning. He was heard from 6:00 to 10:00 a.m. on KSO.

Francis, James   Called "Cincinnati's Morning Mayor," Francis used his quick wit and personal characters to entertain WLW listeners from the mid–1960s through the 1970s. He was heard from 6:00 to 10:00 a.m. daily. Francis also aired a soap opera that became a classic. Patrick O'Neill helped create the fun.

Franklin, Dave   Modern country music anchored Franklin's 6:00 to 10:00 a.m. program on WOKO in Albany, New York, in the 1970s. A radio veteran, Franklin offered a sparkling wake-up commentary interspersed with traffic reports, road conditions, weather and news.

Franklin, Jim   Used a modern country format and provided local news, school lunch menus, swap shops, and great music. His show occupied the airwaves during the 1970s on KRBB in Sallisaw, Oklahoma.

Frederick, Charlie   Was the morning deejay for Lansing, Michigan, station WITL 6:00 to 9:00 a.m. in the 1970s. This humorous former "major market pro" kept his show rolling with the help of his sidekick "Ruda Baga." Frederick played modern country music and featured news twice an hour.

Fredericks, John   Program manager and morning deejay, Fredericks worked for Kansas City's KWKI mornings from 6:00 to 10:00 a.m. in the 1970s. The show consisted of adult-oriented rock music and the broadcasting of Contemporary and FM network news furnished by ABC.

Freeman, James   Took over the 6:00 to 10:00 a.m. slot at WJLD, Birmingham, in the late 1970s where he played rhythm and blues.

Friedberg, Warren   Spent 6:00 to 10:00 a.m. playing current hits and having telephone chats with his audience during the mid–1970s. By the late 1970s the show's format changed over to a straight telephone talk show. Friedberg worked at WLNR, Lansing, Illinois. Roger Triemstra did the weather and traffic.

Fritts, Robby   Preceded Max Meeks on WFMR in High Point, North Carolina, for many years. Fritts aired from 5:30 to 6:00 a.m. playing gospel music. Meeks took over at 6:00 a.m. and continued to 10:00 a.m. with standard music.

Frost, Jack   Played balanced selection of standards and popular hits with no rock 'n' roll. He aired mornings from 6:00 to 10:00 a.m. during the late 1960s for KERN, Bakersfield, California.

Fuller, Mark   Woke up the Mohawk Valley with his own special humor and a blend of adult contemporary music and golden oldies. His "Rise and Shine" show could be heard during the late 1970s at WALY, Herkimer, New York, from 6:00 to 9:00 a.m.

Fulton, Art   Combined phone calls and interviews with adult contemporary music to entertain his KMWX listeners from 6:00 a.m. to 10:00 a.m. with an hour break for news. By the late 1970s he had spent 12 years doing mornings in Yakima, Washington. Fulton doubled as the operations manager.

Fulton, Bob   Delivered lots of news and sports along with contemporary music each day from 6:00 to 9:00 a.m. during the late 1960s on WCOS, Columbia, South Carolina. There was also a fishing report every Friday.

Fusco, Al   Headed up the 6:00 to 10:00 a.m. time slot on WNBF, Binghamton, New York, after John Leslie ended his first stint and before Ted Baer came on the scene in the 1970s. His show had a blend of pop contemporary hits, newscasts, service information and ski and golf reports in season.

Fusco, Dan   Had been "Mr. Morning Man of the Mohawk Valley" for over 16 years by the late 1960s. He entertained his Utica, New York, audience with the best of all music, plus phone discussions with his listeners. He aired from 6:00 to 10:00 a.m. on WBVM.

Gabby and Ken   Aired from 6:00 to 10:00 a.m. on KATT, Oklahoma City, Oklahoma. This album rock station also provided live news five days a week. Audience response was phenomenal during the 1970s.

Gale, Jack   Was the voice behind Lady Hortense, Lope the folk singer, a talking gorilla, the Doctor, Dawson Bells the poet and Traffic Inspector Tom Graff. The entire group, along with a selection of contemporary music, was heard during the late 1960s daily from 6:00 to 9:00 a.m. on WAYS, Charlotte, North Carolina.

Galgon, Paul *see* **Duncan, Dopey**

Gallagher, Joe   Supplied his listeners with the day's information and modern country music. He was heard in the late 1970s from 5:30 to 9:00 a.m. on WOKO, Albany. Joining Gallagher was news director Bryan Jackson.

Gallaher, Eddie   Coordinated a news, talk and information show each morning from 6:00 to 10:00 a.m. Gallaher was heard during the late 1960s on WTOP, Washington, D.C.

Gallegos, Andrea   Hosts the 6:00 to 10:00 a.m. slot Monday through Friday on KABQ in Albuquerque, New Mexico. She appeals to Hispanic youths with both Spanish and English hits.

Galloway, Ed   Played modern country music for Charlotte, North Carolina, while his versatile voice helped him deliver daily features with President Carter, Redd Foxx, Muhammad Ali and more. His late 1970s show was on from 6:00 to 10:00 a.m. on WAME.

Garcia, Jose (Luis)   Used the phone from 6:00 to 10:00 to involve his KAMA, El Paso, listeners in his show. Also featured in his mid–1970s show were Mex-Tex hits, news and sports.

Garcia, Pedro   Hartford, Connecticut, station WLVH featured the "Pedro Garcia Show" from 6:00 a.m. to 12:00 p.m. Garcia started the morning off with the "Así Canta Puerto Rico" from 6:00 to 7:00 a.m. He played country music, mixing in genuine country jokes and dialogue convincing enough for people to believe that there were two Pedros in the station. Garcia's show during the 1970s also included half-hour news programs at 7:00 a.m. and five minute news breaks every hour. He also broadcast a drama at 10:00 a.m., and took music requests at 11:00 a.m. Garcia was also the Spanish director for the station.

Garry, John   Beginning in 1970, Garry took over the morning drive-time show on WIST in Charlotte, North Carolina, disarming listeners with his offbeat humor. Garry's show featured contemporary music from 6:00 to 9:00 a.m.

Gates, Al   Could be heard each morning from 6:00 to 9:00 a.m. on WRKO. "Gatesy" used a combination of his glib humor and contemporary music to entertain Boston in the late 1960s.

Gates, Tony   Played album oriented rock for his listeners daily from 6:00 to 10:00 a.m. During the late 1970s he was heard on WLAV-FM, Grand Rapids, Michigan.

Gatley, George   Used up-tempo country and western music and his "Good morning sunshine, it's great to be in South Florida" greeting to get his listeners moving during the late 1960s. The "Gentleman George Show" was heard from 6:00 to 10:00 a.m. on WIXX, Fort Lauderdale, Florida. Lyle Reeb did the news.

Gay, Brian and Myrick Tom   Provided music, news, weather, sports and banter. Their show was aired during the 1970s on WIXK in New Richmond, Wisconsin.

Gee, Jerry   Used his corny humor and country and western music to entertain Austin, Texas, from 6:00 to 10:00 a.m. on KOKE starting in 1967 and continuing into the late 1970s.

Giese, John   Lansing, Michigan, station WILS featured Giese and Bill Andres from 6:00 to 10:00 a.m. during the 1970s. This duo's focus on humor and human interest kept their show moving as they played adult oriented rock and news hourly.

Gilbert, George   The morning man on WARM in Scranton in the early 1970s, Gilbert was competent but nondescript in style and personality. He later went on to become general manager of WRAK in Williamsport, Pennsylvania, where he completely revamped the station from a traditional 1940s format to a contemporary, pop music format. He currently has an afternoon music program on WARM.

Gilroy, Cranberry   "The Western Jamboree" program headed by Gilroy drew faithful listeners from teens to adults, on WPTS in Pittston, Pennsylvania, in the 1960s. The morning show, which aired from 7:00 to 11:00

a.m., featured Gilroy's "Pick Hit of the Week," weather reports, interviews and sidekick Carol Lee giving household hints.

Glaize, Paul Aired during the 1970s from 6:00 to 10:00 a.m. on WXRI in Portsmouth, Virginia. On this contemporary Christian station, listeners enjoyed sports, news, weather, and good Christian music on "Sonshine Radio."

Gordon, Bill Brought late 1970s Cleveland the "WBBG 1260 Good Morning Cleveland Show." The 5:30 to 10:00 a.m. show was filled with two-way talk between "Smoochie" Bill and his listeners.

Gorgo, Joe Rocked South Jersey with top 40 music, plus news and community happenings during the late 1970s. He was heard from 6:00 to 11:00 a.m. on WDVL-FM, Vineland, New Jersey.

Gould, David Hosted "Radio Reveille" with Ted Besesparis, from 5:30 to 9:00 a.m. during the late 1970s. Their show on WPBR, Palm Beach, consisted of talk, call-ins, news, sports, weather and consumer reports.

Grady, Don Involved his Baton Rouge audience every workday from 6:30 to 9:00 a.m. on WJBO. A 12-year veteran by the mid–1970s, his show included riddles, features, telephone chats, and popular-standard music. Grady also worked as the program director.

Graham, Dodson Lit up WFMF, Baton Rouge, each morning from 6:00 to 10:00 a.m. through the mid–1970s. His show was a well-balanced blend of old and new hits, plus the occasional touch of jazz.

Grant, Barry Could be heard from 6:00 to 10:00 a.m. playing modern country music during the late 1970s at WIRK-FM, West Palm Beach.

Grant, Bruce Could be heard during the late 1960s on WOOD, and in the 1970s on WOOD and WOOD-FM. He began his show at 5:00 a.m. with "RFD 1300," giving Grand Rapids the farm news and weather. He continued from 6:30 to 9:00 a.m. with the local news and current hits and oldies. Grant was also the farm director.

Gray, Fred Began on radio in 1941 and in the late 1970s was on WGNC, Gastonia, North Carolina. His 5:00 to 10:00 a.m. show featured his wit and humor along with local information.

Greaseman Orange, Park, Florida, station WAPE featured the unusual Greaseman from 5:30 to 9:30 a.m. during the 1970s. This one-time truck driver played rock 'n' roll music and reported news every half hour.

Greene, Bob A veteran of radio with wide broadcasting experience, Greene spun country and western hits on WCOP in Boston during the 1970s from 6:00 to 10:00 a.m.

Greene, Charles Brought "Soul At Sunrise" to Columbia, South Carolina, daily from 6:30 to 8:00 a.m. during the late 1960s. His WOIC show consisted of rhythm and blues and the news.

Greer, Charlie   Used a warm, personal touch to entertain Akron in the mid–1970s from 6:00 to 10:00 a.m. on WAKR. News, sports, weather and current hits filled the show.

Gregory, Rex   His wit, charm, humor, and doses of country music awakened Albany in the late 1970s. He could be heard on WGNA from 6:00 to 10:00 a.m. He now is morning man between 6:00 to 8:30 a.m. on WHAZ and WMYY in Albany, New York.

Gregson, Al   From 6:00 to 9:00 a.m. drive-time listeners in York, Pennsylvania, heard Gregson introduce popular standards, news, sports reports and weather in the late 1960s on WORK.

Gregson, Jack   Used the hours from 6:00 to 10:00 a.m. to combine country music with an hour of open phone lines, news, weather and beach reports on WEXY, Miami. He was there during the mid–1970s.

Grieff, June   Indianapolis station WFBQ featured "Glory" June Grieff 6:00 to 10:00 a.m. "Glory" June got the station's listeners off to a good start with her lighthearted ways as she played adult-oriented rock and reported news.

Griffin, Ken   Farmington, Connecticut, station WRCH presented Griffin from 6:00 to 10:00 a.m. in the 1970s. His loony, off-the-wall, impulsive ways drew attention to his show as he created voice characters and even "birthday chickens." This unusual program manager and deejay really got into his own comedy routines and local contests, too. Griffin broadcast three times every hour, and had an hourly comedy serial called "Life is a Big Cookie."

Griffin, Todd   During the 1970s Griffin entertained Memphis, Tennessee, listeners with great contemporary music from the very early hour of 2:00 to 10:00 a.m. on WHBO.

Gunn, Pete   Brought rhythm and blues and soul, along with his "Information Spectrum" of local news and time, to mid–1970s Chattanooga, Tennessee, from 6:00 to 10:00 a.m. on WNOO.

Gunter, Jimmy   A firmly entrenched country and western spinner for 20 years, Gunter served up music for early risers on WBBW in Youngstown, Ohio, in the late 1960s from 5:30 to 6:00 a.m.

Gunton, Dick   Gave his late 1970s listeners a mix of soft rock and local information and news. He could be heard from 5:00 to 10:00 a.m. on WEEI-FM, Boston.

Gutierrez, Ben   Brought Spanish music to Fresno, California, from 6:00 to 8:00 a.m. on KGST during the mid–1970s. In the late 1970s he aired from 8:00 to 9:00 a.m. He was also the station's general manager and operations manager.

Haggert, Mickey   A ten-year veteran in the Easton, Pennsylvania, area, Haggert was at WEEX from 6:00 to 10:00 a.m. during the late 1970s. His light style, area knowledge, and mix of contemporary rock and oldies kept his listeners smiling. He was also the station's program manager.

Halfyard, Jim   Could be heard playing late 1970s contemporary music from 6:00 to 10:00 a.m. on WCGY, Lawrence, Massachusetts.

Halison, Frank   Set his clock five minutes ahead to make sure his Baltimore listeners got to work on time. His 6:00 to 10:00 a.m. "Hot Dog Show" on WEBB featured black rhythm and blues and soul music plus wake-up chatter and creative contests in the 1970s.

Hamberger, George   During the mid–1970s "Hamburger" was on WGRQ, Buffalo, from 6:00 to 10:00 a.m. with news, sports, and lots of hit music.

Hamilton, Bill   Easy listening music and a likeable wit made Hamilton's 6:00 to 10:00 a.m. show popular with listeners of WBNS in Columbus, Ohio, during the 1970s.

Hamilton, Bob   Rocked Grand Rapids in the mid–1970s with his music and charm from 6:00 to 10:00 a.m. on WLAV-FM.

Hamilton, Chuck   Beginning in 1969, "Chucker" joined the KSTT "good guys" playing contemporary pop in Davenport, Iowa. Hamilton's program aired from 6:00 to 10:00 a.m.

Hanauer, Roy   Entertained Central Indiana listeners during the mid–1970s with modern country music from 6:00 to 11:30 a.m. Hanauer was the music manager at WFWR, Fort Wayne, Indiana.

Hanson, Charles   Was a multitalented professional who provided a popular contemporary style format during the 1970s, which included Paul Harvey, local news, sports and traffic. The show occupied the time slot from 6:00 to 10:00 a.m. on WISN in Milwaukee, Wisconsin.

Happy Instant Music   Known as the "cleverest deejay morning man in the Midwest," Happy Instant Music zeroed in on his teenaged and mixed adult audience in the mid–1960s with an alter ego named Maudy in KLEO in Wichita, Kansas. He doubled as KLEO's music director.

Harding, John   With Charlie Martin, Harding formed the "Charlie and Harding Show" from 6 a.m. to 9 a.m. on KHOW, Denver, during the mid–70s. Their format included old and current hits and discussions on almost anything.

Harmon, Hank   Used an up-tempo approach to energize his listeners each morning from 6:00 to 10:00 a.m. His show consisted of the then-current hits of the late 1960s along with news and local information plus Harmon's comments. He aired on KSO, Des Moines, Iowa.

Harper, Bobby   Mixing humor and controversy, "Skinny" Bobby Harper headed up a feature-filled morning show on WIIN, Atlanta, Georgia, in the early 1970s. "20/20 News," and "Eye in the Sky," traffic and sports reports filled the 6:00 to 10:00 a.m. slot.

Harrigan, Irving *see* **Hudson, Mark**

Harris, Don   Intended his country and western show for the young adult market. He could be heard from 6:30 to 9:00 a.m. on WBAP, Fort Worth, during the 1970s. In the late 1960s Harris aired on WBAP from 10:00 a.m. to 12:00 p.m.

Harris, Jack   Hosts a full service non-music morning show in Tampa, Florida, on WFLA with veteran sportscaster Ted Webb.

Harryman, Charles   Harryman's "Wake Up to Music with Charles Harryman" was presented on Kansas City station KXTR 5:00 to 6:00 a.m. during the 1970s. His show featured classical music.

Hawkins, Don   Joined Kris Kane to bring Denver album-oriented rock music in the late 1970s. They could be heard from 6:00 to 10:00 a.m. on KAZY.

Hawkins, Ken   Played his "Soul Sounds" of rhythm and blues for Cleveland during the late 1960s. He aired from 6:00 to 9:00 a.m. on WJMO.

Hayes, Johnny   Was morning man on KRLA, Los Angeles, in the early 1970s.

Haywood, Bill   Brought rhythm and blues to Washington, D.C. during the late 1960s from 5:00 to 9:00 a.m. on WOOK and WOL.

Healey, Jerry   Joined WAKR, in Akron, in the mid–1960s, filling in the 6:00 to 10:00 a.m. slot. He played a selection of popular music and provided news and daily information with his partners Sam and Serena. Before this he was a veteran of Chicago radio and hosted the television show, "Golf with Sam Snead." As of this writing, he is morning man on a satellite network, "Original Hits."

Heckman, Fred *see* **Todd, Gary**

Hendrickson, Fred   During the 1970s from 5:00 to 6:00 a.m. on WKY, Oklahoma City, Oklahoma, Hendrickson's show awakened a large rural audience to contemporary country music.

Henning, Paul   Was on the air during the 1970s from 5:00 to 10:00 a.m. on WTAR, Norfolk. This witty morning man brightened the mornings of his audience with music, news, weather and traffic reports.

Henry, Dan   The 6:00 to 10:00 a.m. shift on WGUL in Palm Harbor, Florida, has been Dan Henry's for several years. WGUL has a "Music of Your Life" format but uses all live, local personalities rather than the canned national format. Besides Henry, there are two other longtime deejays at WGUL: Les Foerrster, who has the mid-day program, and Denny Bateman, who has afternoon drive-time. Each gentleman takes a turn at the 6:00 a.m. to 12:00 p.m. shift every third Saturday. Prior to 1995, Henry and Bateman worked alternate Saturday mornings, while Foerrster alternated Saturday afternoons with Marv Boone, the former evening deejay.

The format for WGUL at virtually all times is "music first." Even during the peak morning period, Henry presents the music in 15-minute sets, with news, weather, and sports sandwiched between. Henry keeps idle patter to a bare minimum; he is no Frank Harden, but occasionally provides us with a personal glimpse or insight. Henry, along with Bateman and Foerrster, also promote a number of big band dances and cruises which they regularly attend, as well as supermarket dedications and other interfaces with the public.

Henry, Ray   Brought a modified top 40 format to his late 1970s 6:00 to 10:00 a.m. show on WLYT, in Cleveland. Henry was also the station's production manager.

Herbert, Jim   Delivered a mix of modern country music, farm reports, ABC news and current sports happenings. From the late 1960s into the 1970s he could be heard from 6:00 to 9:00 a.m. on WHOL, Allentown.

Herendeen, Jim   With Barry Frank and John Doremus, Herendeen put together a warm and informal show of pop standards and news from 6:00 to 10:00 a.m. on WQBK in Albany, New York, in the 1970s.

Herrera, Emiliano   Entertained Albuquerque's Spanish-speaking audience with Latin hits and soap operas twice daily. In the mid–1970s he could be heard from 7:00 to 10:00 a.m. on KABQ.

Herrera, Humberto   Mixed modern Mexican music with news from 8:00 to 10:00 a.m. on KXEX, Fresno.

Hibbs, Dan   Used his numerous character voices to transport his listeners to the unlikeliest places. During the mid–1970s "The Man of a Thousand Voices" could be heard playing the latest hits from 5:00 to 10:00 a.m. on WHBF, Rock Island, Illinois.

Hickok, Bill   Hickok's morning show on WICC in Bridgeport, Connecticut, six days per week, did not have much time for extensive talk, since he played about seven hits per hour. He also worked for WNEW in New York and at stations in several other large cities.

Higgins, Tom   Could be heard in 1977 from 6:00 to 10:00 a.m. on WLTH, Gary, Indiana. His talk show presented listeners with an opportunity to express their varied opinions, comments and gripes. Higgins was also the station's general manager and program manager. By 1978 he was at WWCA, Gary, Indiana, playing contemporary music and supplying local information daily from 5:45 to 11:00 a.m.

Hill, Austin   Stars as morning man on Christian radio station KYMS in

Orange, California, from 6:00 to 10:00 a.m. Traffic, news, sports, and ski and surf reports are provided.

Hill, Norm   Formerly morning man on WXPX in Hazleton, Pennsylvania, Hill plays country and western music on WEMR in Tunkhannock, Pennsylvania.

Hinojosa, Andres   Played Mexican hit songs from 6:00 to 8:00 a.m. on KXEX in Fresno, California, during the mid–1970s. Hinojosa doubled as the news director.

Hiott, Mike   Played the contemporary hits of the late 1960s, with news breaks on the hour. He worked from 6:30 to 10:00 a.m. on WNOK, Columbia, South Carolina, before moving to WCSC in Charleston, South Carolina, in the 1970s, where he also served as operations and program manager. His most famous routine was phone calls around the world.

Hirsch, Peter   Delivered progressive rock music plus plenty of local news and information to his listeners each morning from 6:00 to 10:00 a.m. The late 1970s found him at WOUR, Utica, New York.

Hobbs, Jim   "Morning Show" brought country and western music, news and sports to late 1960s Davenport, Iowa, each day from 6:00 to 9:00 a.m. Hobbs' show on KWNT also featured "Lifeline" and Bob Robinson with "Farm Facts."

Hoffman, Gary   Pasadena, Texas's, AM station KIKK started things early with the "Gary Hoffman Show." Hoffman was on the air from 5:00 to 10:00 a.m. during the 1970s. He played country music, mixing in his keen knowledge of news and other facts that interested listeners.

Holiday, Buddy   Station KMFK out of Houston, Texas, started the early morning hours with Holiday from 6:00 to 9:00 a.m. during the 1970s. The local audience enjoyed Holiday for his comical ways as he played "Jesus" music for them and included local and national news every half hour. He also covered traffic reports during the busy drive time. Holiday was also the station's program manager.

Holland, Eddie   Played the contemporary music of the late 1960s, mixing with it local news, time and temperature reports. He aired between 7:00 and 11:00 a.m. on WMPP, in Chicago. Holland was also the station's program director.

Holley, Jamey   Played a selection of modern country music from 5:00 to 9:00 a.m. on KMAK, Fresno, during the mid–1970s. Holley was also the farm director.

Holliday, Sue   Was the first woman to have a major morning show in Los Angeles, when she took over the morning slot on KRLA in 1974. She also worked in the continuity department there, but her smooth voice was a big asset.

Hollis, Buddy   Aired during the mid–1970s from 5:00 to 9:00 a.m. on WGRD and WGRD-FM out of Grand Rapids, Michigan. He played a selection of popular hits geared toward a young audience.

Holly, Jonathan   Played the contemporary music of the mid–1970s that appealed to all age groups. He could be heard from 5:00 to 10:00 a.m. on WINW, Canton, Ohio.

Hones, Lee   Woke up the drive-time crowd with fast-paced rousing country and western music, weather, traffic reports and news on WSSA, Forest Park, Georgia, in the 1970s from 6:00 to 10:00 a.m.

Hood, Gordy   Began the day with country and western music from 5:00 to 7:00 a.m., then switched over to popular contemporary hits from 7:00 to 10:00 a.m. Hood aired during the late 1960s on WRUN, Utica, New York.

Hooper, Bob   Greenville, South Carolina, station WESC featured Hooper from 6:00 to 10:00 a.m. during the 1970s. His amiable ways mixed well with the new, crisp sounds of modern country. He humorously communicated with his audience about day-to-day living. Local retailers called upon Hooper for personal appearances and promotions because of his successful communication style.

Hopkins, Wes   Beginning around 1950 and continuing for decades, Hopkins kept his 6:00 to 10:00 a.m. show lively with a pleasing mix of contemporary music, news, weather and sports on WCOL in Columbus, Ohio.

Horleman, Bill   Horleman's early-morning "Musical Clock" show from 5:00 to 9:00 a.m. on WDEL Wilmington, Delaware, had a contemporary, easygoing approach to music. With local and network news, weather, sports reports and community events, the 1960s news, weather, sports reports and community events, the 1960s show delivered a wake-up blend with current and past music standards.

Horn, Audie   Supplied stereo rock to Beaumont, Texas, in the mid–1970s from 6:00 to 10:00 a.m. on KWIC.

Horn, Jim   Is co-host of the morning show on WQBK-AM in Albany, New York, from 6:00 to 10:00 a.m., along with Scott Lonsberry. Listener participation is common, and there is a solid half hour of news beginning at 8:00 a.m.

Hornayk, Skip   Could be heard on WHBC, Canton, Ohio, from 5:00 to 11:00 a.m. during the mid–1970s. He opened with his farm market reports and continued through the morning with popular hit music.

Horton, Fred   This cohost of "Breakfast Flakes" on WGNA-AM and FM in Albany, New York, Uncle Fred Horton provides a full-service country and western program between 5:30 and 9:00 a.m.

House, Gerry   Aired the "Gerry House Show" during the 1970s from 6:00 to 9:00 a.m. on WSIX in Nashville, Tennessee. This drive-time show provided a standard format of great music, old and new, news, weather and sports.

Houston, John   Kept his audience laughing during the mid–1970s from 6:00 to 11:00 a.m. on Baton Rouge's WAIL. Houston doubled as the news director.

Howard, Jay   Entertained Albuquerque from 6:00 to 10:00 a.m. on KZIA. He mixed local news and information with the latest hits and album cuts of the 1970s.

Howard, Lowell   Was heard in the late 1960s bringing country and western music to the Philadelphia area. His show aired from 6:00 to 10:00 a.m. on WEEZ, Chester, Pennsylvania.

Howard, Specs   With partner Harry Martin, Howard brought the "Martin and Howard Show" to Detroit in the late 1960s. Using the same comedy that made them so successful in Cleveland, they entertained their WXYZ listeners mornings from 6:00 to 10:00 a.m.

Howe, Nancy   Was a feature writer for a Boston newspaper in 1927, when she saw a classified ad that stated "Girl Wanted Who Can Talk Shopping News." The ad was placed by WNAC, one of Boston's oldest and best radio stations. Howe auditioned and got the job. The term "disc jockey" had not been invented yet. Howe was referred to as "shopping reporter." She was on the air each weekday 6:00 to 8:00 a.m. and from 12:00 to 1:00 p.m. The format consisted of a record followed by a one-minute commercial. There was no idle chatter. All the commercials were live and written by her. (Howe's real name was Nancy Osgood.)

Howell, Jim   The top-rated morning show in Atlanta is "Peach in the Morning" with Jim Howell. Howell sings and tells jokes, and provides vital information. The program airs from 5:30 to 10:30 a.m. The music is adult contemporary.

Hubbard, Eddie   Was morning man on WGN in Chicago in the early 1960s, succeeding Ernie Simon.

Hudson, Bob   Played the rhythm and blues for Cincinnati during the late 1960s while at WCIN. His show aired mornings from 6:00 to 9:00 a.m.

Hudson, Bobby   Energized mornings in Buffalo during the late 1960s with his wit, contests and a mix of country and western music. His "Good Neighbor Jamboree" was on the air from 5:30 to 10:00 a.m. on WWOL. Joining him was news director Mike Waters.

Hudson, Mark   Was half of the Hudson and Harrigan "wake-up team" of Houston, Texas's, AM station KILT from 6:00 to 10:00 a.m. in the 1970s. Their comical ways and their constant stream of characters had them capturing the local audience every day as they played contemporary music and provided news coverage twice an hour.

Hughes, Tom   Hosts a full-service news program from 5:00 to 9:00 a.m. on WGST in Atlanta. The purpose includes the "CBS World News Round-up" and ABC's Paul Harvey news and comments.

Hull, Dave   When KRLA in Los Angeles went to a "hip" format in 1967, Beatles promoter Dave Hull was moved into the 6:00 to 9:00 a.m. slot. It was soon expanded to 10:00 a.m. Hull was best known for creating "Sergeant Red Pepper," with traffic reports from a hot air balloon; "Crazy Harold," a paper boy; and "Big Molly," who pulled on her girdle. Hull later cut a comedy album with "Emperor" Bob Hudson. But by 1969, Hull himself was judged as too square, so his contract was not renewed. He went on to KGBS in Lynwood, California.

Hull, Doc   Used country music and humorous quips to amuse the Los Angeles area during the late 1960s. His show aired from 5:00 to 10:00 a.m. on KIEV, Glendale, California.

Humphreys, Nat   Indianapolis station WXLW headlined Humphreys from 6:00 to 10:00 a.m. Humphrey's quick-moving show included middle-of-the-road music, news every hour, local traffic reports, two-way phone conversations with the station's audience, and telephone calls to intriguing newsmakers around the globe. His program aired in the 1970s.

Hunter, Dan   Was Flint, Michigan's, "Early Bird" beginning in the early 1950s and stretching into the late 1970s. Starting each day at 4:45 a.m. and airing until 10:00 a.m., he knew the right blend of music, news and humor to give his WFDF audience.

Hussey, Chuck   During the 1970s Hussey's show provided listeners with a country and western format, along with news and traffic reports. Hussey could be heard from 6:00 to 10:00 a.m. on WJRB in Nashville, Tennessee.

Irons, Johnny   Used comedy and up-tempo modern country songs to draw Flint, Michigan's, adult audience of the mid–1970s. Heard from 6:30 to 9:00 a.m. on WKMF. Irons was also the program manager.

Jackson, Irv   Played rhythm and blues during the mid–1970s from 6:00 to 10:00 a.m. on KNOX and KNOX-FM, Fort Worth.

Jacobs, Jeff   *see* **Clark, Mike**

Jacobs, Ron   Got things rolling on Honolulu station KKUA from 6:00 to 10:00 a.m. during the winter months of 1978. Jacobs played adult contemporary music, along with the occasional contemporary Hawaiian songs. He also did local celebrity interviews on Fridays. The station also aired adult Associated Press news, and hourly weather and surf conditions, and featured contests and promotions.

James, Bob Could be heard in the mid–1970s on WHLO, Akron, from 6:00 to 10:00 a.m. Joining him was "James Gang," including "Wirt the Janitor," "Our Leader, Mr. President," "Capt. Science" and "Chris the Suburban Housewife."

James, Ernest Played rhythm and blues on WABQ in Cleveland, Ohio, from 7:00 to 10:00 a.m. during the early 1970s.

James, Frank Filled the 6:00 to 10:00 a.m. slot with WISZ's country music format and news for Baltimore listeners in the 1970s.

Jarrett, Hugh Used a mix of top 30 music to add punch to his lively and humorous morning show. He could be heard from 6:00 to 9:00 a.m. on WFOM, Marietta, Georgia, in the late 1970s.

Jarrott, Dave Could be heard from 6:00 to 9:00 a.m. on KNOW, Austin, Texas. Joining him in the mid–1970s were "Goober Hoedecker," "Weather Sheriff Jimmy B. Fuddled" and health specialist "Dr. Quack."

Jay, Hal Jay's show consisted of modern country music punctuated with daily traffic reports. It aired during the 1970s on WMC in Memphis, Tennessee.

Jay & Jolly Started mornings on KILT-FM with "Jolly and Jay" from 6:00 to 10:00 a.m. during the 1970s. This rock 'n' roll station is located in Houston, Texas.

Jay, Larry Aired his gospel show in the 1970s on WYLO in Jackson, Michigan. The format included weather, news, sports, gospel music and programming.

Jefferson, Jim Gave Detroit a comfortable blend of music, new and old, from 6:00 to 10:00 a.m. on WWWW. He was there during the mid–1970s.

Jefferson, Tom Manned the 6:00 to 10:00 a.m. spot on WSNY in Schenectady, New York, in the 1970s, playing the consistent contemporary pop format which aired 24 hours a day on the station.

Johnson, Charlie Was the consummate radio cowboy at KYKR and KYKR-FM. In the mid–1970s he entertained Port Arthur, Texas, with modern country music from 6:00 to 10:00 a.m. six days a week. Mark Stevens joined him at 9:00 a.m. with his "General Store." Johnson was also the program manager at the stations.

Johnson, Irwin Was already a 25-year morning veteran by the late 1960s when he aired on WBNS, Columbus, Ohio. From 6:00 to 10:00 a.m. his deep voice provided suave commentary between the best hits of the day and the past.

Johnson, Jim Could be heard during the late 1970s in Detroit playing a combination of current and golden hits. He was on from 6:00 to 10:00 a.m. on WWWW.

Johnson, Larry   Provided a blend of talk and music on his controversial show from 6:00 to 10:00 a.m. on WZUU in Milwaukee during the 1970s.

Johnson, Mark   Gave Buffalo soul and disco music along with local information and witty conversation. During the late 1970s he was on from 6:00 to 10:00 a.m. on WBLK.

Jon, David   Supplied Denver with a steady stream of classical music and show tunes, along with his current hits of the mid–1970s, from 6:00 to 11:00 a.m. on KADE, Boulder, Colorado.

Jones, Art   Played the contemporary music of the late 1960s for Des Moines, Iowa, mornings from 6:00 to 9:00 a.m. on KIOA.

Jones, Bob   Arrived at WBAL, Baltimore, in the late 1970s from KCRA, Sacramento. His laid-back style and mix of music and news could be heard from 5:00 to 9:00 a.m.

Jones, Bob   During the 1970s, the "Real Bob Jones" combined rhythm and blues with contemporary music. Also featured were comedy, traffic reports and health tips. He occupied the 6:00 to 10:00 a.m. slot on WLOK, Memphis, Tennessee.

Jones, Casey   Could be heard from 6:00 to 10:00 a.m. on WLPL, Baltimore, during the late 1970s. He played a mix of top 40 hits and oldies along with local information.

Jones, Glen   Hosted WLTC's "Getting Up Gang" mornings from 6:00 to 9:00 a.m. Starting in 1972 and running through the 1970s, Jones used a combination of country and western music and humor to entertain Charlotte, North Carolina. Ken Alexander did the sports.

Jones, Lloyd   Entertained the Beaumont, Texas, area in the mid–1970s from 6:00 to 10:00 a.m. with contemporary soul on KJET.

Jones, Red   Was a 26-year radio veteran by the mid–1970s. The last eight years of his career were spent with WFOM, Marietta, Georgia. His show on WFOM was from 6:00 to 9:00 a.m. after which he doubled as the station's sales manager.

Jones, Rhubarb   Hosts the "Morning Zoo Crew" on WYAI and WYAY, two FM stations in the Atlanta area. The format is country and western.

Jones, Terry   Aired on KBUY, Fort Worth, during the mid–1970s. His show was a constantly-moving mix of news, traffic, music and contests from 6:00 to 10:00 a.m. Randy Ryder did the news and Lois Goldswaith the traffic.

Jordan, Ron   Played contemporary music for Indianapolis station WNDE from 6:00 to 10:00 a.m. in the 1970s. Jordan got listeners going in the morning with his quick wit, his familiarity with what was going on, and his sometimes unusual ways. Jordan was once a professional musician with the group the Boxtops, and was also a professional comedy writer.

Jose, Andrade   Was the "Time Keeper" for Albuquerque during the late 1960s on KABQ. Between the hours of 5:00 and 9:00 a.m. he played a selection of Spanish music.

Justice, Larry   Played the top 40 hits for Boston in the late from 6:00 to 10:00 a.m. on WMEX.

Kahoano, Kimo   Honolulu station KCCN has featured Kimo Kahoano for several decades from 5:00 to 10:00 a.m. Kahoano is also a night club entertainer, singer, and fire dancer. He would do all he could to keep his eyes open as he did his show "Kimo's World," which included live interviews, dialogue and humor mixed in with the sounds of Hawaiian music. News was presented on the hour.

Kane, Kris   Joined Don Hawkins to bring Denver album-oriented rock music in the late 1970s. They could be heard from 6:00 to 10:00 a.m. on KAZY.

Karnes, Don   Soft-spoken and slow characterized Karnes, who worked in many different capacities in Long Island radio. He served as morning man on WPAC in Patchogue in the late 1960s and early 1970s.

Karrenbauer, Bill   Popular standards along with news and sports woke up listeners of WHBC in Canton, Ohio, where Karrenbauer reigned from 7:00 to 10:30 a.m. beginning in 1949 and continuing for decades.

Kay, Johnny   Provided Youngstown, Ohio, with local news and traffic information while playing the current top 50 plus six extras. He was heard during the 1960s from 6:00 to 10:00 a.m. on WHOT.

Kaye, Chris   Kansas City, Montana station KBEQ highlighted Chris "Sugar Bear" Kaye's show from 6:00 to 10:00 a.m. in the 1970s. Kaye's airtime was a mix of contemporary music, traffic and news reports. This station's shows were big on contests and promotions, and small on deejay talk.

Kaye, Jeff   Could be found during the late 1970s at WBEN, Buffalo. From 5:30 to 10:00 a.m. Kaye, who replaced the legendary Clint Buehlman, played the day's best music along with news, traffic, ski reports and land and marine forecasts. (Kaye's voice could also be heard in many national advertising campaigns.)

Kaye, Johnny   Started the day for listeners of KUZZ in Bakersfield, California, spinning country and western music from 6:00 to 10:00 a.m. in the 1970s.

Kearns, Jerry   Played the contemporary music of the late 1960s while keeping Charlotte, North Carolina, informed with news and sports. He aired from 6:00 to 9:00 a.m. on WIST.

Keels, Cecil   Teamed with Bob Smith to bring WCSC "Sundial" program to Charleston, South Carolina, in the late 1960s. From 5:00 to 6:30 a.m. they supplied country music, complete farm information, and hunting and fishing reports. Then from 6:30 to 9:00 a.m. they made the transition to the station's all-day popular music format.

Keith, Don   Kept Birmingham moving with his finely-tuned "Wake Up Show" from 5:00 to 9:00 a.m. on WVOK during the mid–1970s. He supplied a mix of current hits, favorite oldies, humor and news. Keith was also the news director. In the late 1970s he moved his show to WVOK-FM where he was the music manager and could be heard from 3:00 to 11:00 a.m.

Kelley, Dan   Aired on Greenville, North Carolina, station WFBC from 6:00 to 10:00 a.m. in the 1970s. Kelley demonstrated a flair for ad-libbing and for great interviews, and his sense of humor was apparent while he played pop and contemporary music.

Kelly, Chris   Standard tunes with unexpected humor characterized Kelly's 6:00 to 10:00 a.m. show on WLNR in Lansing, Illinois, in the early 1970s.

Kelly, Frank   Woke Ohio listeners with a combination of soul, jazz and disco during the late 1970s. He was heard from 6:00 to 10:00 a.m. on WVKO, Columbus.

Kelly, Joe   Could be found in the late 1970s playing modern country music from 6:00 to 10:00 a.m. on KLZ, Denver. A radio veteran, he used his wit and a steady stream of information to supply his listeners with everything they would need to get their day going.

Kelly, Paul   Was heard from 6:00 to 10:00 a.m. on WQFM in Milwaukee during the 1970s. His show contained a contemporary rock format.

Kelly, Tom   Spent the mid–1970s bringing his "Breakfast of Champions" to the Lehigh Valley from 6:00 to 10:00 a.m. on WEEX, Easton, Pennsylvania. An eight-year radio veteran, he was known for his personal style and tight humor.

Kennedy, Bill   Featured middle-of-the-road standards such as Frank Sinatra, Dean Martin, Herb Alpert and Doris Day on his "Wake Up to Music" program. His morning show aired from 6:00 to 9:00 a.m. on WCRT, Birmingham, Alabama, in the 1970s.

Kent, Dick   Kent's "Morning Wake Up" show consisted of the contemporary music of the late 1960s plus his host of characters, including "Grandma," "Ruby Posey," "Gomer," a family of ducks and a weather robot. Originally from St. Louis, Kent was on the air from 5:00 to 9:00 a.m. on WSGN, Birmingham, in the late 1960s.

Kilgo, Jimmy   After a 13-year stint on television, Kilgo returned to radio to head up the morning hours on WAYS, Charlotte, North Carolina. Kilgo's well-known personality was popular with listeners, who tuned in to his pop contemporary format from 6:00 to 9:00 a.m. in the early 1970s.

Kimble, Bill   Presented the "Sound of the City" program each morning from 5:30 to 10:00 a.m. during the late 1960s on WEBR, Buffalo. The sounds included the popular hits of the day along with favorite oldies.

Kines, Gary   Was heard during the late 1960s on WDOD, Chattanooga, Tennessee, where he played country and western music. He aired daily from 5:00 to 9:00 a.m.

King, Danny   Occupied the 5:00 to 9:00 a.m. slot with the "Danny King Show" during the 1970s on WAVE in Louisville, Kentucky. This talented deejay was adept at handling sportscasts and commercials, as well as his morning show. The adult-contemporary style was most conducive to easy listening. Traffic helicopter reports also were included.

King, Dennis   Houston, Texas, station KXYZ started the morning off with Dennis King from 6:00 to 9:00 a.m. during the 1970s. He provided the station's listeners with pop and contemporary music along with news every half hour. Sharon Adams provided traffic reports during King's show.

King, Gary   Played uncontemporary music from 5:00 to 9:00 a.m. on Baton Rouge's WLCS. King, a mid–1970s newcomer, had a shining personality that aided his unorthodox contests.

Kinzbach, Jeff   Spent four years with WMMS, Cleveland, as a producer before taking over the 6:00 to 10:00 a.m. slot in the late 1970s. His up-beat morning show featured contemporary music and Ed "Flash" Ferenc with the news.

Kirk, Steve   Combined the top music of the day with traffic, sports, news and jokes. Joining him on WING, Dayton, from 5:00 to 10:00 a.m. during the late 1960s and 1970s was his longtime sidekick "Walter the Poet." Previously he had spent time on the air at WCOL in Colorado and at WSAI, Cincinnati. One of Ohio's best morning men, Kirk, also a concert promoter, was a real joker with daily "put-ons" for his early audience.

Kithcart, Jim   Aired his "Good Morning Bright Eyes" show from 6:00 to 9:00 a.m. on KBOL and KBVL in Boulder in the mid–1970s.

Klein, Robert   Ran his "Klein Until Nine" program Monday through Saturday from 5:30 to 9:00 a.m. in the 1970s and 1980s on WALK in Patchogue, Long Island, N.Y. The show featured many monologues and skits.

Klobucar, John   Along with a full-time news and sports person, Klobucar plays adult popular music on WNAV from 6:00 to 10:00 a.m. in Annapolis, Maryland.

Knight, Al   Provided contemporary music from 5:00 to 6:00 a.m. on WHOT in Youngstown, Ohio, in the 1960s.

Knight, Jack   Knight's warm and wacky personality drew lots of listeners to WSOC in Charlotte, North Carolina, in the early 1970s. Besides spinning popular standards, Knight sang "Happy Birthday" to celebrants, hawked products for advertisers (they requested his ad-libbed commercials rather than ready-made productions), and gave out advice and information on everything from travel to keeping house. Heavy listener involvement made his 6:00 to 10:00 a.m. morning show a success.

Knight, Jack   Energized late 1960s Charlotte, North Carolina, from 6:00 to 10:00 a.m. with a combination of top 40 and standards, and local information. Two of his favorite tunes were "Tranquilizer Tune" for car pool mothers and "Puppy Posse." He aired on WSOC.

Knight, Joe   Used humor and a mix of standards and the popular music of the late 1960s to fill his 5:30 to 9:30 a.m. time slot. His humor included impersonations, ad-libs and prerecorded bits. He was heard on WFBR, Baltimore. Stu Smith did the traffic.

Knight, Russ   Took over WCUE's 6:00 to 10:00 a.m. show in 1971 (moving from WHK). One of the nation's top deejays according the *Esquire* magazine, Knight brightened Akron's mornings with a pop and contemporary format plus a 45-minute comprehensive news block. Beginning his career in Springfield, Missouri, Knight, the "Original Weird Beard," was rated the number one deejay in Dallas, Texas, from 1960 to 1964. By 1971, he was named one of the top seven rock 'n' roll deejays of all time and was heading up the early morning hours on KBOX in Dallas.

Knowles, Ron   Was at KOAX, Dallas, in the late 1970s playing beautiful music from 6:00 to 9:00 a.m.

Kobernuss, Bob   Brought a smile and a chuckle to early morning listeners to WHLD in Niagara Falls, New York. His program, which aired from 7:00 to 9:00 a.m. in the early 1970s, featured standard popular music.

Kobik, John *see* **Ervine, Jeff**

Kohn, Tom and Sue Finco   Provided an album rock format, making their show one of the most unique in the city. It aired during the 1970s on WZMF in Menomonee Falls, Wisconsin.

Kowa, Brad   Livened the airwaves during the 1970s with a country format. The program could be heard from 6:00 to 10:00 a.m. on WHNE in Norfolk, Virginia.

Kratz, Lyn   Was the only full-time woman on the air in the Lehigh Valley in the mid–1970s. With her knowledge of local events and progressive rock music she entertained her listeners from 7:00 to 10:00 a.m. on WSAN, Allentown, Pennsylvania.

Krauss, Ron   During the 1970s Krauss was the host of the "Sunrise Show" from 6:00 to 7:30 a.m. on WBKV in West Bend, Wisconsin. The show included news, sports and weather.

Krumpak, Mickey   Presented the "Morning Show" from 6:30 to 8:00 a.m. followed by "Coffee and the Morning Show" from 8:30 to 10:00 a.m. The first was a mix of news and local information plus a selection of standards. This was followed by a Polka show that had aired for over 13 years by the late 1960s. Krumpak was heard on WFMJ, Youngstown, Ohio.

Kwesell, Bob   Had an energetic telephone talk show in the mid–1970s. He aired from 6:00 to 10:00 a.m. on WAVI, Dayton. Sports, news and features figured prominently.

LaBar, Frank   Morning man on WYZZ-FM in Wilkes-Barre, Pennsylvania, in the late 1970s and early 1980s, LaBar was an early television pioneer in northeastern Pennsylvania who did everything from playing a clown on a children's show to directing programs. His voice-overs still can be heard on local commercials. With a gravelly but friendly voice, LaBar was easily identifiable. For a while, he did middays on WEMR in Tunkhannock, Pennsylvania. LaBar resides in Jeddo, Pennsylvania.

LaBoe, Art   Bought KRLA in Los Angeles in 1976. He worked tirelessly on the air (as well as off) as a live morning man between 5:00 and 9:00 a.m. His voice tracks were used at many other times of the day. LaBoe's real name was Arthur Egnoion.

Lacey, Bob   Used humor, contemporary music and interesting interviews to entertain his late 1970s Charlotte, North Carolina, listeners. Joining him from 6:00 to 10:00 a.m. on WBT were Harold Johnson with the sports and Jeff Pilot with traffic.

Lacey, Paul   Played soft rock and oldies for his listeners on WLMS, Worcester, Massachusetts. Joining him from 7:00 to 9:00 a.m. during the late 1970s was Bob Morgan with the news.

LaMarca, Don   Supplied local information and adult contemporary music each morning during the late 1970s from 6:00 to 11:00 a.m. on WBVM, Utica, New York.

Lambert, Lou   Got the day started for East Lansing, Michigan, station WFMK during the 1970s. Lambert's lively personality kept things moving as he informed his listeners of the most current happenings in sports and news twice an hour, and played adult contemporary easy rock from 6:00 to 10:00 a.m. Lambert was also the station's program manager.

Lambert, Marty   Played adult contemporary top pop music with a blend of oldies for his listeners on WIST, Charlotte, North Carolina. He was on from 5:00 to 10:00 a.m. in the late 1970s. Lambert was also the program manager.

Lambis, John   Played all-hit music during the late 1970s from 6:00 to 10:00 a.m. on WBCY, Charlotte, North Carolina.

Lambros, Ron   Aired his "Ron Lambros Show" on Jacksonville's WOZN from 6:00 to 10:00 a.m. in the 1970s. He eased listeners into each new day with gospel music. This informative deejay was known as the "Bacon and Eggs" man.

Lange, Bob   Provides a full-service program from 6:00 to 10:00 a.m. as the morning man on KAMX in Albuquerque.

Lanham, Tom   Used his mid–1970s talk show to give his listeners a forum for their views. He could be talked to from 6:00 to 10:00 a.m. on WLTH, Gary, Indiana.

Lanigan, John   Used the popular music of the late 1960s, standards and topical humor to entertain his Albuquerque listeners throughout the 1970s. Lanigan aired from 6:00 to 10:00 a.m. on KDEF before moving to WGAR in Cleveland.

Laquidara, Charles   Played a mixture of progressive rock, jazz and the blues on Boston's WBCN from 6:00 to 10:00 a.m. His 1970s show included sports with Chip Young, weather with Stuart Soroka; Mattress Michegass; and Darrell Martinie the "Cosmic Muffin" with an astrology report.

LaRoche, Phillip   Began the day with "Blues at Sunrise" at WPAL in Charleston, South Carolina, a station devoted to all-day soul music. LaRoche played rhythm and blues from 6:00 to 9:00 a.m. in the early 1970s.

Larson, Paul   Started with WNEB, Worcester, Massachusetts, in 1946 and was still there by the late 1970s. In the late 1960s he filled the hours between 5:00 and 9:30 a.m. with lively popular hits and standards. In the late 1970s he played modern country music. Larson was also the station's operations and program manager.

Latto, Lew   Aired from 6:45 to 9:00 a.m. on WAKZ during the late 1960s, and was the station's president and general manager. During his time slot he played the best of the era's popular music, including Sinatra and Alpert, for his listeners in the Duluth, Minnesota, area. Previously he had worked for WDSM and WEBC as music and promotion director.

Laurello, Johnny   Was morning man on KRLA, Los Angeles, in the early 1970s.

Lawrence, Mike   Brought craziness and up-tempo popular hits to late 1970s Detroit from 6:00 to 9:45 a.m. Lawrence also served as both program and music manager at WBRB, Mt. Clemens, Michigan.

Lawson, Jim   Kept Birmingham shining between 5:00 and 9:00 a.m. through the middle of the 1970s. His home was at rhythm and blues station WJLD.

Layton, Doug   Teamed up with Tommy Charles in the late 1960s to bring top 40 music to the Birmingham area. They were heard from 6:30 to 9:00 a.m. on WAQY. By the mid–1970s Layton was solo and could be found from 5:30 to 9:00 on WERC, in Erie, Pennsylvania. There he combined adult-styled contemporary music, local information and his warm personality. Later that decade he was on from 6:00 to 10:00 a.m. on both WERC and WKXX, in Erie, Pennsylvania.

Ledet, Les   Took his popular wit back to the Port Arthur area after a 6-year absence from the late 60s to mid 70s playing popular music from 6:00 to 9:00 a.m. on KSUZ in Port Neches, Texas (adjacent to Port Arthur). He was also the station's president.

Lee, Bob   Played country and western music for late 1960s Albuquerque from 6:00 to 10:00 a.m. on KRZY.

Lee, Bob   Was much traveled in the Denver area after beginning his radio career in 1953. The late 1960s found him playing top 40 and oldies on KIMN from 6:00 to 9:00 a.m. In the mid–1970s Lee hosted a news show from 6:00 to 9:00 a.m. on KOA. Then, through the summer of 1978, he teamed with Peter B. to play modern country music from 6:00 to 10:00 a.m. on KLAK. Later Lee switched over to KERE where he continued to play modern country music from 6:00 to 10:00 a.m.

Lee, Terry   Combined news, sports, contemporary music, contests with cash prizes and album giveaways. Lee aired during the late 1970s from 6:00 to 10:00 a.m. on WIRK, West Palm Beach.

Leigh, Paul   Aired from 6:00 to 10:00 a.m. on XEROK where he played El Paso the latest hits of the mid–1970s.

Lemon, Dick   Played the standard-popular music of the late 1960s for his listeners on KCBC, Des Moines, Iowa. Joining him from 5:00 a.m. to 12:00 p.m. were Ed Sheppard with news and Ralph Vogel with farm news.

Lennen, Mike   Started each morning with a joke, lots of information and modern country music. He was on WCRV, Washington, New Jersey, from 6:00 to 10:00 a.m. After six years in broadcasting, in 1977 he became WCRV's program director.

Leonard, Mitch   Anchored WRNG "All News in the Morning" along with cohost Bruce Bartley. During the late 1970s they conversed with listeners and kept Atlanta informed from 6:00 to 9:00 a.m. daily.

Lewis, Bob   Contemporary rhythm and blues, news and special features of general appeal comprised Lewis' 7:00 to 10:00 a.m. program on WCIN, Cincinnati, Ohio, during the early 1970s.

Lewis, Dick   Hosted an all news, sports and weather show from 5:30 to 9:00 a.m. on WJLK and WJLK-FM during the late 1970s. His Asbury

Park, New Jersey, show also included local interviews. Lewis doubled as station manager.

Lewis, Fred   Brought his "country style" to the Syracuse area daily from 6:00 to 9:00 a.m. on WSEN. His late 1960s show featured country and western music along with news, weather, sports and farm reports. In addition to being an on-air personality, Lewis was also a singer, performer and recording artist.

Lilligren, Chuck, Glenn Olson, and Howard Vilen   Provided early risers with farm information, news, music, and weather reports. They aired during the 1970s on WCCO in Minneapolis, Minnesota.

Lindsey, Charlie Byrd   Played plenty of country music, accepted requests and added news, occasional country guests and interesting talk to his show. Lindsey was heard during the mid–1970s from 6:00 a.m. to 12:00 p.m. on WEZL, Charleston, S.C., and doubled as the station's operations manager.

Lindsey, Tempie   Was the only woman on-air personality doing mornings in the Dallas/Fort Worth area in the late 1970s. From 6:00 to 10:00 a.m. on KTXQ, Dallas, she delivered album oriented rock and comedy features, including the "Dreaded Morning Oldie." Mitch Carr did the news.

Lloyd, Jim   Took over WEEX's morning show in 1967, after moving from Allentown's WAEB. Continuing into the 1970s, Lloyd developed a personable style mixing humor with present and past hits for listeners in Easton, Pennsylvania. His program aired from 6:00 to 10:00 a.m.

Lobdell, Dave   Hosts a telephone talk show from 6:00 to 9:00 a.m. on KENI in Anchorage, Alaska.

Logan, Lee   Was the early morning deejay and the program manager for Indianapolis station WIFE. "Logan in the Morning" aired from 6:00 to 9:00 a.m. Logan's show featured a sports trivia quiz, sports education, the "Breakfast Serial," Nikki's traffic reports, and the "comedy cut." Logan played contemporary music on his show during the 1970s.

Logsdon, Jimmy   Was heard from 6:00 a.m. to 12:15 p.m. on "Country Time," a show bringing Cincinnati modern country music during the late 1960s. Logsdon aired on WCLU.

Lomas, Joe   Presided over the 6:00 a.m. to 12:00 p.m. time slot on WCLU, Cincinnati, Ohio, during the early 1970s with his "Country Time" program. WCLU adhered to an all-day format of modern country and western music.

London, Gery   Played a mix of mid–1970s top 40 hits, album cuts and oldies from 6:00 to 9:00 a.m. on North Charleston's WKTM.

London, Jim   Was featured on Kansas City station KCMO between the hours of 6:00 and 10:00 a.m. in the 1970s. His lighthearted, bright style kept his show moving as he played adult contemporary music and broadcast news, weather, traffic and sports reports. His show also included Paul Harvey news and the "Breakfast Serial."

London, Joe   Mixed local information with current hits on WIBR, Baton Rouge. Working from 5:00 to 9:00 a.m., his local knowledge and comments made him popular with the young adult listeners of the mid–1970s. London doubled as the music manager.

London, John   Played contemporary music with Ron Engelman during the late 1970s for Denver each day from 6:00 to 9:00 a.m. on KTLK.

Long, Bob   Aired his show "Soul at Sunrise" from 7:00 to 10:00 a.m. on WCIN, Cincinnati during the mid–1970s. His show featured rhythm and blues plus top 40 music. In the late 1970s he was still at WCIN, but was playing adult contemporary music while delivering local information.

Long, Gene   Plays rhythm and blues pop music on WANN in Annapolis, Maryland.

Lonsbury, Scott *see* **Horn, Jim**

Love, Michael   Played rhythm and blues and popular music for WJMO's primarily black Cleveland audience from 6:00 to 10:00 a.m. during the mid–1970s.

Lovett, Don   Supplied the Birmingham area with old time country music and the latest information. During the late 1970s he could be heard on WYAM, Bessemer, Alabama, mornings from 5:00 to 9:00 a.m. and then on a call-in talk show from 10:00 to 11:00 a.m. Lovett was also the station's program manager.

Lowe, Jim   Served Dallas a selection of the current popular hits while excluding rock 'n' roll. He started in the mid–1950s in the 6:00 to 9:00 a.m. time slot at WRR, running his comedy line through the usual pop standards, time, weather and traffic reports. The show ran for decades.

Loyd, Dave   Was Charleston, South Carolina's "Morning Mayor" during the late 1960s when he aired from 5:00 to 9:00 a.m. on WTMA. Still in Charleston in the mid–1970s, he had moved over to WQSN where he kept his listeners entertained from 6:00 to 9:00 a.m. with modern country music, news, and weather and traffic reports. He was also WQSN's operations and program manager.

Luber, Frank *see* **Marr, Tom**

Luczak, Michael   Was heard from 5:00 to 9:00 a.m. on WXGT, Columbus, Ohio, where he played the current hits of the late 1970s. Mike Perkins joined him with the news twice an hour.

Lujack, Larry   Ad-libbed his way through the 5:00 to 9:00 a.m. morning slot on WLS in the 1970s, delighting Chicagoans with his unpredictability. Doing whatever came to his mind, "Super Jock" Lujack featured the "Klunk Letter of the Day," contemporary music, news, traffic, sports and weather reports plus the unexpected. The time of the broadcast later changed to 5:30 to 10:00 a.m.

Luke, Keith   Combined his pleasant personality with popular music and local information to entertain his listeners during the late 1970s. He was heard from 6:00 to 8:00 a.m. on WJJL, Niagara Falls, N.Y.

Lund, Howie   Hosted the "Morning Watch" program on WERE in Cleveland, Ohio, from 5:30 to 10:30 a.m. during the early 1970s. The show featured talk, information and news. The final 90 minutes of each show featured guest interviews with open phone lines.

Lupton, John   Combined his off-the-wall humor with news, sports, stock market reports and hits, both old and new, on his show. He was on the air from 6:00 to 10:00 a.m. on WFTL, Ft. Lauderdale. By the late 1970s he had been with WFTL for 16 years, though in the late 1960s he had done afternoons.

Lynn, Tony   Hosts a country music show in KRZY-AM and KRST-FM that has the only helicopter traffic report in Albuquerque.

Lyons, David   Could be found in Wheeling, West Virginia, during the late 1970s at WNEU. There the energetic program director could be heard from 6:00 to 10:00 a.m. playing soft rock music. Before this Lyons had been program director at WGCL, Cleveland, and had worked in Phoenix, Louisville and Jacksonville.

Lyons, Joe   Presented "The Lyons Den" from 6:00 to 10:00 a.m. during the mid–1970s. His high-energy show provided popular music and biting humor. Lyons gradually slowed the show down for the listening Canton homemakers. Bill Allen did the news and sports. Lyons was WNYN's program manager.

McCain, Bob *see* **Smith, Dave**

McCain, Doug   Took over the 5:00 to 9:00 a.m. slot at WYDE, Birmingham, in the late 1970s. He supplied his listeners with the latest information and country and western music.

McCarren, Dale   For decades, has brought news and information to Chicago from 6:00 to 10:00 a.m. on WBBM, including sports with Brent Musburger and Brad Palmer, outdoor news with Art Mercer, and John Madigan on politics. In the mid–1970s he teamed up with Donn Pearlman, who was later replaced by Frank Beaman.

McCoy, Steve   During the 1970s the "Steve McCoy Calls the World" show aired from 5:30 to 9:00 a.m. on WBYQ in Hendersonville, Tennessee. Steve McCoy made comical telephone calls worldwide to inquire about strange occurrences or off-beat hobbies, occupations, etc. From there he went to WORD, as program manager. From 6 a.m. to 10 a.m., Spartanburg, South Carolina, McCoy played contemporary music and gave local news reports. The station constantly supported local peoples' involvement in promotions. Now McCoy can be heard in the mornings from 6:00 to 10:00 a.m. on WSTR in Atlanta, an FM station playing adult contemporary music.

McCuen, Mike   Used a unique blend of music and local information to entertain Denver from 6:00 to 10:00 a.m. on KLZ during the mid–1970s.

McCulloch, Don   Rocked mid–1970s Denver from 6:00 to 10:00 a.m. on KLZ-FM with his pranks and music.

McDaniel, Grant   Was known to the Yakima, Washington, area as "Mr. Radio" for over 20 years by the late 1970s. News, farm information, weather, sports and local events were mixed with up-tempo music each day from 5:00 to 10:00 a.m. "The Grant Mac Show" was heard on KIT.

McDonough, Joe   Delivered his pep and Boston's super country fresh sound every morning from 6:00 to 10:00 a.m. on WCOP. He also kept his mid–1970s audience informed with a supply of environmental information.

MacDougall, Dave   Played the contemporary music of the mid–1970s from 6:00 to 10:00 a.m. on WCOS while keeping his Columbia, South Carolina, listeners informed of local news and events. Ken Willmott did the news, weather and sports.

McFarland, David   Off-the-cuff wit was a trademark of McFarland's modern country music show on WONE in Dayton, Ohio, which aired from 5:00 to 9:00 a.m. in the early 1970s. His career started in the mid–1960s.

McGann, Max   Program manager and a.m. deejay for Lansing, Michigan station WILS during the 1970s. McGann's lighthearted approach kept his audience tuned in for the fun. He played adult contemporary music from 6:00 to 10:00 a.m. His show included news every hour, and sports reports.

McGovern, Terry   Took over the 5 a.m. to 9 a.m. slot at Los Angeles' KRLA in February 1982. Radio critic Bill Earl liked McGovern's "low key, witty mellowness." McGovern's claims to fame were his Marlon Brando impersonations, his "Rude Awakenings" random phone calls to listeners, and call-ins from real comedians, as well as a generous sprinkling of comedy record cuts.

McGrath, Dan   Supplied Wheeling, West Virginia, with the best albums plus time, temperature, traffic and news. He could be found on WOMP-FM from 6:00 to 10:00 a.m. during the late 1970s.

McGrew, Terry   Terry McGrew provided listeners with in-depth local and national news during the 1970s from 6:00 to 8:00 a.m. on KOCY, Oklahoma City, Oklahoma. From 8:00 to 10:00 a.m. country music filled the airwaves, along with lively comments.

Mack, Bill   Was heard in the early and mid–1960s playing country and western music from 6:00 to 10:00 a.m. on KBUY, Ft. Worth. Mack then moved to Dallas and featured country and western music during his 5:00 to 9:00 a.m. time slot on KPCN. A veteran of country music, he had previously worked in San Antonio and Wichita Falls. Mack also enjoyed success as a singer and songwriter.

McKai, Missy   Used her warm personality and a pleasing mix of music to help listeners start their day. During the late 1970s she was heard from 6:00 to 10:00 a.m. on KNYO-FM, Fresno.

McKay, Dick   Put a step in the morning for Grand Rapids with his mixture of humor, talk and music hits. In the mid–1970s he aired from 7:15 to 10:00 a.m. on WMAX.

McKay, Gene   Took the air from 5:00 to 10:00 a.m. with news and the current musical hits. His show, which ran from the late 1960s to the mid–1970s, on WIS, Columbia, South Carolina, included Bob Bailey's agriculture report and Don Rollins with the news.

McKay, John   Gave his Wichita, Kansas, audience a pleasing blend of top 30 music plus mass appeal oldies. During the late 1970s he aired from 6:00 to 9:00 a.m. on KLEO.

McKay, Mike   Hartford, Connecticut station WTIC-FM highlighted Mike McKay from 6:00 to 9:00 a.m. in the late 1970s, after Bob Steele's decades-old program was no longer simulcast on FM. The station's music was top 40 hits, with religious and educational programs airing on Sundays.

McKee, Bob   His "Wake Up Atlanta" show delivered an entertaining mix of humor, rhythm and blues, news and contests. From the late 1960s through the 1970s he was heard from 6:00 to 9:00 a.m. on WAOK.

McKee, Gary   Could be heard through the 1970s from 6:00 to 10:00 a.m. on WQXI and WQXI-FM, Atlanta. His show included news with David Collins and Gary Corney, sports extras by Jack Hurst, and sidekick Willis the Guard.

McKinnon, Ellen   Gave Albany, New York, album-oriented rock from 6:00 to 10:00 a.m. during the late 1970s. Her show on WQBK-FM included Brian Keegan's astrology forecast and twice a week, Susan Berkely's natural food recipes.

McLaine, Joe   Delivered album-oriented rock on his show during the late 1970s. Airing each morning from 6:00 to 9:00 a.m. on WSAN, Allentown, Pennsylvania, McLaine also supplied local information and gave away movie tickets and albums.

McLean, Bill   Presented "Bill in Kakeland" during the 1950s and 1960s from 6:00 to 9:00 a.m. for KAKE, Wichita, Kansas. He gave his listeners a pleasing blend of standards and popular hits along with the news every half hour. By the late 1970s he had switched over to afternoons and was known as "Kakeland's Living Legend," having been with KAKE for over 30 years. McLean was also the station's operations manager.

McLean, Marty   Worked the 6:00 to 10:00 a.m. slot at WAYE, Baltimore, Maryland, in the mid–1970s, where he played a progressive blend of top 40 hits mixed with album cuts. He also included Associated Press news at the top of the hour and traffic reports as needed.

McShane, Jim   Settled in as morning man of WQUA in Moline, Illinois, in the fall of 1971. His program aired from 5:30 to 10:00 a.m. and featured pop contemporary music.

McShea, Greg   Delivered consistent contemporary music and plenty of news to the Mohawk Valley during the late 1970s from 6:00 to 10:00 a.m. on WTLB, Washington Mills, New York.

McWilliams, Bob   Hosted a call-in talk show that featured interviews which aired from 8:00 to 10:00 a.m. on KGMC, Englewood, Colorado, during the mid–1970s.

Magwyre, Ray   Worked as a newsman at WARM in Scranton before becoming general manager and morning man at WEJL in Scranton when the station went to a "music-of-your-life" format in the late 1970s. Magwyre, a native of Old Forge, Pennsylvania, whose real name is Ray Toro, has a good, deep voice and a pleasant personality.

Malesky, Bob   Was already a seven-year radio veteran by the late 1960s when he aired from 6:00 to 10:00 a.m. on WENE, Binghamton, New York. He combined popular-contemporary music with easygoing banter that his listeners enjoyed.

Maloney, Wayne *see* **Wayne, Larry**

Manley, Don   Played the hits of the day and oldies while bringing news, weather and sports reports to Davenport, Iowa, in the late 1960s. He aired from 5:00 to 9:00 a.m. on WOC.

Mann, Gary   Brought his unique style to WEAL in Greensboro, North Carolina, during the 1970s from 6:00 to 10:00 a.m. This early morning rhythm and blues deejay was also a production manager for the station.

Marcum, Dave   Is the host of the traditional rock 'n' roll show between 5:30 and 10:00 a.m. on WGRX in Baltimore. The cohost is Teresa Blythe.

Margis, Johnny   Entertained Wilkes-Barre, Pennsylvania, with a mixture of popular hits and the standards. Included in his late 1960s show were traffic reports, and birthday and anniversary announcements. He was heard from 6:00 to 10:00 a.m. on WBAX.

Marino, Dave Brought a mix of popular and country music to York, Pennsylvania, each morning from 6:00 to 10:00 a.m. during the late 1970s. "Marino in the Morning" also supplied local news, weather and sports along with "Cash Call." He was also WNOW's program manager.

Markert, Phil Like his older counterparts, Markert's on-air trademark was his piano, but he did not play sentimental ballads. Markert used the piano for gags and humor, and even school lunch menus were recited in rhyme. Beginning at a small radio station in Fulton, New York, Markert's radio and television career took him to Syracuse, Florida, and Binghamton. His morning slots were at WHEN in Syracuse in the 1970s, and at WINR in Binghamton in the 1980s. Markert was also well known for his live performances at upscale upstate New York piano bars.

Marks, Johnny Gave his Corpus Christi, Texas, listeners local information plus a complete early morning fishing report. From 5:00 to 9:00 a.m. he also played the popular hits of the late 1960s on KEYS.

Marlin, Ray In the late 1960s, when Don Russell switched from WSTC, Stanford, Connecticut, to WGCH, Greenwich, Connecticut, WSTC hired Marlin (né Marlitz) to replace him. Marlin's rich baritone voice was every bit as pleasing to Russell's more nasal tone, and he also had a winsome personality. During the 6:00 to 10:00 a.m. shift Monday through Friday, Marlin played music similar to Russell's but preferred anecdotes about his family and friends to discussing the music. In the 1970s, WOR hired Marlin as a staff announcer, thus ending his career as a disc jockey and morning man.

Marr, Denton Rocked Cincinnati every morning from 6:00 to 10:00 a.m. on WEBN during the mid–1970s, where he also served as the news director. The "Free Electric Classified" was featured every day at 9:55. By the late 1970s he was moved to the 10:00 a.m. to 2:00 p.m. slot and became the program and promotional manager.

Marr, Tom From 5:00 to 9:00 a.m., Marr and cohost Frank Luber host an audience participation show focusing on controversial issues over WCBM in Owings Mills, Maryland.

Martin, Charlie Could be heard on "The Charlie and Harding Show" with John Harding from 6:00 to 9:00 a.m. on KHOW, Denver during the mid–1970s. The format included old and current hits and discussions on any subject. In the late 1970s it became the "Hal and Charlie" show with Hal Moore.

Martin, Harry Brought the "Martin and Howard Show" to Detroit in the late 1960s with partner Specs Howard. Using the same comedy that made them so successful in Cleveland, they entertained their WXYZ listeners mornings from 6:00 to 10:00 a.m.

Martin, Joe   Could be heard from 5:00 to 10:00 a.m. during the late 1970s, bringing top country hits to the Fort Worth area on KSCS.

Martin, Michael   Combined his unique humor and a mixture of contemporary hits and country music to make his deep voice easily recognizable to his Chattanooga audience. Martin could be hard from 6:00 to 10:00 a.m. on WFLI in the mid–1970s.

Martindale, Wink   Everyone associates Winston "Wink" Martindale with network game shows, but Martindale got his start as a radio morning man and a local television dance program host in Los Angeles. Beginning at M.O.R. format KHJ, Martindale was traded to top 40 KRLA in 1960, bringing with him his "rubber duckie" and Wink Awake contests. In 1962, when Dot records offered Martindale a better job, he did an unusual stunt: have the listeners vote for his replacement! The winner was Bob Eubanks, another future game show host, who at the time had the all-night show on KRLA. Martindale later joined KFWB in Los Angeles.

Martinez, Walter   Walter Martinez and Omar Aquilera were hosts of "The Voice of Latin America" on Newington, Connecticut, station WRYM during the 1970s. They played Spanish music from 5:30 to 11:45 a.m. The program included news and sports, short features about law, medicine, social events, and a novella at 10:30 a.m.

Masatus, Jamie   Aired in the 1970s from 6:00 to 10:00 a.m. on KDWA in Hastings, Minnesota; format included news, road-weather reports, and other informational tidbits.

Masingill, Luther   In the summer of 1971, WDEF in Chattanooga, Tennessee, proclaimed Masingill "first by far, in all surveys, for more than 25 years — longer than any other morning program now in existence in America." His "Sundial" program ran from 6:00 to 10:00 a.m. and featured popular standards. The show continued for many years.

Mason, Bill   "Mason's Mixer" was the morning program on WDBQ in Dubuque, Iowa, from 1958 to 1967. Mason played a mixture of popular and big band music, polkas, marches and lots of ad lib observations of life. Mason tracked the daily doings of his young family as they grew. He was a master at ad libbing and maintained strong ratings throughout the entire period. After 1967, Mason went into sales and sports. His last job was a general manager of Teleprompter Cable TV of Dubuque. Mason died in 1988.

Mason, Jerry   Blended country and western music, humor, weather, and news together on Mason's 6:00 to 10:00 a.m. show on WUBE in Cincinnati during the early 1970s.

Mathey, Jeff   Supplied a top 40 soul format to arouse listeners, and included weather, traffic, news items and features. The show aired during the 1970s from 6:00 to 10:00 a.m. on WVOL in Nashville, Tennessee.

Matlock, Stan   Beginning in 1953, from 6:00 to 10:00 a.m. Matlock would amuse listeners on WKRC, Cincinnati, with entertaining stories on "Magazine of the Air." Chuck Bolland and his caustic humor joined him during the mid–1970s. Their 6:00 to 10:00 a.m. "Daybreak" show included Lt. Heinlein with traffic, Paul Sommercamp on sports and news with Doug Anthony, plus new and old hits. By the late 1970s Matlock had moved over to WLQA, Cincinnati, where his "Magazine of the Air" reappeared and was heard from 6:00 to 8:30 a.m.

Matthews, Sean   Brought his special magic to WWMM, Arlington Heights, Illinois, from 5:00 to 10:00 a.m. daily. He played a mix of current and past hits and delivered the news, sports and weather. Matthews was the station's music manager during the mid–1970s.

Maule, Tom   Played modern country music in the late 1970s for Fresno, California, from 6:00 to 9:00 a.m. on KARM.

May, Dave   Used the first hour of his 5:00 to 8:00 a.m. show for farm and agricultural reports, then he played a selection of music from various fields while giving all the local information. He was heard on WGSA, Lancaster, Pennsylvania, during the late 1960s.

Maynard, Dave   Found a diverse audience for his humor and popular blend of music. In the mid–1970s he could be heard on Boston's WBZ from 8:00 a.m. to 12:00 p.m.

Meador, Dale   Aired from 5:00 to 9:30 a.m. in the early 1970s on WDOD, Chattanooga, Tennessee. His show featured country and western music plus news, weather, time checks, shopping tips and community events.

Meadows, Bob   Combined easy listening music with in-depth news from 6:00 to 9:00 a.m. for KXOL, Fort Worth, during the mid–1970s.

Means, Gene   Called "King of the Country" in the 1970s because of his modern country format. This pleasant show aired from 6:00 to 10:00 a.m. on WWOR in Miami.

Medina, Alex   Played Mexican hit songs of the late 1970s for his listeners on KXEX, Fresno. He was heard from 6:00 to 8:00 a.m.

Meeks, Max   One of the longest running live morning programs in the South, "Max in the Morning" has been broadcast on WFMR in High Point, North Carolina, since 1947. Meeks is a warm grandfatherly type who wears a suit and tie and promotes worthy causes and events. The music leans toward the old, pre rock 'n' roll style, and there is ample local and national news. Saturday programs follow an entirely different format, with Meeks doing a live remote from a restaurant with different listeners invited to join him for breakfast.

Merchant, Bill   Aired in the Grand Rapids, Michigan, area for over 10 years by the late 1960s. From 5:00 to 9:00 a.m. he was heard on WLAV playing the top popular and contemporary hits. He also did a daily television show.

Merrell, Johnny   From 6:15 to 8:30 a.m., Merrell's "Morning Mayor Show" drew listeners in the sixties with his knowledge of records, bands and vocalists. The program aired on KFH in Wichita, Kansas, followed by "Contact" from 8:30 to 10:00 a.m. Contact was a call-in show that touched on a variety of subjects, many controversial.

Merritt, C.   A veteran of South Florida radio, he worked 7:00 to 11:00 a.m. on WRBD, Ft. Lauderdale, playing rhythm and blues. Starting with the station in 1969, by 1978 he was the station's program director.

Merz, Curt   Kansas station KMBZ in Shawnee Mission, presented Curt Merz in the morning between 6:00 and 10:00 a.m. during the 1970s. Curt kept his show alive with humor, mixing it in with traffic and news reports.

Meunier, John   Served as morning man on WVPO AM and FM in Stroudsburg, Pennsylvania, for many years during the prolonged reign of owner Ron Drescher. Drescher was a traditionalist who believed in talkative deejays and traditional standard music. Meunier worked from 6:00 to 11:00 a.m. Monday through Friday and 6:00 a.m. to 12:00 p.m. on Saturdays. When Drescher died, the new owners quickly dropped this traditional format and all of WVPO's deejays were dismissed.

Meyer, Bob   Played a blend of late 1970s contemporary music and standards, plus all the latest news, to entertain and inform his Ohio listeners. He was heard from 6:00 to 10:00 a.m. on WELW, Willoughby, Ohio.

Michaels, Bob   Station WPOP aired news for the Hartford, Connecticut, area. Newscasters from 5:30 to 10:00 a.m. during the 1970s included Bob Michaels, traffic reporter Bill Callahan, business news reporter Pete Southwick, and sports reporter Jerry Brooks. Norm McDonald came on every half hour with the weather. Wall Street Journal hourly reports aired on the station, as well as the CBS World News Roundup and the CBS Sports Roundup.

Michaels, Jay   Mixed news, traffic and the current late 1970s adult contemporary hits to entertain Grand Rapids, Michigan. He was heard from 6:00 to 10:00 a.m. on WZZR where he was also music director.

Michaels, Johnny   Played contemporary music for late 1970s Dallas from 5:30 to 9:00 a.m. on KNUS. Bob Richman did the news, Doug Vair sports, and Jan Bishop traffic.

Michaels, Ken   Supplied his WYDE listeners with "Skywatch 85," the only air traffic reports in Birmingham during the mid–1970s and played country and western music. He was also the station's farm director. By the late 1970s he had joined WVOK and was part of the Johnny Davis "Wake Up Show."

Michaels, Lee   Michaels hosts a gospel music program aimed at black audiences between 5:00 and 10:00 a.m. on WCAO in Baltimore.

Miles, Kenny   "Miles in the Morning" got things rolling for Houston, Texas, station KRBE from 6:00 to 9:00 a.m. during the 1970s. Kenny's sense of humor and character guests kept things alive as he played contemporary top 40 music. Mike Martin and Jay Sorrentino came in with news and reports.

Millard, Mike   Was heard from 6:00 to 10:00 a.m. on country music stations WVBE AM and FM in Cincinnati, and in Denver from 6:00 to 9:00 a.m. during the mid–1970s. By the late 1970s he was at KFJZ, Fort Worth, where he mixed adult contemporary music with his quick wit. Joining him were Martha Martinez with current events and traffic, plus Mark Oristano with the sports.

Miller, Howard   Mixed his own interesting viewpoints with a selection of popular music and standards. He spent over 20 years doing mornings for WIND, Chicago, beginning in the 1950s.

Miller, Jack   "The Breakfast Club" was a favorite of women listeners of WRPL in Charlotte, North Carolina. The program, which aired from 5:00 to 10:00 a.m. in the early 1970s, featured rhythm and blues.

Miller, Neal   Was an eight-year veteran of Birmingham broadcasting by the late 1960s when his "Wyde-A-Wake Show" aired. He could be heard from 5:00 to 9:00 a.m. on WYDE where he played modern country music and supplied news and local information.

Miller, Tom   Motivated Greensboro, North Carolina, people with the sounds of gospel music from 5:00 to 6:00 a.m. during the 1970s on WGBG. The "Tom and Jim Show" took over the air from 6:00 to 10:00 a.m. Cohosts Tom Miller and Jim Bryan used outlandish, comical behavior to keep audiences in stitches with phone calls and played adult contemporary hits.

Mills, Denny   Mixed the adult contemporary music of the mid–1970s with odd-ball robbery and accident reports, street interviews, traffic and weather. Mills was assisted by Bill Patterson and Roger Fowler. Aired between 5:30 and 10:00 a.m. on WSOC, Charlotte, North Carolina.

Mircos, Gus   Used his "Morning Report" to supply Denver with the news, weather and information. He was heard from 6:00 to 10:00 a.m. on KOA during the 1970s.

Mitchell, Alan   Brought the easy-listening sounds of WBBM-FM to Chicago from 6:00 to 10:00 a.m. during the late 1970s.

Mitchell, Jim   Filled his late 1960s 6:00 to 10:00 a.m. time slot on WEXL, Detroit, with personable comments on the country and western music he played and the news and weather.

Mitchell, Rick Was heard from 5:30 to 9:00 a.m. on WTRY, Latham (Troy), New York, during the late 1970s. He gave his listeners contemporary music along with all the local information.

Mitchell, Rick Mitchell is morning man on WKLI in Albany, New York, presenting music of the 1960s through the 1990s with cohost Lisa Walker from 6:00 to 10:00 a.m.

Mitchell, Robert "Real Robert Mitchell" aired in the 1970s from 6:00 to 9:00 a.m. on WTIX, New Orleans. Its contemporary format included news, weather and sports.

Moline, Don Bristol, Connecticut, station WBIS jump-started their airwaves with their operating manager and early morning deejay Don Moline from 6:00 to 9:00 a.m. The station featured adult contemporary music, weather, news, and sports.

Mollett, Mike *see* **Rider, Mark**

Monache, John Delle Presents a full-service show from 6:00 to 10:00 a.m. on WAAM in Ann Arbor, Michigan.

Montgomery, Monty Aired a straightforward morning show in KAFY in Bakersfield, California, in the early 1970s. The 6:00 to 10:00 a.m. program featured pick hits, million sellers, and phone requests.

Moore, Bob Worked during the mid–1970s for KDKO, Denver's only all-soul station. He was heard mornings from 5:00 to 9:00 a.m.

Moore, Hal Teamed up with Charlie Martin in the late 1970s to form the "Hal and Charlie" show on KHOW, Denver. From 6:00 to 10:00 a.m. they delivered the hits of the past and present plus humor of all sorts.

Moore, Harv Known as both "The Boy Next Door" and "The Morning Mayor," Moore supplied the top hits of the day to the Washington D.C. area during the late 1960s. He aired from 6:00 to 10:00 a.m. on WPGC, Bladenburg, Maryland. He moved to WYSL AM and FM in Buffalo, New York, with the same time slot.

Moore, John Began his 5:00 to 10:00 a.m. shift on WSB, Atlanta, with the "Dixie Farm and Home Hour." He then supplied the "WSB Merry-Go-Round" with a mix of popular music, celebrity guests, and the news and traffic. After going solo in the mid–1970s, Moore was later joined by Jim Howell in the late 1970s. During the late 1960s he had been WSB's afternoon deejay.

Moore, Lee Was morning man for many years on WNLK in Norwalk, Connecticut. He was less talkative than most deejays in the 1950s and 1960s, although talkative by today's standards. The show was simulcast on WDRN-FM and aired Monday through Saturday from 6:00 to 9:00 a.m., and 10:00 a.m. to 12:00 p.m. Dick Bee hosted "The Sign Post" between

9:00 and 10:00 a.m., with exhaustive information about community events.

Moore, Terry   Originator of the "Old Commuter" program on WSTC in Stamford, Connecticut, Moore was known for his distinctive, mellifluous nasal tone, his fast wit, and his good taste. Before airing a recorded Midas commercial, Moore would quip, "It's kind of cold outside today, you'd better put your muffler on." When Moore left, WSTC chose Don Russell, who sounded almost identical to Moore, thus assuring a smooth transition.

Moos, Bill   During the 1970s, Bill Moos's easy listening style combined a blend of favorite music, news and weather. It was on the air from 6:00 to 11:00 a.m. on WEZW in Milwaukee, Wisconsin.

Moran, Joe   Moran was the only country and western format morning man in the New York area in the 1960s and 1970s, hosting on WJRZ, Hackensack, New Jersey. However, he did little besides providing basic information for the commuter.

Morgan, Al   Used his humor and a combination of contemporary music and news to amuse his Dayton listeners from 5:00 to 9:00 a.m. on WTUE.

Morgan, Chris   Broadcasts from 6:00 to 10:00 a.m. playing contemporary music on WCKF in Canton, Georgia.

Morgan, George   Played modern country music from 6:00 to 10:00 a.m. on WISZ and WISZ-FM, Glen Burnie, Maryland, during the mid–1970s. There was American Entertainment network news on the half hour plus local information and contests. In the late 1970s he could be heard on WJRO, Glen Burnie, Maryland, playing adult contemporary music.

Morgan, Jack   Aired from 6:00 to 10:00 a.m. on Bloomfield, Connecticut's WDRC. Jack's amiable, warmhearted ways earned him awards as the number one top-40 deejay in the country and the top contemporary morning slot in Hartford in the 1970s. He created and used comic voice characters as part of his show.

Morgan, Jeffery   Played great hits while solving his listeners' problems with "Dear Jeffery." Heard during the mid–1970s from 6:00 to 10:00 a.m. on WRFD, Columbus.

Morgan, Roger W.   Working many of the nation's top radio markets, Morgan settled into WSGN's morning position in the early 1970s, spinning contemporary sounds interspersed with crazy antics and humorous bits known as Morganizings. His program aired from 6:00 to 9:00 a.m. in Birmingham, Alabama.

Morley, Russ   Slipped his special brand of humor around the adult contemporary music he played each morning from 6:00 to 10:00 during the late 1970s. News director Steve Armstrong joined him at WJNO, West Palm Beach. Morley wore several hats at the station, serving as the program manager, farm director and promotions manager.

Morris, "Michael" George   Played late 1970s contemporary album rock from 6:00 to 10:00 a.m. for his Boston audience on WCOZ.

Morrow, Larry   Brightened up Cleveland every morning from 6:00 to 10:00 a.m. during the mid–1970s with contemporary hits and special stories of special people on WWWE. In the late 1970s Morrow's slot was moved to afternoons from 2:00 to 7:00 p.m.

Morrow, Weaver   Weaver aired traffic reports, local news and rock and roll from 6:00 to 10:00 a.m. on Houston, Texas, station KAUM during the 1970s.

Morti, John Hernandez & Juan   Livened up the 1970s with great music, along with "The Worst Joke of the Day" feature. It aired from 6:00 to 10:00 a.m. on WMJX in Miami, Florida.

Munyon, Roger   Spent the 1970s keeping the Grand Rapids area both entertained and informed while on WYGR, Wyoming, Michigan. In the mid–1970s he aired the ungodly shift from 6:00 a.m. to 3:00 p.m. During this time he was also the program manager. In the late 1970s he moved over to the late afternoon shift.

Murphy, B.J.   Co-hosts the morning show with Jean Ross on WXYV in Baltimore from 5:00 to 9:00 a.m.

Murphy in the Morning   Brought late 1970s contemporary music to Charlotte, North Carolina, from 6:00 to 9:00 a.m. on WAYS and WROQ.

Murphy, Tom   Took over the morning slot at KRLA, Los Angeles, in early 1971. Sarcastic and hip, "World Famous" Tom Murphy had a strong personality, too strong, in fact, for the new program director who took over later that year. Murphy moved to a less prominent shift at 9:00 a.m.

Murrey, Dave   Delivered a top 30 and country mix to Atlanta through the mid–1970s. Murrey was heard from 6:00 to 10:00 a.m. on WYZE, Atlanta, with hourly UPI news and Georgia network news on the half hour.

Mussen, Dave   Brought a pleasing blend of easy-listening country music to Buffalo during the late 1970s. His show was on from 6:00 to 10:00 a.m. on WWOL-FM.

Myers, Gene   In the late 1950s the "KLEF AM" show was featured on Houston, Texas, station KLEF from 6:00 to 9:00 a.m. Myers kept the show fast paced with classical music, traffic reports, and news twice an hour.

Nealon, Al   Handled the 6:00 to 10:30 a.m. slot of KBIS, Bakersfield,

California, in the late 1960s and early 1970s. His program featured contemporary music plus newscasts, sports and "Dear Abby."

Neaverth, Dan   Started in 1962 at WKBW, Buffalo, and aired with his cast of characters, including "Artie the Dum Dum," "The Perpetually Engaged Woman," and "Pierre Puck," beginning at 6:00 a.m. His show featured top 40 music plus sports, traffic, skiing and boating reports. Neaverth was also the announcer for the Buffalo Bills and Buffalo Braves.

Neilson, Bob   Conservative political commentary is the trademark of Neilson's 30-year-old wake up show which features easy-listening and big band sounds from 5:00 to 10:00 a.m. on WNAK, Nanticoke, Pennsylvania.

Nelson, Art   Spontaneous humor and brisk up-tempo country and western tunes greeted morning listeners of WJJD in Chicago during the early 1970s. Nelson, a top-rated morning man who began in 1951 on a number of the nation's leading stations, headed up the 6:00 to 10:00 a.m. time slot.

Nelson, Avi   Kept Boston informed with his late 1970s all-talk show from 6:00 to 10:00 a.m. on WITS, Boston.

Nelson, Jerry   Lively country and western music plus weather and traffic reports comprised Nelson's 5:00 to 8:30 a.m. program on WYDE in Birmingham, Alabama, in the 1970s.

Nelson, Larry   Was heard during the late 1970s playing adult contemporary music throughout South Jersey. Nelson's enthusiasm filled the airwaves for WWBZ, Vineland, New Jersey, between the hours of 6:00 and 9:30 a.m.

Nesbitt, Bill   Works from 5:00 to 10:00 a.m. at KEZY in Anaheim, California. This is a hit music station, but shuns rap music.

Nichols, Guy   Went from afternoon drive-time to morning man in the early 1970s on WENE in Endicott, New York. His program, which aired from 5:30 to 9:30 a.m., featured a mix of contemporary hits, time checks, weather and lots of wit. Nichols also served as program director.

Noesch, John   Amarillo, Texas, station KAKS-FM features its program director John Moesch from 6:00 to 10:00 a.m., playing current hit music.

Nolan, Lee   Played contemporary music on Greenville station WQOK from 6:00 to 10:00 a.m. during the 1970s. The station also featured local and national news, and local, regional, and national sports.

Norman, Teri   Was the featured morning deejay for Honolulu station KQMQ from 6:00 to 10:00 a.m. during the 1970s. The station played mellow rock with a nice blend of contemporary and traditional island music. The station also featured Earth News, weather and surf reports on a regular basis.

Norris, Steve   Was the witty morning deejay and operating manager for

Winston-Salem, North Carolina's WAIR and WSEZ in the 1970s. His comical approach got the day rolling along with top 40 music, news and weather.

Norteno, Ranchero   Played Spanish music for late 1970s Central California each day from 6:00 to 8:00 a.m. He was heard on KGST, Fresno.

North, Bob   Woke listeners up with contemporary music from 6:00 to 10:00 a.m. on WNCI in Columbus, Ohio, during the early 1970s. North moonlighted during the weekend as host of "Midnight Sunshine," a heavy rock show.

Novak, Mike   Used energetic humor and contemporary music to delight his mid–1970s audience from 6:00 to 10:00 a.m. on KYNO, Fresno, California. Novak had previously worked at KFRC in San Francisco and K100 in Los Angeles.

O, Harry   Opened the airwaves at Houston, Texas, station KMLQ at 6:00 a.m. and finished at 10:00 a.m. He played adult contemporary music with a little disco, jazz and local news mixed in during the 1970s.

O'Bannon, Gene   Provided Ft. Worth, Texas, with a mix of standards and the popular music of the late 1960s, plus plenty of news, time and short features. His show aired from 6:30 a.m. to 9:00 a.m. on WBAP.

O'Banyon, Roger   Brought "Kings Kastle" to late 1960s Chattanooga each day from 6:00 to 8:30 a.m. on WNOO. Besides supplying local information, he played a mixed music selection of popular, standards and rhythm and blues.

Oatman, Mike   Played country music for the Wichita, Kansas, area from the late 1960s through the 1970s. Oatman blended the music with his humor, philosophy and candid interviews. He aired from 6:00 to 9:00 a.m. on KFDI. Oatman was also the station manager.

O'Brien, Dale   "O'Brien in the Morning" is a long-running program on WSB-FM in Atlanta. The format is adult contemporary.

O'Brien, Ed   Provided a contemporary format, along with humor and a warm, refreshing personality during the 1970s. The show aired from 6:00 to 9:00 a.m. on WDWD in St. Paul, Minnesota.

O'Brien, Joe   Served as morning man on WNBC, New York, after "Big" Wilson moved to Florida. He later worked for several radio stations in Westchester County, New York. He was not as colorful as his predecessors.

O'Brien, Shawn   Filled his 6:00 to 10:00 a.m. show with plenty of news, sports, time and weather, plus golden oldies and some current on WEIF, Moundsville, West Virginia. O'Brien doubled as both operation and program manager.

Ochs, Charlie   FM station KIKK featured Charlie Ochs from 5:00 to 10:00 a.m. This well-informed Vietnam vet played modern country music with local and international news every hour. Charlie worked at this station in the 1970s.

O'Dell, Morey   Containing some of the longest discussions currently on morning radio, O'Dell talks incessantly with his newsmen, sportsmen, and others on the "Great Morning Wake-Up" program on WPTF in Raleigh, North Carolina. Topics concern current events and local political issues. The show is a full service program, but do not expect to hear much music.

O'Donnell, Charlie   When KRLA in Los Angeles fired "Emperor" Bob Hudson in 1966 for defying management, they slid mid-morning host Charlie O'Donnell into Hudson's 6:00 to 9:00 a.m. slot. O'Donnell, who had been Dick Clark's sidekick on "American Bandstand," ironically was not deemed hip enough when an appeal to a young audience became the management's top priority the next year.

O'Gara, Dave   Used his easy style and adult contemporary music to entertain Worcester, Massachusetts, during the late 1970s. He could be heard from 5:00 to 10:00 a.m. on WORC.

O'Hara, Russ   Worked at KMEN in Baseline, California before coming to KRLA in Los Angeles as the new morning man in 1969. His most famous line: "How's your head?" He did not last long because the station wanted a faster-talking personality. O'Hara was better known as an emcee and concert promoter.

Oldag, Ben   "The Farm Report" with Ben Oldag and Bill Zak was presented on Houston station KTRH 5:30 to 6:30 a.m. in the 1970s. The show included information and audience participation for the farmer and gardener, and agri-business. Ben Oldag was also the farm director.

Olson, Glenn   Heard from 6:00 to 10:00 a.m. during the 1970s on WRRD in St. Paul, Minnesota. The format included new country music, along with news, traffic watch, weather, and sports.

O'Neil, Sean   Aired on WKAP in Allentown from 6:00 to 10:00 a.m. during the mid–1970s. He used quick wit and personality, plus a selection of adult contemporary music, to entertain his listeners.

O'Neill, James   Provided contemporary tunes, 10-minute news segments, weather, sports and helicopter traffic reports from 6:00 to 10:00 a.m. on WLW in Cincinnati, Ohio, in the early 1970s.

O'Neill, Jimmy   Pasadena's KXLA became KRLA in September 1959 and switched to a top 40 format. Owners Jack and Donald Cooke selected 19-year-old Jimmy O'Neill as the new morning man between 7:00 and 10:00 a.m. He lasted only a few months, switching to afternoons when Perry Allen took over.

O'Shea, Michael   Nudged listeners awake with a pleasant patter and happy sounds from 6:00 to 9:00 a.m. on KLIF in Dallas, Texas, during the early 1970s.

O'Toole, Tom   Brought mid–1970s Detroit the very latest in hits and albums from 6 a.m. to 10 a.m. on WRIF.

Owen, Zack   Hosts a country and western morning program from 6:00 to 10:00 a.m. on WIKX in Birmingham, Alabama.

Owens, Loren   Played the top 40 hits of the late 1970s from 6:00 to 9:00 a.m. on KIMN and KIMN-FM, Iron Mountain, Michigan. His morning team included Greg Jarret with news, Dick Dillon with traffic and Jerry Castro with sports.

Owens, Pete   Served as morning man for WFOM in Marietta, Georgia, in the late 1960s and 1970s, and as program and production director. A native of Fayetteville, North Carolina, Owens started his radio career in 1959, working at WFLB, WFBS, WHFL and WSMA. This production expert played contemporary music from 6:00 to 10:00 a.m. in the early 1970s, with a straightforward, informative style.

Painton, Keith   Was operating manager and early morning deejay following Charles Harryman on Kansas City's classical music station KXTR from 6:00 to 10:00 a.m. Painton's show featured early bird news, the morning edition, morning tabloid news, the fine arts page and the stock market report.

Paolucci, Jimmy   Could be found on WFFX, Grand Rapids, Michigan, during the late 1970s. He filled his 6:00 to 10:00 a.m. slot with the very best album material available.

Parker, Al   Brought soul to Buffalo in the mid–1970s with his selection of rhythm and blues. Parker was heard from 6:00 to 11:00 a.m. on WUFO, Buffalo.

Parr, Shawn   Presents country hits from 6:00 to 10:00 a.m. on KIKF in Orange, California.

Parris, Bill   Played the hits from the 1950s, 1960s and 1970s, from 6:00 to 10:00 a.m. on WLYT, Cleveland Heights, Ohio. Local news, weather and sports, plus a touch of humor added to his mid–1970s show.

Patrick Bill   Was a broadcast veteran in the Albany area. In the mid–1970s Patrick could be heard from 6:30 to 9:30 a.m. on WHRL where he gave his listeners pertinent information along with easy listening wake-up music.

Patrick, Don   With Joe Donovan, his show supplied Detroit with a complete package of news, sports, traffic and features during the late 1970s. They could be heard from 5:00 to 10:00 a.m. on News Radio WWJ. Farm news was given each day at 5:55 a.m.

Patrick, Jim   Woke-up Birmingham, Alabama, on WLPH featuring modern country and western music, news, sports and weather from 6:00 to 8:30 a.m. in the 1970s.

Patterson, Ismond   Has run the "Break a Day" program from 5:00 to 10:00 a.m. on WAOK in Atlanta since the 1970s. Gospel music is the format.

Paul, Dave   Provides inspirational religious music and talk over WRBS in Baltimore. This show runs from 6:00 a.m. to 12:00 p.m.

Paul, Larry   Brought modern country music to Baton Rouge during the mid–1970s from 5:00 to 8:30 a.m. on WYNK and WYNK-FM. Paul also worked the 11:00 a.m. to 1:00 p.m. shift.

Pauley, Rich   Played a mix of popular music chosen to appeal to a diverse mid–1970s Birmingham audience. He could be heard from 5:30 to 10:00 a.m. on WAPI and WAPI-FM.

Pavelka, Kent, Don Cole, Tom Johnson   Provided listeners music, temperature, time and weather during the 1970s on KFAB in Omaha, Nebraska. Their Editorial Voice feature (speaking out on important issues of the day) was winner of broadcasting awards for many years.

Payne, Lloyd   Started in the late 1940s with WDXB, Chattanooga, and lasted for decades. "Neighbor Payne" aired from 6:00 to 9:00 a.m. with news, weather, time checks and a pleasing combination of popular hits and standards.

Pearlman, Donn   Teamed up with Dale McCarren in the mid–1970s to bring news and information to Chicago from 6:00 to 10:00 a.m. on WBBM.

Pearson, Bill   Aired from 6:00 to 9:00 a.m. on WWCK in Flint, Michigan; by the mid–1970s he was a 9-year veteran.

Peck, Allen   Produced "Peck 'n' Penny in the Morning" with Penny Reeves. Their humorous country music show was on from 6:00 to 10:00 a.m. on KBOX, Dallas, during the 1970s.

Perkey, Wayne   Aired during the 1970s from 5:00 to 9:00 a.m. on WHAS in Louisville, Kentucky. A talented deejay with a strong personality, he encouraged audience involvement and included "good 'n' gold" music, news, and traffic reports.

Perkins, Al   Charmed Detroit while delivering rhythm and blues music as well as black-oriented news. "The Perker" was heard in the 1970s from 6:00 to 10:00 a.m. on WJLB.

Perry, David   Played mostly rock, but blended in an interesting mix of jazz, country and classical. During the mid–1970s he was heard from 7:00 to 11:00 a.m. on WABX, Detroit.

Perry, Rick   Aired in the 5:30 to 11:00 a.m. slot during the 1970s on

WINR, Binghamton, New York. The show was a sophisticated program of pop standards, newscasts on the half-hour, community service reports, time checks and complete weather and highway conditions, along with women's commentary by Dottie Baker Robinson.

Peters, Jim Alton and Shirley Were hosts of a unique talk show on WKAT in Miami from 6:00 to 10:00 a.m. during the 1970s. Their in-depth investigative and research format included topics ranging from the serious to the hilarious. WKAT played standard popular music from the 1930s, 1940s and 1950s.

Peterson, Jack Entertained New England during the 1970s with a blend of the modern top 40, along with news, sports and weather. His program was on WLLH, Lowell, Massachusetts, from 6:00 to 11:00 a.m. He doubled as the program manager.

Phillips, Guy Aired in the summer of 1978 with Mike Wall at KYNO in Fresno, California. Their 6:00 to 10:00 a.m. show featured contemporary hit music and crazy humor.

Phillips, Richie *see* **Horton, Uncle Fred**

Pierce, Bill Completely dominated the Scranton area market for the 1940s generation with his folksy, casual style on WQAN (now WEJL).

Pierce, Joe Entertained mid–1970s El Paso with the current easy-listening hits while informing them with news, weather and traffic. He was heard daily from 5:00 to 9:00 a.m. on KTSM.

Pippet, Paul Brought Wichita, Kansas, the "Great Plains Farm Show" along with Howard Tice, during the late 1970s. From 6:00 to 8:30 a.m. they delivered the latest farm information, weather and commentary, along with good country music, on KFRM. News director Mark Allen joined them with the news. Pippet was also the station's farm director.

Pitts, Charlie Aired on WOKO, Albany, from 6:00 to 10:00 a.m. Cheerful Charlie brightened up the day with a mix of country music and regularly scheduled information breaks.

Pluckett, Sam Brought a unique blend of everything to his late 1970s Fresno listeners. The show included modern country music, contests, prizes, remedies, insights on the true lives of the stars plus the treasures of his world-famous garage. His show aired from 6:00 to 10:00 a.m. on KMAK.

Pobuda, Ron Brought in-depth news coverage to drive-time listeners on WTAG in Worcester, Massachusetts, in the 1960s. His mixed adult audience, which tuned in for a blend of lively and soft music, was punctuated by a younger audience when his campaign for a new zoo at the Worcester Science Museum brought in more than 5,000 poems and essays about animals from young children.

Pompey, Harold   Used his 6:00 to 10:00 a.m. slot at WWIN, Baltimore, to play rhythm and blues during the late 1970s.

Porter, John   Kept the morning rolling from 6:00 to 9:30 a.m. with a combination of friendly talk and contemporary music. He aired in the mid–1970s on WION, Ionia, Michigan.

Price, Tony   Played soul music during the mid–1970s in Dayton from 6:00 to 9:00 a.m. on WDAO.

Pupule, Akuhead   Aired on Honolulu station KGMB from 5:00 to 10:00 a.m. "The King of Hawaii Radio" played pop music and broadcast news and helicopter reports. He was number one with the island listeners, and in showmanship and sales.

Purcells, Jackie   *see*   **Rydell, Rick**

Purtan, Dick   Mixed popular music with loads of laughs for Detroit in the late 1960s from 6:00 to 9:00 a.m. on WKNR. By the mid–1970s he had switched to WXYZ, where he aired from 6:00 to 10:00 a.m. Favorite targets of his humor were Detroit's prominent figures. The late 1970s found him at CKLW, Southfield, Michigan. Purtan mixed up-tempo popular hits with a humorous combination of characters and one liners.

Putnam, Brock   Handled the 6:00 to 10:00 a.m. slot on WPSB in Bridgeport, Connecticut, in the early 1970s. The station's album standards format also included features such as "Passport," a travel tips show plus shows on gourmet cooking and "Better Living."

Quave, Mackie   Entertained drive-time listeners with modern country music, wit, and cheer on WQXL in Columbia, South Carolina. Quave's show aired from 6:00 to 9:00 a.m. during the early 1970s.

Quay, Bill   Lit up the Charlotte, North Carolina, morning from 6:00 to 10:00 a.m. on WAME during the mid–1970s. Tom Browne did news.

Quigley, Paxton   Played contemporary music for York, Pennsylvania, listeners during the late 1970s. He aired from 5:00 to 9:00 a.m. on WZIX.

Quillin, Ted   Served late 1960s Los Angeles listeners a selection of popular music from 6:00 to 10:00 a.m. His show on KEZY, Anaheim, included "Arnold Palmer Golf Tips" and sports with Bill Brundige.

Quinn, Bill   Last morning man on WNEW in New York, Bill Quinn had a pleasant voice but lacked the imaginative "shticks" of his predecessors. He continued to play the fine jazz music of the 1940s and 1950s right to the end.

Radka, Al   Used top 40 music and oldies plus his wit and the telephone to amuse the Fresno, California, area during the late 1960s. His telephone bits included zany calls and giveaway contests. The "Morning Line" aired from 7:00 to 11:00 a.m. on KFRE.

Raiford, Bob   Kept Charlotte, North Carolina, informed during the mid–1970s. His show aired from 7:00 to 10:00 a.m. on Talk and News station WIST.

Railey, Jay   Aired music by black singers from the 1960s, 1970s and 1980s from 6:00 to 10:00 a.m. on WIGO in Atlanta.

Raleigh, Bob   Took over the 6:00 to 10:00 a.m. slot at WPOC, Baltimore, during the late 1970s. He played modern country music and supplied the news every half hour.

Raleigh   Brought Akron "Raleigh in the Morning" daily from 5:00 to 10:00 a.m. on WCUE, during the late 1960s. He played an up-tempo, carefully selected group of old standards, popular vocals, instrumentals and included time, temperature and local news.

Ratchford, Bob   Hosts "Joy in the Morning" from 5:00 to 9:30 a.m., a Christian contemporary music program on WTJC in Birmingham, Alabama. The music sounds contemporary, but contains religious lyrics.

Raub, Ted (Edwin Raub)   Was best known as a beloved magician and horror flick host on "Uncle Ted's Ghoul School," on WNEP-TV 16 in Avoca, Pennsylvania, but also had a distinguished radio career, including morning man on WYZZ-FM in Wilkes-Barre, Pennsylvania, in the early 1980s. Raub usually did the morning stint on Thursdays, Fridays, and Saturdays, with Frank LaBar hosting on Mondays, Tuesdays, and Wednesdays. Raub's style was low-key to the point of soporific, with his husky, whisper voice and slow delivery. "Here's Jo Stafford; she just came out of a haunted house and will now sing 'I Don't Stand a Ghost of a Chance with You.'" Raub resides in Dallas, Pennsylvania.

Ray, David   Brought Denver a unique mix of jazz, rock, folk and blues between 6:00 and 9:00 a.m. Roy could be heard on KBPI during the mid–1970s.

Ray, Ron   Used the 6:00 to 9:00 a.m. slot at WXFM to bring Chicago light classical music during the mid–1970s.

Raymond, Hal   Played the popular hits of the late 1970s for his York, Pennsylvania, listeners from 6:00 to 10:00 a.m. on WSBA.

Read, B. Mitchell   Was morning man at KRLA in Los Angeles in 1972.

Reed, Dale   Entertained mid–1970s Cleveland with impersonations of popular figures plus a combination of popular music and standards. Joining him from 6:00 to 10:00 a.m. on WJW was Gib Shanley with the sports and Dick Goddard with the weather. By the end of 1978 he could be found in the Detroit area playing modern country music from 5:00 to 9:00 a.m. at WDEE, Southfield, Michigan.

Reed, Jon   Played modern country music, and reported news and traffic for Kansas City, Missouri's station KAYQ from 6:00 to 10:00 a.m. during the 1970s. Reed was also operating manager and program manager.

Reed, Les   Was Atlanta's "Good Morning Man" in the mid–1970s. His bright personality, quick wit, local information and country and western music could be heard from 6:00 to 11:30 a.m. on WSSA, Forest Park, Georgia.

Reeves, Penny   Was co-host of "Peck 'n' Penny in the Morning," a humorous country music show on from 6:00 to 10:00 a.m. on KBOX, Dallas, during the 1970s.

Reid, Chuck   Played black oldies music from 6:00 to 10:00 a.m. on WSID, Baltimore, during the late 1970s.

Reilly, Pat   Used a contemporary format to entertain his audience and impersonations during the 1970s. His show aired from 5:00 to 9:00 a.m. on WLAC in Nashville, Tennessee.

Reineri, Mike   Was heard in the 1970s from 5:30 to 10:00 a.m. on WIOD in Miami, Florida. This pleasant show includes bright, adult contemporary music, news, traffic reports, Paul Harvey News and Comments, Jack Anderson's Commentary, movie, theater and concert reviews.

Reineri, Mike   Used a unique combination of contemporary music and callers to entertain Cleveland during the 1960s. He aired from 6:00 to 10:00 a.m. on WIXY.

Reinhart, Rob   Led the ratings with a rock-and-roll full-service show from 6:00 to 10:00 a.m. on WIQB AM and FM in Ann Arbor (Saline, Michigan) in the early 1990s.

Reno, Walt   Gave his listeners on KRNT, Des Moines, Iowa, plenty of news and local information, along with a selection of standards and popular music. He aired from 5:30 to 9:00 a.m. during the late 1960s. Bud Sobel did the sports.

Reynolds, Elgin   Used rhythm and blues plus local information to wake up Cleveland in the late 1970s from 6:00 to 10:00 a.m. on WJMO.

Rhea, Don   Was the music manager and early morning deejay for Kansas City's country music station KFIX in the 1970s. Rhea combined fun with birthday and anniversary announcements as he played country music from 6:00 to 10:00 a.m. News and sports reports were broadcast hourly.

Rice, Don   Played country and western music for Dallas during the late 1960s. He was heard mornings from 5:30 to 9:00 a.m. on KBOX.

Rice, Ken   Aired country music from 6:00 to 10:00 a.m. in the 1970s on WBCS-FM. News, sports and weather were also heard on this Milwaukee station.

Rich, Craig   Spent most of the 1970s doing a morning show. The late 1970s found him at WZND, Zeeland, Michigan, from 5:00 to 11:00 a.m. The show featured news, traffic and weather plus country music requests from his listeners. Rich was also the station's program director.

Rich, Gary   Airs a two-part morning show on WJLD in Birmingham, Alabama. From 6:00 to 8:00 a.m., he plays rhythm and blues music, but from 8:00 to 10:00 a.m., the program is all talk.

Richard, Sweet   Gave Akron a blend of topical humor, humorous phone calls and entertaining music. Renowned for his personal appearances, he could be heard on WCUE from 6:00 to 10:00 a.m. during the mid–1970s.

Richards, Mark   Plays country hits from 5:30 to 9:00 a.m. on WAXT in Anderson, Indiana.

Rider, Mark   Played beautiful music, and included traffic reports every fifteen minutes from 6:00 to 10:00 a.m. on Houston, Texas's AM and FM station KODA. Mike Mollett informed the audience with news twice an hour.

Riedy, Matt   Supplied the late 1970s Miami area with album-oriented rock music each day from 6:00 to 10:00 a.m. His show aired on WSRF and WSHE, Ft. Lauderdale.

Riggins, Bob   Aired on KTOK during the 1970s from 6:00 to 10:00 a.m. in Oklahoma City, Oklahoma. The "Bob Riggins Show" used a 'middle of the road' format containing a lot of news and commentary, including Paul Harvey with "The Rest of the Story," ABC News, Red Rover News and weather, Howard Cosell, Bill Boren sports and traffic reports.

Riley, Shotgun   Gave his listeners rhythm and blues, news, sports and contests. During the late 1970s he was heard from 6:00 to 10:00 a.m. on WBUL, Birmingham.

Rippy, Dick   Could be heard during the late 1970s playing modern country music for Wichita, Kansas. Joining him from 6:00 to 10:00 a.m. were Cecil Carrier with weather and Ken Softley with sports. Rippy was also the operations manager at KFH.

"Rise and Shine With O'Henry"   Was the opening show for Honolulu station KISA from 6:00 to 9:00 a.m. This station aired Filipino music with some English adaptations, local and international news, and weather reports.

Robb, Stew   Was heard from 6:00 to 10:00 a.m. on WMC-FM in Memphis, Tennessee, during the 1970s. A former assistant program and music director, he was an exciting Star Rock a.m. personality.

Robbin, Earl   Played popular standards for early risers and insomniacs in Washington, D.C. on WWDC in the 1960s from 5:00 to 6:00 a.m.

Robbins, George   Airs each morning on New Age station WHRL-FM in Albany, New York, between 5:30 and 10:00 a.m.

Robbins, Jack   Aired between the hours of 6:00 and 10:00 a.m. in the 1970s on Lansing, Michigan's station WJIM. Robbins shared his in-depth musical knowledge with listeners as he played middle of the road music ranging from 1950 through 1978. He broadcast sports, with an emphasis on local news, and he also did interviews.

Robbins, Jim   On KASH in Anchorage, Alaska, Robbins and co-host Mike Ford play country music and present contests and "wiseguy awards" from 5:00 to 9:00 a.m.

Roberts, Art   Aired in the early 1970s from 6:00 to 10:00 a.m. on WCFL in Chicago and featured pop contemporary music. Roberts' signatures were "deep masculine voice" and "brief but meaty comments."

Roberts, Bob   Used his personality and popular music to entertain Ft. Lauderdale during the late 1960s. His show on WFTL featured the "Fishing Show," "Challenge and Response," "Arnold Palmer Golf Tips" and "Community Calendar of the Air." He could be heard from 6:15 to 10:00 a.m.

Roberts, Don   Played contemporary top 40 in the 6:00 to 9:00 a.m. slot on WEEF in Memphis, Tennessee. His witty personality and informative style made him an excellent morning man during the 1970s.

Roberts, Don   Featured popular hits and standards, news, weather and time, along with "Word of the Day" and "Sound of Money." He was heard during the late 1960s from 6:30 to 9:00 a.m. on KLZ, Denver. Lee Berg did the traffic.

Roberts, Frank   Made waking up fun for listeners of WMNI in Columbus, Ohio, during the early 1970s. "The Grey-Haired Dirty Young Man" aired from 5:30 to 9:00 a.m. and featured modern country plus news, weather and traffic reports.

Roberts, Greg   Used contemporary 1970s music and a pleasant personality to warm Bakersfield, California, from 6:00 to 10:00 a.m. on KAFY.

Roberts, Jim   Could be heard during the late 1970s from 6:00 to 10:00 a.m. on both WKWK and WKWK-FM playing top 40 music. Prior to this "Mr. Radio" had done afternoons for the Wheeling, West Virginia, station for 10 years. Bill Murdock did the news. Roberts was also operations and program manager for WKWK.

Roberts, Lan   Broadcasted from 6:00 to 10:00 a.m. in the 1970s on Honolulu's KORL. Lan's unique style was highlighted by segments such as the Stupid News, various special games and comments, and the Freeway Game. Lan played contemporary rock and roll and the Hawaii top ten. He was also the news director for KORL.

Roberts, Lou Came to Baltimore from the mid–West in the late 1970s. His easy style and mix of contemporary music could be heard from WCAO from 6:00 to 10:00 a.m.

Roberts, Mike Was co-host of "Your Morning Smiles" with Carol Blackmon between 5:30 and 10:00 a.m. on WVEE, Atlanta. The format consists of fusion jazz, top 40 crossover, soul and dance music. The music is not normally heard on most radio stations.

Roberts, Nathan Woke up Atlanta with a bright combination of late 1960s popular music and standards. He was heard from 5:30 to 10:00 a.m. on WGST, Atlanta.

Roberts, Ray and Jeff Hug Aired during the 1970s from 6:00 to 10:00 a.m. on WSMB in New Orleans, Louisiana. The standard format included breezy reporting on current events in New Orleans. Roberts and co-host Jeff Hugg held conversations with entertainment, sports, and political personalities and reported weather, news and traffic.

Roberts, Rick Was the early morning deejay and program manager for Houston, Texas, station KYOK. He aired from 6:00 to 10:00 a.m. in the 1970s. Houston's alarm clock since 1966, Roberts kept the rhythm and blues music flowing while Charles Porter reported national and local news every hour.

Roberts, Ron Presented a blend of contemporary hits and oldies. Features on his 6:00 to 10:00 a.m. show included "The Comedy Guest Spot," "Traffic Radar Reports" and "Chickenman." Roberts could be found in the late 1970s on KCFI, Cedar Falls, Iowa.

Roberts, Stan Was heard from 6:00 to 9:00 a.m. on WKBW in Buffalo during the late 1960s. The 1970s found him still in Buffalo, but on WGR from 6:00 to 10:00 a.m.

Roberts, Steve Provided listeners with country and western music and local, state and national news. The program occupied the drive-time slot during the 1970s on WCMS in Norfolk, Virginia.

Robin, Ron Aired fresh contemporary sounds from 5:00 to 9:00 a.m. on WMEX in Boston during the 1970s.

Robinson, Bill Played "Alive Country" music for his listeners on KENE and KENE-FM, Toppenish, Washington, during the late 1970s. News director Dale Carpenter and farm director James Thompson were also heard on the 5:00 a.m. to 12:00 p.m. show. Robinson has been named a CMA country western "Disc Jockey" of the Year.

Robinson, Bill Aired modern country music on Indianapolis station WIRE from 5:00 to 9:30 a.m. in the 1970s. His warm sense of humor and well-informed approach kept his interviews and phone calls with listeners interesting to hear. Bill was selected as the 1977 deejay of the year by the CMA. His syndicated show was heard in every part of the United States.

Robinson, Jay   Rocked the Orlando area with the rhythm and blues his listeners requested. His "Tiger in the Morning" show aired during the late 1960s from 6:00 to 10:00 a.m. on WOKB, Winter Garden, Florida.

Robinson, John   Delivered a carefully prepared blend of past and present hits for his adult audience in the mid–1970s. He could be heard on KLYD and KLYD-FM in Bakersfield, California, from 6:00 to 10:00 a.m.

Rohmer, Ron   Was morning man for many years on WELI in New Haven, Connecticut. Rohmer varied between Jonathan Winters-style quick humor and sardonic critiques of people and conditions. "Ron Rohmer's Morning" aired Monday through Friday from 5:30 to 9:00 a.m.; Saturday until 10:00 a.m. Canadian-born Rohmer played professional hockey before starting in radio in the 1950s.

Rose, Don   Mixed humor and popular and contemporary music for his late 1960s audience in Atlanta. He aired from 6:00 to 9:00 a.m. on WQXI.

Rose, Jack   Was host of a 5:00 to 6:00 a.m. contemporary music show on WARM-AM in Wilkes-Barre, Pennsylvania. The show featured farm reports, weather and sports capsules.

Ross, Al   Was "Your TimeKeeper" for the Washington, D.C. area during the late 1960s. His format was a selection of bright standards with frequent "live" ukelele interruptions. Features included early morning farm reports, "The Joe Garagiola Sports Show" and news. Ross aired from 5:30 to 10:00 a.m. on WRC.

Ross, Dave   Played a pleasing combination of top 40 album cuts and singles. Through the late 1970s he could be heard from 6:00 to 10:00 a.m. on WAYE, Baltimore.

Ross, Don   Joined WCKY in Cincinnati in 1965 where he could be heard from 6:00 to 9:00 a.m. playing a mix of popular music and standards. Previously he had held a variety of positions while at several stations throughout Illinois and Kentucky.

Ross, Jean   *see* **Murphy, B. J.**

Ross, Steve   Could be heard following Bob Sanders at Grand Rapids, Michigan, station WGRT from 6:00 to 9:00 a.m. Steve was known for calling entertaining people from around the world and creating characters to share his air time as he played music and covered sports in the 1970s. News reporter Gordon Graham covered news twice an hour.

Rudolph, Jeff   Entertained South Florida in the lat 1970s with a mixture of big band swing, dixieland and a touch of jazz. He also included local information and beach reports. Rudolph aired from 6:45 a.m. to 12:00 p.m. on WSBR, Boca Raton where he was also news director.

Rumore, Duke   Played country and western music in the late 1970s for WZZK, Birmingham from 6:00 to 9:00 a.m.

Rump, Gene   Delivered in an energetic morning start in Wichita, Kansas, with his personality and adult contemporary music. During the late 1970s "Rump in the Morning" could be heard from 6:00 to 9:00 a.m. on KAKE. Rump was also program director at KAKE.

Runyon, Jim   Aired local humor about Cleveland and its people from 6:00 a.m. to 10:00 a.m. on WKYC during the early 1970s. The program featured listener involvement, national and local news plus traffic reports.

Russell, Bill   Worked from 6:00 to 11:00 a.m. on WIQT in Elmira, New York, before it changed its dial position and went to a religious format. The morning shift was unusually long, and followed by Bill Miller in the afternoon. Miller often did the Saturday morning broadcast, and even for regular listeners it was difficult to tell them apart.

Russell, Charlie   Mixed contemporary music with news on the half hour and sports once an hour to entertain listeners on KELP, El Paso, Texas, from 5:00 to 9:00 a.m. during the late 1960s. By the mid–1970s he was morning man at KHEY in El Paso. He played country and western music while supplying the news, farm reports and local information. Russell had over 18 years experience by the mid–1970s.

Rutledge, Ned   Had entertained the York, Pennsylvania, area for over 25 years by the late 1970s. He gave his listeners a blend of popular hits, oldies and easy-listening selections. He aired from 6:00 a.m. to 12:00 p.m. on WHVR, Hanover, Pennsylvania.

Ryan, Bruce   Aimed his show at the Grand Rapids young adult market during the mid–1970s. He entertained them with a mixture of current hits and local information from 6:00 to 10:00 a.m. on WLAV. In the late '70s, he played a heavy mix of contemporary music during his 5:00 to 9:00 a.m. slot on WKRQ, Cincinnati.

Ryan, Dan   Aired from 6:30 to 10:00 a.m. on WBBW in Youngstown, Ohio. For the first hour and a half, Ryan played a combination of albums and show tunes. He then switched over to a call-in talk show for the rest of his time slot. Ryan had been with WBBW for 17 years by the late 1960s.

Ryan, Dan   Was heard during the late 1960s playing country and western music from 5:30 to 10:00 a.m. on WKOP, Binghamton, New York.

Ryan, Steve   Gave Buffalo local information along with modern country music during the late 1970s. He could be heard from 6:00 to 11:00 a.m. on WWOL.

Rydell, Rick   Airs from 5:00 to 9:00 a.m. in KBFX in Anchorage, Alaska. Rydell and co-host Jackie Purcell play classic rock and tell jokes.

Ryel, Floyd   Broadcasted from 5:30 to 9:00 a.m. on WHHH in Youngstown, Ohio. Popular standards, easygoing personality and goodnatured comments about people and happenings in the Mahoning Valley drew a large audience of early morning listeners.

St. James, Jerry   Entertained late 1970s Detroit with his special brand of humor. Included in his 5:00 to 10:00 a.m. show on WDRQ were "Billy Biceps with Sports," the "Breakfast Serial" and "Guido, the Famous Italian Lover."

St. John, Don   Used a soulful approach with little talking to bring rhythm and blues to 1970s Chicago from 6:00 to 10:00 a.m. on WJPC.

St. John, Steve   Used up-tempo hits to prepare Detroit for the day ahead. Heard from 5:00 to 9:00 a.m. on WCAR during the mid–1970s.

Sainte, Dick   Worked with Doug Dahlgren in the mid–1970s to bring Chicago "The Dick and Doug Show." They combined contemporary music with humor and relevant local information to keep listeners informed. The show aired from 6:00 to 10:00 a.m. on WCFL.

Sampson, Roy   Played uptempo rhythm and blues from 7:00 to 11:00 a.m. on black station WILD in Boston during the 1970s.

Sanders, Bob   Played inspirational music over the airwaves of Grand Rapids, Michigan's, station WGRT. Sanders aired between 5:00 and 6:00 a.m. in the 1970s and was also Spanish director.

Sanders, Fred   Played popular and standard music, including show tunes, for a sophisticated Tampa-area audience. He aired from 6:30 to 10:30 a.m. at WAZE, Clearwater, Florida.

Sanders, Mozell   Played gospel music during his program which aired 5:00 to 6:00 a.m. in the late 1970s on Indianapolis's station WTLC. Reverend Sanders' show also included dedications for the sick and shut-in.

Sands, Jay   Was known as the "Clockwatcher" and filled the hours between 6:00 and 10:00 a.m. in the 1960s and 1970s with contemporary music and a pleasant personality. He aired on WAEB, Allentown, Pennsylvania.

Santella, Jim   Could be found in Buffalo during the late 1970s playing adult album rock from 6:00 to 10:00 a.m. on WGRQ.

Saunders, Dave   Was already a long time country music personality in the Buffalo area when he took over the 6:00 to 10:00 a.m. slot at WXRL in the late 1970s. He kept his listeners informed with news, sports and weather. Saunders was also the station's news director.

Schaden, Chuck   Played the current hits of the mid–1970s plus oldies from 7:00 to 10:00 a.m. on WLTD, Evanston, Illinois. He now hosts a radio nostalgia show in the evening.

Schader, Con   Had spent 13 years by the mid–1970s playing modern country music and entertaining Denver each day from 6:00 to 10:00 a.m. on KLAK and KLAK-FM.

Schaefer, Dan   Used pop-contemporary music to entertain listeners on WKLO, Louisville, during the 1970s.

Schneider, Jim   Was morning man on WTOB in Winston-Salem, North Carolina, in 1967 and 1968. Schneider was influenced heavily by Dr. Don Rose and developed a fast-paced, manic delivery, and a crazy collection of characters. After leaving WTOB, Schneider went to WKEE.

Schroyer, David   Helped WSUM in North Royalton, Ohio, bring contemporary gospel music to the Cleveland area. Schroyer, the station's program manager, was heard from 6:00 to 9:00 a.m.

Scott, Bob   Started the day in Windsor, Connecticut, with rhythm and blues music, along with traffic, weather, and important events of the day. The morning deejay and program manager for station WKND was known for his contagious, comical ways during the 1970s.

Scott, Bob   Used an invigorating mix of modern country music, quick one-liners and boundless energy to get Charleston, South Carolina, moving from 6:00 to 9:00 a.m. He was heard on WSQN during the late 1960s.

Scott, Jay   Gave Albany, New York, the day's vital information while bringing his listeners a smile with his humor and a selection of country music. During the mid–1970s he could be heard from 6:00 to 10:00 a.m. on WGNA.

Scott, Jay   Played mid–1970s contemporary top 40 with a full mix of local news and information from 6:00 to 10:00 a.m. on Port Arthur, Texas, station KOLE. Scott was also the program manager.

Scott, Jim   Broadcast in the 6:00 to 10:00 a.m. time slot on WSBA in York, Pennsylvania, in the 1960s with bright, carefully-selected music, "Cash Call" contests and audience participation games. Scott went to Cincinnati where he was well-known for his radio campaign to drain the Ohio River and build a nine-lane super highway. His show aired in the early 1970s on WSAI from 6:00 to 10:00 a.m. and featured contemporary music.

Scott, Joe   Brought "Scott's Coffee Shop" to northeastern Pennsylvania each morning from 6:00 to 10:00 a.m. during the 1960s. His show featured up-beat music with no rock 'n' roll. He aired on WBRE, Wilkes-Barre with humor, news and sports. Scott also did two local tv shows.

Scott, Mike   Aired on Houston, Texas, station KQUE 6:00 to 10:00 a.m.

in the 1970s. This highly-experienced radio personality played standard pop music with news every half hour. Scott's credentials include being a program director at Detroit's WDEE and San Diego's KCBQ. He also worked at KLIF in Dallas and KERC in San Francisco. Well-known for his commercials, he was pursued for commercial work. Scott also had a small role in the movie "Future World" that featured Peter Fonda.

Sebastion, Dave   Concentrated on contemporary music with a little information on an uptempo, 6:00 to 10:00 a.m. program on KPAR, Albuquerque, New Mexico, in the 1970s.

Seneca, Nick   Played modern country music for Buffalo during the mid–1970s from 6:00 to 10:00 a.m. on WWOL and WWOL-FM. Dick Spaulding did the news and sports.

Shafer, Dave   Began his radio career in Dover, Delaware. In 1963 he joined CKLW, Windsor, Ontario, where he initially worked afternoons. By the late 1960s he could be found playing the popular hits from 6:00 to 9:00 a.m.

Shallcross, Bill   Airs on WROW AM/FM in Albany, New York from 5:00 to 9:00 a.m. where he presents easy listening records.

Shannon   Spun pop-contemporary music for WGY, Schenectady, New York, in the early 1970s. "Shannon in the Morning" listeners with his "Line of the Day," salutes to deserving New Yorkers and relevant comments from 6:00 to 10:00 a.m.

Sheen, Bob   Used popular music, lots of information and interesting features to get his listeners moving. The late 1970s found him at WION, Ionia, Michigan, from 6:30 to 9:30 a.m. Sheen was also general manager.

Sheldon, Jim   Mixed plenty of humor with wild tracks and up-tempo music to entertain Ventura, California, during the late 1960s. He aired from 6:00 to 10:00 a.m. on KVEN.

Shelley   Combined his high energy style with rhythm and blues to get Birmingham started. In the late 1970s he could be heard from 6:00 to 8:00 a.m. on WATV.

Shelley, Bob   Greenville, South Carolina, station WMRB presented Bob Shelley from 6:00 to 9:00 a.m. in the spring of 1978. Shelley played beautiful music and featured local and national news. He was also the Spanish director for the station.

Sheman, Bethina   Station KBUK out of Baytown, Texas, featured Bethina Sheman from 6:00 to 9:00 a.m. in the 1970s. The early morning audience quickly developed a liking for this amiable deejay. Bethina played modern country music.

Shepard, Gary   Could be heard during the mid–1970s mixing rhythm and blues music with service announcements and local information daily from 6:00 to 10:00 a.m. Shepard was also sports director at WCHB, Inkster, Michigan.

Sheridan, Jack   Salutes to citizens, horoscopes and contests were some of the unusual components of Sheridan's 6:00 to 10:00 a.m. morning show. He aired on WYSL in Buffalo, New York, in the early 1970s.

Sherman, Ralph   Could be heard from 6:00 to 9:00 a.m. playing late 1970s contemporary hits while supplying a lively mix of humor, news and sports. Sherman was also the vice president and general manager at WJRC, Joliet, Illinois.

Sherwood, Lee   Played a selection of hits that stretched from 1955 to the late 1970s. Heard from 6:00 to 9:00 a.m. on WAXY, Miami, in the late 1970s. He was joined by Sherbert the Wonder Dog.

Sherwood, Lee   Spent 6 to 10 each morning on WMAQ in Chicago. He gave his 1970s listeners Country music, news and traffic reports, "Big Farmer Magazine Farm Reports," and sports with Tim Weigel. Sherwood was the program manager during the mid–70s.

Shore, Moe   Delivered a mix of news, music and information on his "Cambridge Morning Record Show." In the late 1970s from 6:00 to 10:00 on WCAS, Boston. Joining him was Dave Johnson with the weather. Shore was the station's operations manager.

Showers, Ken   Could be heard during the late 1970s from 5:00 to 9:00 a.m. on WHTC and WHTC-FM, Holland, Michigan. He gave his listeners all of the popular hits plus lots of local news and information.

Sievers, Bob   Opened his mid–1970s show at 5:00 a.m. with farm director Jay Gould and their "Little Red Barn." From 7:00 to 10:00 a.m. he continued with a selection of his music on WOWO, Fort Wayne, Indiana.

Silva, Joe   An average deejay without a strong personality, Silva took over Bill Pierce's slot on WEJL, Scranton, Pennsylvania, when Pierce passed away.

Sims, Charles Cusack & Mike   During the 1970s, KOMA in Oklahoma City, Oklahoma, station was fun to wake up to and provided great music, fun, news, and traffic tips. The credo was "get you up and keep you going!" This show aired from 6:00 to 10:00 a.m.

Simms, Lee   Began as a substitute for Sue Holliday in 1975 at KRLA, Los Angeles, using the pseudonym, Matthews Frail. His favorite contest involved dropping coins and having listeners guess their value. The show ran from 6:00 to 9:15 a.m.

Simon, Ernie   Simon was a zany and colorful morning man on WGN, Chicago, in the early 1950s, playing the popular songs of the pre rock 'n' roll era He was #1 rated for many years.

Sirott, Bob   Headed up the 5:30 to 10:00 a.m. slot on WBBM in Chicago, a station devoted to contemporary rock music. His program aired in the early 1970s.

Sisneros, Phil *see* **Biondi, Joe**

Slade, Scott   Hosts Atlanta's morning news from 5:00 to 9:00 a.m. on WSB. The program is full service, including two traffic helicopters, a full-time meteorologist, and a full-time sportscaster. Farm news is provided between 5:00 and 5:30 a.m.

Slane, Terry *see* **Claveria, Moses**

Slauhter, Regina   Hosts the "Good Morning" show on WYZE in Atlanta between 6:00 and 9:00 a.m. The gospel music show is directed towards a primarily black audience.

Sloan, Bill   Got things going for station KFRD in Rosenberg, Texas, from 9:30 a.m. until 12:00 p.m. in the 1970s. Sloan provided country music along with local news and a bulletin board for local people.

Smiley, Mike   This bright personality played country and western selections, along with news, traffic and sports. He was one of the top morning men in the area during the 1970s and filled the 6:00 to 10:00 a.m. time slot on WIZO in Franklin, Tennessee.

Smith, Bob   Teamed with Cecil Keels to bring their WCSC "Sundial" program to Charleston, South Carolina, in the late 1960s. From 5:00 to 6:30 a.m. they supplied country music and complete farm information along with hunting and fishing reports. From 6:30 to 9:00 a.m. they made the transition to the station's popular music format.

Smith, Dave   Presented "Outdoors with Dave" on Houston, Texas, station KULF from 5:00 to 6:00 a.m. Smith's specialty was in sharing hunting and fishing information with his audience. The "Bob McCain Show" followed Dave's air time from 5:30 to 9:00 a.m. in 1978. MOR music and comedy were the format of his show. McCain also informed listeners with traffic reports and five-minute news on the hour.

Smith, Doug   Blended modern country music with some older favorites to entertain his Flint, Michigan, listeners during the late 1960s. His "Country Music Time" aired from 7:00 to 10:00 a.m. on WKMF.

Smith, Frank   Could be heard during the late 1970s playing contemporary music from 6:00 to 10:00 a.m. for WVBF, Framingham, Massachusetts.

Smith, Lloyd   Smith is morning man on full-service WCSS in Amsterdam, New York, between 6:00 and 10:30 a.m. The music featured is from the 1960s, 1970s, and 1980s.

Smith, Roger   Played a mix of standards and the current 1970s hits, along with frequent local information, from 7:00 to 9:00 a.m. on WHLD, Niagara Falls, New York. Smith was also the program manager.

Smith, Sandy   Played album-oriented rock for Dayton in the late 1970s. He was heard from 6:00 to 9:00 a.m. on WVUD.

Smythe, Pete   Used his quiet, folksy humor and a selection of standards and the top hits of the late 1960s to entertain Denver. He aired from 6:00 to 10:00 a.m. on KOA. Chuck Miller did "Farm and Ranch Time."

Snow, Les   Presents easy-listening music and encourages audience participation on KHAR in Anchorage, Alaska, from 6:00 to 11:00 a.m.

Soltero, Jesus   Did a Spanish language and music program for the El Paso, Texas, area during the late 1960s. His show featured language instruction plus news, crop reports, weather and sports. He aired from 5:00 to 8:00 a.m. on XELO.

Sommers, Lee   Used irreverent humor and top 40 music to entertain Schenectady, New York, during the late 1970s. His 6:00 to 10:00 a.m. show on WWWD also had extensive local news. Sommers also served as the station's program manager.

Spitler, Patty   Aired news and progressive rock music from 6:00 to 9:00 a.m. each morning. WVUD had Dayton's only female deejay in the mid–1970s. She moved over to WTUE in the late 1970s.

Stack, Jack   Aired from 5:30 to 10:00 a.m. during the late 1960s on WAVI, Dayton, Ohio. His show included country and western music, news, sports and "Five Minute Mysteries."

Stagg, Bud   Hosted "Morning World," where he entertained listeners with news stories, talk and music favorites. Stagg was heard during the 1970s from 6:00 to 9:00 a.m. on WLYK, Milford, Ohio.

Stagg, Paul   During the 1970s this show consisted of adult contemporary music, news, weather and other informational segments. It was on the air from 6:00 to 9:00 a.m. on WCCO-FM in Minneapolis, Minnesota.

Staley, Bob   Served up KLVD's standard California format from 6:00 to 10:00 a.m., entertaining early risers in Bakersfield, with contemporary music plus hits of the past and album cuts of well-known artists in the early 1970s.

Steadman, Bill   Supplied Chicago with album rock during the late 1970s from 6:00 to 10:00 a.m. on WKQX. Joining Steadman with the lighter side of world events was Steve Thom.

Stebbins, Therman   A 25-year veteran of WSBA's "On the Farm" show, Stebbins served up early-morning news coverage of agricultural happenings including weather, market reports and guest interviews in the 1960s. This old, respected agricultural program aired in York, Pennsylvania.

Steele, Richard Drew Chicago drive-time listeners to WGRT with his rhythm and blues format from 6:00 to 9:00 a.m. during the early 1970s.

Steele, Ted Worked at WBAL, Baltimore, Maryland, during the 1950s, 1960s and 1970s, from 5:00 to 8:30 a.m. Steele's background included stints as a vocalist, a background musician for soap operas, a musical director, and a TV teen dance party host, plus 12 years with NBC's "Monitor." Steele was also an A.S.C.A.P. composer of the song "Smoke Rings."

Stephens, Jim Brought contemporary rhythm and blues, plus jazz, to Cleveland in the late 1970s. His show was heard from 6:00 to 10:00 a.m. on WABQ. Joining him at 7:00 a.m. was astrologist Delores O'Bryant with an hour of listener calls on "The Stars Write the Script."

Stevens, Eric On KQ12-FM in Amarillo, Texas, Stevens and co-host Jill Christie play hit music, make animal noises, quiz listeners on strange noises, and take listener polls. They are on from 6:00 to 10:00 a.m.

Stevens, Jay Was hired as morning man in 1970 at KRLA, Los Angeles. He was best known for his imaginary animal sidekick Moby Dick. Later Stevens added the nickname "Jaybird."

Stevens, Lee Combined necessary local information with phone calls from high school and college students in the Washington, D.C. area and the latest of popular music from the late 1960s. He aired from 6:00 to 9:00 a.m. on WEAM, Arlington, Virginia.

Stevens, Paul Was early morning deejay on WCOG during the 1970s. Stevens helped get Greensboro, North Carolina, off to a good start with continuous music and a little wit, news and weather.

Stewart, Bill Brightened the mornings in Columbus, Ohio, during the late 1970s with his special humor. He was joined on WRFD from 6:00 to 10:00 a.m. by Paul Cox with the news.

Stewart, Jimmy This veteran deejay was heard from 5:00 to 9:00 a.m. playing rhythm and blues to Charleston, South Carolina, during the late 1960s on WPAL.

Stewart, Sam Played popular contemporary music for his Bakersfield, California, listeners. Stewart aired from 6:00 to 9:00 a.m. and was also copy and production manager at KBIS. He had been with the station for 4 years by the late 1960s.

Stewart, Shelley Brought Birmingham the "Big D Wake Up Show" each day from 6:00 to 8:00 a.m. on WJLD. His late 1960s show featured his own special brand of rhythm and blues music.

Stingley, Roy Had 15 years of experience as a country and western deejay by the late 1960s which allowed him to tie historical events to the oldies he played. He aired from 5:00 to 9:00 a.m. on WJJD, Chicago.

Stout, Cal   Brought mid–1970s Des Moines a bright, quick-paced show with easy music from 5:00 to 10:00 a.m. on KRNT.

Strait, Terry   Presents rock music and a character known as "the 612 pound newsman" with his co-host "Radio Phill" from 5:00 to 9:00 a.m. on KHWL in Anchorage, Alaska.

Stratton, Steve   Served up a blend of hit music, humor and local news. During the mid–1970s he was heard on WOIO, Canton, Ohio, from 6:00 to 10:00 a.m. Stratton was also the station program manager.

Streeter, Dan   Played a musical medley of standards, popular, jazz and show tunes. Streeter was heard from 5:00 to 10:00 a.m. on WGL, Fort Wayne, Indiana, during the mid–1970s.

Stuart, Dave   Stuart's format included a unique blend of local news, farming information, and gospel music. This very popular deejay delighted all age groups during the 1970s on WKBL in Covington, Tennessee.

Sugarman, Jerry Prouty   Brought Rome, New York, plenty of the contemporary music of the late 1970s along with news, weather and sports. Prouty aired from 5:30 to 9:00 a.m. on WKAL.

Sullivan, Marty   Played the best-selling albums of the El Paso, Texas, area during the late 1960s. He was heard from 7:00 to 10:00 a.m. on KROD.

Sullivan, Paul   Was the morning deejay in the 1970s in Jeffersonville, Indiana. The format included ABC Information Network news on the hour, local news on the half hour, weather, sports, and traffic reports.

Sullivan, Tim   Known as the "Clockwatcher," Sullivan played a selection of standards plus albums of the late 1960s for KDEN, Denver. Included in his 6:00 to 9:00 a.m. show were news, weather, time and his "History Quiz" shorts.

Summers, Ken   Gave his mid–1970s audience music, news and information from 5:30 to 10:00 a.m. on WFAA, Dallas.

Sweeney, Vince   Sweeney is best known as the weatherman on WBRE-TV Channel 28 in Wilkes-Barre, Pennsylvania. In the early 1970s, Sweeney was a morning man on WWPA in Williamsport, Pennsylvania, playing popular music and offering lively chatter. His gregarious personality in real life as well as on-air has attracted a large following.

Tainter, Larry   Aired in the 7:30 to 9:00 a.m. time slot on WBKV in West Bend, Wisconsin, during the 1970s. Tainter's contemporary show included music, games, and call-in guests.

Talbot, Len   Talbot came to WORC in Worcester, Massachusetts, in 1964 with his 5:00 a.m. to 12:00 p.m. "Farm Round Up." This show featured agricultural tips, market reports and general advice for a mixed adult audience.

Talbot, Mario The morning deejay on KWIZ in Santa Ana, California, Talbot, known on the air as "El Gato," presents Hispanic hits and jokes.

Tanner, Bill Aired with sidekick Jim Reihle to give South Florida the best hits and big money giveaways. Through the 1970s they could be heard from 6:00 to 10:00 a.m. on WHYI, Hollywood, Florida.

Tate, Buddy This energetic show mixed modern country and western music with local news, information and shopping tips. Tate could be heard from 5:00 to 10:00 a.m. on WDOD and WDOD-FM, Chattanooga, during the mid–1970s.

Tatum, John Could be found in the late 1970s bringing Flint, Michigan, the black top 40. Tatum's "Wake Up Flint" show aired from 6:00 to 10:00 a.m. on WAMM.

Taylor, Bill Delighted his Duluth, Minnesota, listeners during the late 1960s with contemporary music and humor. He aired from 6:00 to 10:00 a.m. on WEBC.

Taylor, Bob Played popular music during the late 1960s to entertain the Fresno, California, area. His show aired from 6:00 to 9:00 a.m. on KYNO.

Taylor, Chuck Spent the late 1970s playing a mix of contemporary music and golden oldies from 5:30 to 10:00 a.m. on WPTR, Akron.

Terrell, Bill Gave mid–1970s Columbia, South Carolina, a steady mix of soul sounds, local news and information from 6:00 to 10:00 a.m. on Black-oriented WOIC.

Terry, Chem Brought late 1960s Dallas the "AM News Front" from 6:30 to 9:00 a.m. and "Clockwatch" from 9:00 to 10:00 a.m. The first was a constant stream of news and local information while "Clockwatch" brought a selection of standards. Terry was heard on KRLD.

Thomas, Bill Delivered a blend of late 1970s rock and golden oldies to Waterloo, Iowa, each morning from 6:00 to 9:00 a.m. "Captain" Thomas aired on KLEU.

Thomas, Jay Worked the 6:00 to 9:00 a.m. slot for WAYS, Charlotte, North Carolina, in the mid–1970s. He mixed plenty of contemporary music with his own brand of topical comedy. Thomas was also the station program manager.

Thomas, Jerry Played the top hits of the late 1970s plus oldies. Thomas was notorious for his improvisations and characterizations. He aired from 5:30 to 10:00 a.m. on WKRC, Cincinnati.

Thomas, Jim Gathered a host of characters around him when he aired his "Jim Thomas Organization" morning show on WDXB, Chattanooga,

Tennessee, in the early 1970s. The program, which aired from 6:00 to 9:00 a.m., featured the adventures of Bobby Duck and Mouth to Mouth interviews.

Thomas, Kris   Aired the "Memphis in the Morning Show" from 6:00 to 9:00 a.m. during the 1970s. Local news, stock reports, and features were emphasized on this pleasant, drive-time program on WWEE.

Thomas, Mike   Gave his listeners a blend of old and new hits plus plenty of talk and contests. During the late 1970s he aired from 5:00 to 9:00 a.m. on WFGL, Fitchburg, Massachusetts.

Thomas, Tommy   Began and ended his late 1960s 6:00 to 11:00 a.m. time slot with "Western Roundup," an hour of country and western music. Between them was "Timekeeper," with popular hits of the day. By the mid–1970s he was on from 6:00 a.m. to 12:00 p.m., playing contemporary music and standards along with the top 40. He aired on WNIA, Buffalo.

Thompson, Bill   Played adult contemporary music from 5:30 to 10:00 a.m. over Honolulu station KGU during the winter months of 1978. This intelligent, humorous, Hawaiian native had done a lot in the entertainment business. His areas of experience included radio, TV, record production, and talent management. Thompson was big on promotion and kept his radio show going with music, humor, and local news.

Thompson, H. A.   Mixed contemporary music and his quick wit to entertain the Charlotte, North Carolina, area from 6:00 to 10:00 a.m. on WBT during the mid–1970s. By the end of the decade he had moved to the 10:00 a.m. to 3:00 p.m. slot.

Tice, Howard   Brought Wichita, Kansas, the "Great Plains Farm Show" during the late 1970s with farm director Paul Pippet. From 6:00 to 8:30 a.m. they delivered the latest farm information, weather and commentary, and good country music. News director Mark Allen joined them with the news on KFRM.

Tidwell, John   Was known to mid–1970s Birmingham as "Brother John" and kept his show jumping with a selection of rhythm and blues. Charlie Harraway did the sports.

Tipton, Mike   Gave Cincinnati a heavy dose of album rock during the late 1970s. He was heard on WSAI-FM from 6:00 to 10:00 a.m.

Todd, Bill   Houston, Texas, station KRLY featured Bill Todd from 6:00 to 9:00 a.m. in the 1970s. Bill played album-oriented rock, and Barry Bennett did the news. Bill was also the operating manager for the station.

Todd, Gary   Was featured on Indianapolis, Indiana, station WIBC along with the "Fred Heckman News" from 6:00 to 9:00 a.m. in the 1970s. Their show was filled with contemporary music, with importance placed on news and sports, and traffic and farm reports.

Tom, Allen   Was featured from 6:00 to 10:00 a.m. on Jacksonville station WVOJ in the summer months of 1977. This seasoned deejay was considered top in his field, and was especially well known in Boston and Washington, D.C. His intelligent personality and booming voice penetrated the airwaves as he played modern country music and aired CBS news every hour. Featured during his show was Robbie Rose with his "Spirit of 1320" skyway traffic reports. Tom was also the station program manager.

"Tom Dynamite Show"   Honolulu station KIOE featured the "Tom Dynamite Show" from 5:00 to 10:00 a.m. during the 1970s. The music was adult contemporary along with country and western, but the primary focus was telephone conversations with the audience. The station also aired AP Wire Service news, Paul Harvey news, local news, local and national sports broadcasts, and traffic updates.

Tommy Stone, T.   Modern country music plus "morning madness" reigned on WAME, Charlotte, North Carolina, in the early 1970s. Stone aired from 6:00 to 10:00 a.m. His show also featured Whitey Kelley with sports and local news with Don Frye.

Trane, Simon   Played pop contemporary hits during the 1970s on WQXI, Atlanta, Georgia, while regaling his audience with his comedic style. Trane also worked as a comedy writer and actor.

Traver, Clay   Added school lunches and aviation weather to his mix of modern country music. Heard from 6:00 to 9:00 a.m. on KWNT, Davenport, Iowa, during the mid–1970s.

Treadway, Bob   Brought a comfortable feel to KFYE from 6:00 to 10:00 a.m. daily. During the mid–1970s he charmed Fresno, California, with his personality and a selection of his music. By the late 1970s he was off the air, having been promoted to general manager.

Trevis, Kenny   Brought soul music in the late 1970s each day from 6:00 to 10:00 a.m. on WDAO, Dayton, Ohio.

Tripp, Steve   Gave his Bakersfield, California, listeners the latest popular music of the late 1960s. He was heard from 6:00 to 10:00 on KAFY.

Truesdell, Eddie   Played standard and popular music with no rock and roll for Corpus Christi during the late 1960s. He aired from 6:00 to 9:00 a.m. on KSIX. Included in his show was "Corpus Christi Chapel" and "World News Roundup."

Tucker, Bob   Got his Greensboro, North Carolina, audience moving with adult-oriented rock and soul, local and business news, sports and weather from 6:00 to 10:00 a.m. in the winter of 1978. Tucker was one of the most well-known morning disc jockeys of the Greensboro area. He was also the station program manager and news director for WQMG.

Tucker, John   With his comforting voice and popular music selections, Tucker would coax Boston awake each morning from 6:00 to 9:00 a.m. during the 1970s. He worked for WCAP out of Lowell, Massachusetts.

Turk, Al   Was morning man on WALK in Patchogue Long Island, New York, in the 1960s where he played traditional standards of the 1930s, 1940s and 1950s. His theme song was an obscure Otto Cesana composition, "Fancy and Free."

Tyler, Jim   Delivered a mix of mid–1970s contemporary music, dry humor, sports, and news from 5:30 to 9:00 a.m. on WSGN, Birmingham.

Ullman, Debbie   Could be found on WMMS from 6:00 to 10:00 a.m. She played the latest rock music of the mid–1970s while enlightening and entertaining Cleveland with her unique storehouse of memories.

Underhill, Dave   Aired light classical music from 6:00 to 9:00 a.m. on WCRB in Boston during the 1970s. The format included marches, waltzes and concert favorites plus news, weather, and time checks.

Underhill, Leo   Started in Cincinnati radio in 1951 and provided both laughs and jazz from 5:45 to 9:00 a.m. Underhill later moved to WNOP, Newport, Kentucky, where he aired from 6:00 to 11:00 a.m. He was well known for his love of, and failures at, the horse track.

Valentino, Leo   Spent the late 1970s bringing adult contemporary music to the Albany area on WKOL, Amsterdam, New York. He could be heard from 6:00 to 9:30 a.m. Neal Seavey talked to listeners on local issues for 30 minutes at 8:30.

Valenzuela, Paco   Brought Spanish music to Bakersfield, California, from 7:00 to 11:00 a.m. on KWAC. By the mid–1970s he was a 20-year veteran of radio.

Vallardies, Ricardo   This ethnic variety show combined sports, music, news, weather, traffic and humor during the 1970s. It was on the air from 6:00 to 10:00 a.m. on WOCN in Miami.

Van Camp, Bob   Hosted the "WSB Merry-Go-Round" with pop standards, 15-minute newscasts, and traffic reports from mobile units from the late 1940s to the mid–1970s. Van Camp's program aired from 6:00 to 9:00 a.m. in Atlanta.

Vernon, Bob   Teamed with Nick Fanady to lighten up late 1970s Detroit with their special brand of humor. Their cast of characters included "Buzz and Jugs," "Uncle Lenny's Wake-Up Stories for Grownups" and "The Graffiti Lady." They performed from 6:00 to 10:00 a.m. on WCAR.

Vincent, Pat   Played a carefully blended mix of music in the late 1970s from 6:00 a.m. to 12:00 p.m. on WADV, Buffalo.

Wagner, J.   Greeted Albany, New York, each morning during the mid–1970s with "Good Morning Dear Hearts." Contemporary music, humor and the latest information filled the hours between 6:00 and 10:00 a.m. on WPTR. Wagner was also the station program manager.

Walker, Ed   Played popular standards from 6:00 to 9:30 a.m. on WEEF, Highland Park, Illinois, during the early 1970s.

Walker, Jerry J.   Followed Reverend Mozell Sanders' show from 6:00 to 10:00 a.m. Walker played rhythm and blues and offered consumer tips during his lively, successful show on Indianapolis station WTLC.

Walker, Joe   Woke up Port Arthur, Texas, with modern country music, news, traffic reports and commentary on hot topics. Walker aired from 6:00 to 10:00 a.m. on KCAW in the 1970s.

Walker, Johnny   Aired on WFBR from 6:00 to 10:00 a.m. with Charley Eckman on sports. His unique voice and crazy escapades kept Baltimore guessing what radio's bad boy of the 1970s would do next.

Walker, Lisa *see* **Mitchell, Rick**

Walker, Rusty   Aired on WQIK, Jacksonville, Florida's, modern country station from 6:00 to 10:00 a.m. during the summer of 1978. Ron Morgan joined Walker with local news three times an hour.

Wall, Mike   Aired with partner Guy Phillips in Fresno, California, in the summer of 1978. Their 6:00 to 10:00 a.m. show on KYNO also featured contemporary hit music.

Wallace, Scott   Played the softer hits of the day plus oldies, and gave local information to Wilmington, Delaware, during the late 1960s. He aired from 5:00 to 9:00 a.m. on WAMS.

Walton, Art   Signed on each weekday morning in the late 1960s with "The Musical Clock" on WBRC. The hour between 5:00 and 6:00 a.m. brought the "Alabama Farm Hour." From 6:00 to 9:00 a.m. Walton played a combination of standards and popular hits.

Wamsley, Bill   Delivered local information along with a blend of popular music. In the late 1970s Wamsley could be heard from 5:30 to 10:00 a.m. on WCKY, Cincinnati.

Warner, Jeff   Doubled up two morning shows on WOKE in Charleston, South Carolina, in the early 1970s. "Wake Up with WOKE" aired from 5:00 to 7:00 a.m. and blended contemporary music with local calendar items, weather, temperature and time checks and sports. "Low Country Musical Clock" aired from 7:00 to 9:00 a.m. and sent listeners to work with national and local news plus contemporary music. Both shows aired in the early 1970s.

Warren, Al Supplied menus of the day plus recipes three days a week. His show during the 1970s included current hits plus detailed local news, weather and information. He aired from 5:30 to 10:30 a.m. or 6:00 to 10:00 a.m. on WICC, Bridgeport, Connecticut.

Warren, Don Brought the current hits, plus news, weather and sports to WHO, Des Moines, from 6:30 to 9:00 a.m. daily. He aired from the late 1960s through the mid–1970s.

Washington, Reuben Aired a rhythm and blues show for his Ft. Worth, Texas, listeners. "Blues at Sunrise" was heard from 6:00 to 9:00 a.m. on KNOK during the late 1960s.

Waterman, Kent Brought his listeners in the San Francisco area a pleasing blend of the best music and local information. He aired from 6:00 to 9:00 a.m. on KPAT, Berkeley.

Watson, Doc Gave late 1970s Cincinnati traditional country music programming with a more current approach. On the air from 6:00 to 10:00 a.m., Watson was also operations manager and music manager for WCLU.

Wayne and Wally Broadcast adult contemporary music in Winston-Salem, North Carolina, for WSJS from 5:00 to 8:00 a.m. during the 1970s. They also aired NBC World and National news, local news, agricultural information, weather and sports. The "George Brown Show" continued from 8:00 to 10:00 a.m. with adult contemporary music after Wayne and Wally. George Brown was the station program manager.

Wayne, Larry Broadcasts "The Strange Waynes" with co-host Wayne Maloney over KFOT in Anchorage, Alaska, from 6:00 to 10:00 a.m. The music is contemporary.

Weaver, Cal Aired rhythm and blues plus drive-time information, time and weather checks, local social and community news, and sports reports. Weaver's program aired on KJET in Beaumont, Texas, in the 1960s and 1970s.

Webb, Mike Entertained the Fresno, California, area between 6:00 and 10:00 a.m. with a selection of popular music. Mike was also music manager in the mid–1970s and program manager in the late 1970s at KFRE.

Webb, Ted *see* **Harris, Jack**

Weber, Bill This Columbus native and former TV personality delivered modern country music and easy humor to Columbus, Ohio, each morning from 5:30 to 9:45 a.m. He was joined by his dog "Spot" and Martin Petree with the news on WMNI.

Weber, Clark   A morning deejay since 1960, Weber presided over the 6:00 to 10:00 a.m. time slot on WMAQ. He entertained Chicago natives with popular standards, national and local news, weather, sports and traffic reports.

Webster, Chuck   Aired from 6:00 to 10:30 a.m. on Winston-Salem, North Carolina, station WSNX during the 1970s. Webster's creative approach kept his audience going with modern country music, weather, news, traffic conditions and sports. Chuck Webster was also general manager and program manager at WSNX.

Wells, Pauline   Aired "Inspiration Time," a morning gospel program on WSID. Aired in Baltimore from 6:00 a.m. to 12:00 p.m. in the 1970s.

Wendelken, Carl   Delivered a fast-paced show that included news, traffic, weather, time, humor, and country and western music to Columbus, Ohio, in the late 1960s. His show aired from 6:30 to 9:00 a.m. on WMNI. Wendelken was also the station's program director.

West, Clark   Has an unusually long morning program, from sunrise until 1:00 p.m. on WBMD in Baltimore. The format is religious gospel music.

West, Gary   Began each day at WBUF, Buffalo, with a combination of weather, news, cultural happenings and music from 7:00 to 8:00 a.m. Museum and art followed at 8:30 a.m.

West, Don   Played contemporary music for late 1970s Chicago on WEFM. Joining him from 6:00 to 10:00 a.m. with the news was P.J. Morgan.

West, Harry   Was morning man on WARM in Scranton, Pennsylvania, from the mid–1970s to 1992, WILK in Wilkes-Barre, Pennsylvania, in 1993, for one year, and WEJL, Scranton, beginning in 1994. West was influenced by Gene Klavan, which inspired him to create zany characters such as "Emerson, the Main-tain-ance Man."

Western, Dave   Was on Albuquerque's KRKE from 6:00 to 10:00 a.m. In the mid–1970s he played a blend of contemporary music, oldies and selected album cuts while also delivering local news and market reports.

Whalen, Tom   Was morning man on WICC "Service Six" in Bridgeport, Connecticut, for many years. The show was done jointly with meteorologist Walt Davanas. Whalen enjoyed poking fun at Davanas, all in good taste. He worked a crushing schedule, Saturday and Sunday evenings at WNEW in New York, as well as mornings on WICC.

White, Dave   Rousing country and western sounds and on occasional spiritual song greeted morning risers in Birmingham, Alabama. White's 5:00 to 10:00 a.m. program aired on WYAM in the 1970s.

White, Joe   Supplied Boston with rhythm and blues during the 1970s. He could be heard from 7:00 to 10:00 a.m. on WILD, the only black station in New England. "Sunny" Joe was also the program manager.

White, Paul   Was once voted the Number One radio personality in America by NATRA. "Tall" Paul's Morning Show ran from 6:00 to 8:00 a.m. on Birmingham's WENN and WENN-FM from the mid–1960s until 1976, when programming changes were made at both stations. White's personality and rhythm and blues selections made him popular with teens while his news and sports attracted adult listeners.

White, Paul   Played a mix of country and western music, top 40, a number of "hot extras," plus an album cut and several oldies each hour. He aired from 6:00 to 10:00 a.m. on WMOC, Chattanooga, during the late 1960s.

Whittaker, Tom   Was host of the "Morning Watch" program on WFAS AM/FM in White Plains, New York, in the 1960s and 1970s. His personality was bland, but professional. The program aired six days a week from 6:00 to 10:00 a.m.

Whitten, Jim   Headed up the "Early Risers Club" which aired from 5:30 to 9:00 a.m. on WAPI in the 1970s. Whitten's pop standards appealed to a large audience in Birmingham, Alabama.

Whittinghill, Dick   A fixture at KMPC in Los Angeles, Whittinghill had his listeners make up short stories leading into a record's title.

Wickline, Jerry   An interviewer and deejay, Wickline opened WFIS's airwaves at 6:00 a.m. for Fountain Inn, South Carolina, people. His show aired during the winter of 1978 and included modern country music, local news, and interviews with local people in the news.

Wilburn, George   Bright wakeup music was the hallmark of Wilburn's 5:00 to 10:00 a.m. program on WKBB in Wichita, Kansas, in the 1960s. The format blended current songs with hourly NBC newsbreaks, school lunch menus, birthday salutes, secretary of the day and community calendar.

Wilenski   Could be found in the late 1970s playing adult contemporary music and delivering information from 6:00 to 10:00 a.m. on WKAP, Whitehall, Pennsylvania. He was joined by newsman Alan Raber.

Williams, Danny   Aired from 6:00 to 9:00 a.m. in the 1970s on WKY. Danny brought humor and top contemporary hits to thousands of listeners enroute to work. He also hosted his own daily show on KTVY TV.

Williams, Dean   Presents a full-service program and modern music from 6:00 to 10:00 a.m. on KNIK in Anchorage, Alaska.

Williams, Fred   Played upbeat pop standards for morning listeners of WAZL in Hazleton, Pennsylvania, from 5:30 to 8:00 a.m. Williams broadcast music, news, and information to a mixed adult audience in the late 1960s. Today, Williams is a top-rated conservative talk show host between 9:00 a.m. and 12:00 p.m. on WILK/WGBI-AM in Wilkes-Barre, Pennsylvania.

Williams, Jerry   Orchestrated a late 1960s telephone talk show that covered local and national issues of the day. His show aired from 6:00 to 10:00 a.m. on WBBM, Chicago.

Williams, Sam   Played contemporary black music from 6:00 to 10:00 a.m. during the mid–1970s at WAMM, Flint, Michigan. By the late 1970s Williams had left the air to become the community relations director of the station.

Williams, A.C. and Theo Wade   This spiritual and gospel show had been a favorite morning show of the mid–South. It aired from 6:00 to 9:00 a.m. on WDIA in Memphis, Tennessee, during the 1970s.

Williams, Tom   Was already a radio veteran when he came to WMEE, Fort Wayne, Indiana, in 1968. He was still there in the mid–1970s where he could be heard playing the latest hits from 5:00 to 9:00 a.m.

Williams, William F.   Began in 1962 at KMEN in San Bernadino, Califiornia, a new top-40 station which had been KITO. He moved to KBLA, then back to KMEN, before joining KRLA in Los Angeles in 1967. He became morning man at KRLA in 1969. Williams was outrageous. His jokes were suggestive and his attitude suave. This irked management, who kept sending him memos defining what he could do on the air. One morning, Williams read all the memos on the air. It was a great stunt, but led to his dismissal.

Williamson, Art   Played music and gave information, while Nancy Cherry provided news and traffic reports.This team is a simulcast of two stations licensed for different cities. This unique show in the late 1970s from 5:00 to 10:00 a.m. was based on WMYK in Norfolk, Virginia, and nearby WZAM.

Willoughby, John   Joined with Tommy Charles in the late 1970s to bring contemporary music and wacky humor to Birmingham, where they could be heard from 6:00 to 10:00 a.m. on WSGN. Willoughby was also the farm director.

Wilson, "Big"   Throughout the 1960s served as the witty, smooth as silk morning man on WNBC in New York. He played the piano live on the air, but did not sing. Traffic reports were done by N.Y.C. traffic commissioner Henry Barnes, and were drawn out and loquacious. The folksy, slow-paced format was already an anachronism in "sin city"; Wilson was the last WNBC deejay to follow that tradition. He moved to Florida and continued working in radio until his death.

Wilson, Michael J.   Popular with the modern adult audience in Buffalo, New York, Wilson's program on WGR mixed pop standards with free-spirited conversation and humor plus the usual news, weather, sports and traffic reports. On the air in the early 1970s.

Wilson, Joe   Was heard playing top 40 rock during the late 1970s on WRUN, Oriskany, New York. His time slot was 5:30 to 10:00 a.m.

Wilson, Marcellus   Used his personable style and "Scrambled Time Breaks" to help get listeners out of bed. His 6:30 to 10:00 a.m. show on WAMM, Flint, Michigan, featured the contemporary music of the late 1960s.

Wilson, Royce   This deejay has a good audience and knows gospel music well. He was heard from 5:00 to 6:00 a.m. on WKBL in Covington, Tennessee, during the 1970s.

Windham, Woody   Featured unique segments such as challenge rounds, fishing reports and telephone interviews with sports personalities and lots of listener involvement. The 6:00 to 10:00 a.m. program had a format of contemporary music and aired on WCOS in Columbia, South Carolina, in the early 1970s.

Winner, Bill   Brought a bright mix of pop country favorites mixed with telephone contests, and other features such as the "Birthday Corner," to listeners in the late 1960s. Winner's show ran from 6:00 to 9:00 a.m. on WNOW in York, Pennsylvania.

Winston, Fred   Aired a high energy show in the mid–1970s from 6:00 to 10:00 a.m. on WLS, Chicago. In the late 1970s, he had moved over to WFYR, where he encouraged audience participation through contests and call-ins while delivering outrageous humor and contemporary hits. Joining him at WFYR with news and information were Lyle Dean, Red Mottlow and Harry Volkman.

Winters, Bill   Aired bright, happy gospel from 5:00 to 8:00 a.m. on KDAZ in Albuquerque, New Mexico, in the 1970s. Winters had kept morning listeners entertained and informed since 1956.

Wise, Bob   Indianapolis's 24-hour country station WFMS started its morning air time with Bob Wise. "Captain Bob" played country music during the 1978 winter months as Dave Foor covered the news and sports. Also, Deputy Chief Ron Tuttle did traffic reports twice an hour.

Wolfe, Al   Began in the early 1950s and ended in the late 1960s on WILK, Wilkes-Barre, Pennsylvania. Wolfe's show featured popular hits plus golden oldies as well as time checks, weather, news, sports and comedy from 6:00 to 10:00 a.m.

Wolken, Bob   Woke up Bethlehem, from 6:00 to 10:00 a.m. on WGPA. His show featured oldies with the news and sports and ran for decades, beginning in the early 1950s.

Womack, Jerry   Aired during the 1970s from 6:00 to 9:00 a.m. on WSHO in New Orleans, Louisiana. Womack played modern country music and included Mutual Network News, local news and weather.

Wood, Robin   Used a combination of adult-oriented rock and trivia tidbits to fill the hours between 6:00 and 10:00 a.m. "The Springer Memorandum" was featured two mornings a week. Her late 1970s show aired from 6:00 to 10:00 a.m. on WEBN, Cincinnati. Craig Koop did the news.

Wood, Steve   This very popular morning man was heard from 6:00 a.m. to 12:00 p.m. on WKBL-FM in Covington, Kentucky, in the 1970s. His vast audience enjoys his country music format.

Woodside, Scott *see* **Chase, Barry**

Wright, Tommy   Entertained Bakersfield, California, through the mid–1970s from 6:00 to 10:00 a.m. with fictitious traffic reports and humorous horoscopes. Hal Leffoon, a 20-year radio veteran, joined him on KUZZ and KUZZ-FM with local news.

Yancey, Arch   The Arch Yancey Show was presented on Houston, Texas, station KNUZ from 5:30 to 9:00 a.m. each week-day morning during the 1970s. Yancey played country music and featured news twice an hour.

Yeager, Bill   Blended a host of features into his morning show on KGGM, Albuquerque, New Mexico. The format included cuts from pop albums, local and national news, "Our Changing World," and "Point of Law" plus school menus and sports scores. His program ran from 6:00 to 10:00 a.m. in the 1970s.

Young, Art   Combined current hits of the mid–1970s and golden oldies from 6:00 to 9:00 a.m. on KRMH, Austin, Texas.

Young, Bill   Hosted a lively talk-radio show that concentrated on current events. He was on from 6:00 to 8:00 a.m. on KISO, El Paso, during the mid–1970s.

Young, Charles   Lots of top 40 contemporary sounds kept this bright show rolling along from 5:00 to 9:00 a.m. on KOLE, Port Arthur, Texas, in the late 1960s and 1970s.

Young, Cy   Ran a fast-paced country and western show from 5:30 a.m. to 10:00 a.m. in the late 1960s on KOAH, Duluth, Minnesota.

Young, John   Was on the air from 6:00 to 8:00 a.m. during the 1970s on WSM, Nashville, Tennessee.

Young, Preston   Opened the airwaves from 6:00 to 10:00 a.m. for

Honolulu station KIKI in the 1970s. Preston played adult contemporary music and included local music on occasion. He broadcast news 20 minutes after and 20 minutes before the hour during heavy traffic hours and 20 minutes after the hour the rest of the time.

Zak, Bill *see* **Oldag, Ben**

Zebrowski, A.   Was Cleveland's "Polka Baron" and entertained WZAK's Polish audience with polkas, waltzes and obereks from 5:30 to 8:30 a.m. daily through the 1970s.

Zipf, Dick   Aired with partner Jack Evans to entertain Columbus, Ohio, listeners in the late 1970s. They also added adult contemporary music and local information to their 5:30 to 10:00 a.m. show on WBNS.

Bibliography

"Archives Center Register of the George H. Clark Radioance Collection, c. 1880–1950," Washington, D.C., Smithsonian Institution, 1990.

B. F. Communication Services, Inc., *Radio Programming Profile*, Woodbury, NY, 1967 (various editions through 1993).

Birchard, John, "Those Drive Time Morning Men," *Connecticut*, October, 1981.

"Blood Disease Claims Detroit Radio Legend," *Detroit Free Press*, August 17, 1995, page 7A.

"Bob and Ray," *The New Yorker*, September 24, 1973.

Brook, Jill, and Phil Mushnick, Arts and Entertainment Column, *New York Post*, June 24, 1991.

Bryan, Garry, and Ross Brittain, "Radio Suffers a Mid-Life Crisis," *New York Times*, July 28, 1991, Section 2, page 1.

Carroll, D., "Morning Man Phil Markert Plays People," *The Sunday Press*, 3/8/82, p. 2.

Colvin, Geoffrey, "Fred Silverman," *Fortune*, July 14, 1980.

Dougherty, Philip H., Arts and Entertainment Column, *New York Times*, July 1, 1980.

Douglas, George H., *The Early Days of Radio Broadcasting*, Jefferson, NC, McFarland, 1987.

Duncan, Bernadette, Arts and Entertainment Page, *Daily News*, October?, 1991.

Earl, Bill, *Dream House,* Montebello, California, Desert Rose, undated.

Eberly, Philip K., *Music in the Air: America's Changing Taste in Popular Music, 1920 to 1980*, Hastings House, NY, 1982.

"Fifty Years of Unique Radio," WJR Radio (private printing), 1972.

Fornatale, Peter, and Joshua E. Mill, *Radio in the Television Age*, Penguin, 1990.

Franklin, Joe, & R. J. Marx, *Up Late with Joe Franklin*, N.Y., Scribner, 1995.

Gambling, John, *Rambling with Gambling*, Englewood Cliffs, Prentice-Hall, 1972.

Gray, Barry, *My Night People*, New York, Simon & Schuster, 1975.

Kaikowski, Geri Ann, "Time for the Female Morning Drive Deejays to Finally Wake Up," *Citizens Voice*, Wilkes-Barre, PA, May 16, 1993, p. 14.

Klavan, Gene, *We Die at Dawn*, Garden City, Doubleday & Co., 1964.

LA Times, Entertainment Column, January 3, 1992.

Lang, Joel, "Our Man in the Morning," *Northeast*, August 29, 1982, p. 8ff.

Maksian, George, Entertainment Page, *Daily News*, June 20, 1991.

Moskowitz, Jane, *Bob Steele's 50th Anniversary: An Affectionate Memoir*, Hartford, Conn., Spoonwood Press, 1986.

New York Daily News, Arts and Entertainment Column, October 15, 1991.

New York Daily News, Entertainment Section, January 12, 1992, p. 2.

New York Magazine, March 13, 1989, page 50.

New York Post, Arts & Entertainment Column, September 3, 1991.

_____, Arts and Entertainment Column, December 13, 1991.

New Yorker, April 15, 1991, page 78 to 93.

Passman, Arnold, *The Deejays*, New York, Macmillan, 1971.

"Radio Personality Honored" (Thomas Grunwell), *The News*, Frederick, Maryland, January 19, 1993.

Rothwell, Kate, "Good Morning Frederick," *The News*, undated, pp. 35–38.

Routt, Edd, Jones B. McGrath, and Fredric A. Weiss, *The Radio Format Conundrum*, New York, Hastings House, 1978.

Sanger, Elliott M., "Rebel in Radio, the Story of WQXR, NY," Hastings House, 1973.

Sklar, Rick, *Rocking America*, NY, St. Martin's Press, 1984.

Smith, Buffalo Bob, and Donna McCrohan, *Howdy and Me*, NY, Plume Books, 19xx.

Smith, Dinitia, "Morning Mouth," *New York Magazine*, June 24, 1991.

Steele, Bob, *Bob Steele: A Man and His Humor*, Hartford, Spoonwood Press, 1980.

Sterling, Jack, and William C. Vance, *So Early in the Morning*, New York, Crowell, 1958.

Time, April 15, 1989, pp. 88-89.

Wolfman Jack, *Have Mercy*, NY, Warner Books, 1995.

WOR: The First 60 Years, private publisher, undated.

York, Jeffrey, *The Washington Post*, Arts and Entertainment Page, June 18, 1991.

"Z Morning Zoo," business page, *Newsweek*, March 25, 1985.

Index